Reemerging Jewish Culture in Germany

Acknowledgments

We would like to thank the German Academic Exchange Service (DAAD), the Institute for European Studies (Cornell University), and the Goethe Institute (New York) for their generous support of the conference from which this book took its genesis. Ned Brinkley, Ted Nasser, and Alison Orton provided us with editorial assistance in the initial stages of this project. A special thanks to Colleen Duncan for her expertise in getting the final draft into camera-ready form. And lastly, our heartfelt appreciation to Despina Papazoglou Gimbel at NYU Press for her patient and expert guidance.

Contributors

Y. MICHAL BODEMANN teaches sociology at the University of Toronto and at Humboldt University in Berlin. He has done extensive research in Sardinia, and has written on sociological theory, patron clientage, underdevelopment, German elites, the Green Party and more recently on Jews in postwar Germany. A paper, "Priests, Prophets, Jews and Germans: Max Weber's Conception of Ethno-National Solidarities," has just appeared in the *Archives européennes de sociologie*. A book, *Jews, Germans, Memory: State and Ethnicity in the Construction of a New German Jewry* will appear with University of Michigan Press next year.

ESTHER DISCHEREIT was born in 1952 in Heppenheim (Germany) to a Jewish mother and a non-Jewish father. She studied German literature and political science at the University of Frankfurt. She worked at various jobs in the tool and die and printing industries. Since 1985 she has published numerous newspaper articles and given radio broadcasts about current events. In 1986 she published her first book, *Anna macht Frühstück*, for children. Subsequent publications include the children's book, *Südkorea—Land für friedliche Spiele* (1988), a collaboration with other authors; the novel *Joëmis Tisch* (1988); a jazz and poetry project with Johannes Niebergall on bass and Bülent Ates on drums; the novel *Merryn* (1992); various theater and radio plays; and two books of poetry, *Red Shoes* and *I Am Pulling the Colors out of My Skin*. In 1993 she made a speaking tour of the United States.

SANDER L. GILMAN is the Goldwin Smith Professor of Humane Studies at Cornell University and Professor of the History of Psychiatry at the Cornell Medical College. A member of the Cornell faculty since 1969, he is a cultural and literary historian and the author or editor of over forty books, the most recent in English—*Freud, Race, and Gender* (Princeton) and *The Case of Sigmund Freud* (Johns Hopkins)—having appeared in the fall of 1993. He is the author of the basic study of the visual stereotyping of the mentally ill—*Seeing the Insane*—published by John Wiley and Sons in 1982 as well as the standard study of *Jewish Self-Hatred*, the title of his Johns Hopkins University Press monograph of 1986. During 1990–1991 he served as the Visiting Historical Scholar at the National Library of Medicine, Bethesda, Maryland. He has been the Northrop Frye Visiting Professor of Literary Theory at the University of Toronto, the Old Dominion Fellow in the Department of English at Princeton University, and the Visiting B. G. Rudolph Professor of Jewish Studies at Syracuse University. He also served as a visiting professor at Colgate University, Tulane University, the University of Paderborn and the Free University of Berlin (Germany) and has been a Guggenheim Fellow. He is the president-elect of the Modern Language Association.

MARION KAPLAN is Professor of Modern History at Queens College and the Graduate Center of the City University of New York. Her research interests include the history of Jews in Germany and European Women's History. She has written *The Making of the Jewish Middle Class: Women, Family, and Jewish Identity in Imperial Germany* (Oxford University Press, 1991), and *The Jewish Feminist Movement in Germany: The Campaigns of the Jüdischer Frauenbund, 1904–1938* (Connecticut, 1979). She has also edited *The Marriage Bargain: Women and Dowries in European History*, and co-edited *When Biology Became Destiny: Women in Weimar and Nazi Germany.*

SUSAN NEIMAN studied philosophy at Harvard and the Free University of Berlin, and is currently Associate Professor of Philosophy at Yale. Her book *Slow Fire: Jewish Notes from Berlin* (Schocken, 1992) won a PEN Citation for a Distinguished First Work of

Nonfiction. She is also the author of *The Unity of Reason: Rereading Kant* (Oxford, 1994).

KATHARINA OCHSE is a free-lance journalist for German television and radio. She is currently completing her dissertation on the confrontation with anti-Semitism between 1918–1939 in the works of German-writing Jewish authors.

ROBIN OSTOW is a Research Associate at the Centre for Russian and East European Studies at the University of Toronto. She lived in West Berlin for six years during the 1980s and early 1990s, and she has published extensively on eastern German Jewry. Her book *Jews in Contemporary East Germany: The Children of Moses in the Land of Marx* appeared in 1989.

JEFFREY M. PECK is an Associate Professor of German in the Center for German and European Studies at Georgetown University. Developing from his interest in the relationship between anthropology and literary studies, his work in cultural studies focuses on national and minority identities in Germany, the representation of the "foreign(er)," and inter-German relations since unification.

KAREN REMMLER is an Assistant Professor of German at Mount Holyoke College. Her research includes articles on the relationship between postmodernist discourse and the representation of the body in torture, the structures of remembrance in the *Todesarten* by Ingeborg Bachmann, and body politics in the former GDR. She is currently engaged in research on the relationship between sites of memory and Jewish cultural identity in Berlin.

RAFAEL SELIGMANN was born in 1947 in the Palestinian Mandate and moved to Munich at the age of 10 with his parents. Educated in Munich as a political scientist, he is the author of two novels, *Rubensteins Versteigerung* (1989) and *Die jiddische Mama* (1990). As of 1985, he has been a lecturer in political science at the University of Munich.

KIZER WALKER is a doctoral candidate in German Studies at Cornell University. He grew up in California's San Joaquin Valley and received his Bachelor or Arts from the University of California at Santa Cruz. He is currently living in Berlin with his wife and son.

JACK ZIPES is Professor of German at the University of Minnesota and has published numerous articles and books on fairy tales, folklore, drama, children's literature, and German culture. Among his major publications dealing with German-Jewish topics are: *Germans and Jews Since the Holocaust: The Changing Situation in West Germany* (1986), edited with Anson Rabinbach, and *The Operated Jew: Two Tales of Anti-Semitism* (1991). He is also one of the founding editors of the journal *New German Critique* and editor in chief of the series *Modern German Voices*, published by Holmes and Meier.

Introduction

This volume is the outcome of an interdisciplinary conference on "The Reemergence of Jewish Culture in Germany" that brought together scholars and writers from North America and Germany.[1] The timeliness of the topic, confirmed by the intensity of the debates that ensued at the conference, warrants further discussion. The rise of xenophobic attacks in Germany since unification and a more pronounced atmosphere of internal anxiety among Germans and non-German residents also raise many questions about the feasibility and desirability for a renaissance of Jewish culture in Germany. By presenting various historical, cultural, and personal perspectives, this collection contextualizes the debates about whether or not a (German) Jewish culture is possible in today's Germany. The renewed self-awareness among Jews living in Germany is certainly not a sudden occurrence but one that has become more articulated in the last decade. The events of the 1980s—beginning with the Bitburg affair, continuing with the "Historikerstreit," the debate over Rainer Werner Fassbinder's play *Garbage, the City and Death* (both in 1985), and Philipp Jenninger's controversial speech commemorating the fiftieth anniversary of the November pogrom (*Kristallnacht*) of 1938 that led to his immediate resignation—are perhaps the major catalysts for a reevaluation by Jews of their place in a German society in which the majority of the population has never met a Jew. The fall of the Berlin Wall on November 9, 1989, a date that also marked the fifty-first anniversary of the November pogrom, and the subsequent call by major politicians and many German citizens for a new era free of the burden of the past—complicated by attempts in all political sectors to establish a new, prouder German national identity—have been received with mixed feelings by Jews living in Germany. Despite protests against violence by thousands of Germans in candlelight vigils and in public outrage, the politically sanctioned restriction of immigration and the continuation of violence against those deemed foreign by groups of neo-Nazis and other right-wing extremists, has created not just alarm among Jews but also a desire to redefine their own Jewish identity within German culture. Whereas some Germans struggle to lay a foundation for a positive, inclusive German identity, their Jewish neighbors and coworkers are speaking out publicly and debating what constitutes Jewish culture in Germany today.

The articles in this volume attest, on the one hand, to the increased interest in things Jewish among Germans expressed by the proliferation of television programs, museum exhibits, and events centered around Jewish issues. On the other hand, they document the growing self-definition among Jews manifested in the establishment of Jewish cultural centers in major German cities, an increasing number of Jews choosing to live in Germany (particularly those from the former Soviet Union), and lively debates in Jewish circles about the dilemma of being Jewish in Germany. Not all of these phenomena can be taken as a sign of "normalization" of German-Jewish relations. On the contrary. Despite the increasing visibility and self-perception of Jews as citizens and residents of Germany, the ever-present memory of the Shoah and its repression in German society, combined with Germany's growing pains induced by unification, demands attention.

At the same time as Jews in Germany are facing and even arguing for a recognition of the fragmentation and diversity among members of the Jewish community in Germany, they confront a continued consolidation of their differences by a German public that apparently finds dealing with Jews easier in museums than on the streets. How do those who choose to remain in Germany, or indeed to emigrate to the country that may have persecuted and killed their ancestors, see their future in Germany? Is the possibility of a thriving Jewish culture in Germany a chimera in light of the rise in xenophobia, open anti-Semitism, and parliamentary decisions to restrict the previously guaranteed constitutional right of political asylum? Can the German economy, taxed by the cost of unification, accommodate the rising unemployment and thus dissatisfaction and scapegoating among disgruntled "German" Germans? Who are the Jews living in Germany today? How are they defining their Jewishness? What pitfalls do they encounter in seeking to establish their presence in German society? And conversely, how are Jews seen by non-Jewish Germans? How are they represented in the media, in literature, and in museum exhibits? What are the responses of the Jews to this representation in their literature and discussions?

With Jews both absent and present in Germany after the Shoah, the evocation and repression of Jewish visibility is central to those young writers who understand themselves as Jewish writers in Germany. Jews in contemporary reunited Germany come to acknowledge their simultaneous visibility and invisibility, their sense of belonging and their sense of difference, and they represent this ambiguity in their literary work. This is not necessarily a result of the fall of communism and the unification of the two German states, but it is heightened by this historical context. The growth of a new Jewish culture in both eastern and western Germany would have taken place without the fall of the Wall, but it would have certainly taken very different form and direction. The sense of being "integrated foreign bodies" (*integrierte Fremdkörper*), as Esther Dischereit's protagonist describes herself at the close of her recent novel *Merryn* (1992), is definitely not a result of the collapse of communism. The difference is the cultural context in which these young Jewish writers now begin to articulate their sense of belonging and yet not belonging.

Dan Diner, the most articulate social critic in the Jewish intellectual community in Germany, has labeled this phenomenon a "negative symbiosis." Accepting, on one level, Gershom Scholem's dismissal of the "German-Jewish symbiosis" as a fantasy on the part of Jews in Germany before the Shoah, Diner asks how Jews can live in Germany today. His answer is that Jews exist in a "negative symbiosis" to German culture, aware of and forced to deal with their own difference from the "German." Thus Rafael Seligmann, taking the American case as exemplary, can write about the Jews in Germany as the "Indians of Germany," in analogy to the "vanished American" who is not black (like the "real" minority) in the United States and present more in myth than in reality.

These writers have a complex relationship to their audiences. It is evident that the greater reading and viewing audience in Germany is non-Jewish and yet maintains a very special relationship to things Jewish. But there is also a Jewish audience in Germany for or against which these writers often define themselves. Jewish journals such as the muckraking *Semittimes*, the intellectual *Babylon*, the student journals such as *Tachles* (in Frankfurt) or *Nudnik* (in Munich), official or quasi-official newspapers of the Jewish communities, such as the *Frankfurt Jewish News* or the *General Paper of the Jews in Germany* provide a Jewish response to writers who represent Jewish life in contemporary Germany. The audience sees them as Jewish because they have chosen to label themselves Jews and write on themes from contemporary Jewish life, but their non-Jewish audience "sees" them as representative Jews, while their Jewish audience often fears such heightened visibility. The complexities increase when we compare the intense visibility of Jews in contemporary Germany with their essential invisibility.

German law on ethnic difference can only replicate the ambiguities of Jewish German identity. The constitutional reform commission of the upper house of parliament, the *Bundesrat*, decided on May 14, 1992, that a clause in regard to "national and ethnic minorities" should be included in the revision of the "basic law" (the *Grundgesetz*, Germany's constitution) and should "specifically apply to the Danish, Sorb, and Frisian populations, the German Sinti and Roma ["Gypsies"] and—as far as a specific sense of themselves as a minority ["ein entsprechendes Minderheitenselbstverständnis"] exists—the Jewish population." Jews are both ethnic "minorities" and not "minorities," while the other groups are distinctly minorities. The law might bracket the Jewish question simply because of the old difficulty of defining the Jew: is this a social, cultural, racial or religious designation? It is clear that the unique sense that Jews and Germans share a long history also plays a part: a history that encompasses both the Enlightenment promise that Jews could identify as Germans and that Germans would also identify them as such, and the Nazi reversal of this promise. The Jews are not like other minority (or "out") groups in Germany, who are all defined in terms of a static, homogeneous German center. The reciprocal instability of Jewish and German identity is at the very heart of the literary self-representation of the Jewish writer in Germany.

The essays in this volume address these issues in a historical context. First, to what extent can the German Jewish presence in Germany be seen as a reestablishment of pre-1933 German Jewish relations? Can we speak of a continuity with the German Jewish culture of the Weimar Republic? The influx of Soviet Jewish immigrants, in particular to Berlin, in some ways recreates pre-Shoah differences between German Jews and the less assimilated Eastern European Jews. Secondly, how can we speak about a German Jewish culture, when the majority of Jews living in Germany are not of German descent? The differences within both the official and unofficial Jewish communities in Germany are the subject of heated debate within Jewish circles and publications such as *Babylon* or *Semit*. For example, in a critical response to the annual 1991 Jewish Cultural Festival (*Jüdische Kulturtage*) sponsored by the *Jüdische Gemeinde* in Berlin, an alternative Jewish group held a series of open panel discussions at the Humboldt University. The panel discussions were organized to protest what the Jewish group saw, in part, as a coopting of critical voices and a stereotypical representation of Jewish culture during the officially sponsored cultural festival. Third, how do second- and third-generation Jews living in Germany define their Jewishness vis-à-vis their parents who survived the concentration camps, went into hiding or lived in exile? What do younger Jews see as their role in unified Germany as a whole and in relation to other minorities in German culture in particular?

Although the essays that follow do not claim to give answers, they do provide a first attempt to describe the relationship between the complicated process of unification and a reemerging Jewish culture from a variety of insider and outsider perspectives. The four sections of the collection provide historical, cultural, literary, and personal overviews of the issues in the debate about the possible reemergence of Jewish culture in Germany. Each contribution addresses the issues within a particular field of inquiry or against the backdrop of personal experience. In addition to scholarly readings of the phenomenon, two German Jewish writers, Esther Dischereit and Rafael Seligmann, offer their personal experiences and observations on the vicissitudes of being Jewish in Germany. As Jack Zipes points out in his article on "The Contemporary German Fascination for Things Jewish," the postwar discussion of German Jewish relations has been ongoing. The German government's relations with Israel or the conflation of anti-Zionism with anti-Semitism on the Left are only two examples of postwar Germany's stance toward Jews. What makes the current situation different?

The difference lies in the changing definition of what it means to be Jewish in a Germany that is redefining its role in Europe and in the world while, at the same time, facing internal economic and social crises that have already taken lives and that continue to threaten the very fabric of German society. Zipes examines the historical context of Jewish culture today and the participation of Jews in this process. The fall of the Wall and the establishment of a unified Germany on October 3, 1990, became a sign of a process of reassessment that had already begun in the 1980s. Although Zipes is perhaps the most optimistic of the contributors in supporting the view that a reemergence of Jewish culture is possible, he notes that the small number of Jews actually living in Germany does not constitute a thriving community.

Susan Neiman concludes the volume by recalling her long-term stay in Berlin and her return after the fall of the Wall. The sharpness of her observations and polemical stance on the necessity of Jewish culture in Germany for Jews and Germans expresses many of the same concerns addressed in the other essays, but also advances a tentative optimism about the vitality of Jewish culture in unified Germany. As Neiman and other contributors in this volume warn, however, the role of Jews living in Germany is by no means uncomplicated or even safe. Yet the continuing emigration of Jews to Germany, the establishment of Jewish-owned businesses, and the frequent debates among and between Jewish groups mark the reemergence of Jewish culture. Some of the contributors in this volume, tellingly those who live in Germany, cautiously call for a vigilant critical stance toward a reobjectification of Jewish culture into a separate enclave. Could it become a vital part of German society and engage in transforming German culture from one monolithically self-defined to one more multifarious? For the reemergence of Jewish culture, as Michal Bodemann suggests in his article, brings with it a transformation in the "ideological labor" of the Jews living in Germany, a turn away from the focus on Auschwitz to one aimed at reestablishing a pre-1933 German Jewish culture. At the same time, the arrival of Soviet Jews in substantial numbers since the mid-1970s suggests a different development, a new cultural definition of what it means to be Jewish in Germany. Zipes relates this change to the conflicts and differences manifest in the split in the Jewish communities in Berlin and between Jews of German versus Eastern European descent. What emerges is the heterogeneity of the Jewish community, estimated by Bodemann to be well above the official count of 40,000 (as of early 1993), yet hardly significant enough to constitute a thriving Jewish culture.

Robin Ostow and Katharina Ochse question not only the subsumption of Jews under the term "foreign"—in the case of Jewish German citizens a false representation—but also the lack of attention paid to the difference between Jews in the former East and West Germanys. In her article, Ostow describes the situation of Jews in the former GDR and the complicated relationship between those Jews who did not acknowledge their Jewish heritage but identified themselves foremost as socialists. Today they are caught up in the dilemma of having to justify their role as high officials in the Stasi or GDR government and reclaiming a Jewish identity. Ostow questions the motives of some former GDR citizens whose more recent reconnection to their Jewish heritage "provided a release from the ranks of an increasingly unpopular elite and a new status as a victim of socialist, European and German history." Ostow warns against decontextualizing the experience of Jews living in Germany. Similarly, Ochse comments on the tensions within the Jewish communities and raises questions about assuming that Jewish culture in Germany signifies German Jewish culture. But what does "German Jewish" mean in today's

Germany? Despite the possible parallels to pre-1933 German Jewish culture, it has taken on a new meaning as a term for Jews living in Germany regardless of their ethnic background.

Kizer Walker's analysis of the responses to the Persian Gulf War by different factions within a no longer clearly delineated right and left end of the German political spectrum suggests that the reemergence of Jewish culture must be seen within the context of a rising anxiety in Germany about its status in the "new world order." Walker analyzes the propensity of different constituencies on the Right and Left to reenact an irrational anxiety in response to the Persian Gulf War, through which many Germans positioned themselves as victims. Walker's detailed documentation of the debates surrounding the Gulf War by German intellectuals and media supports the notion that neither the Right nor the Left responded in a way that would suggest a differentiated view of their own anti-Semitism. As Walker shows, the Gulf War was for many Jews a final straw in the ever-growing series of events that demonstrated the fissure between Germans and Jews in unified Germany. Yet as Marion Kaplan's essay demonstrates, many Jews continue to live and thrive in Germany, though with some apprehension. Many of the younger generation are making their presence felt and asking themselves what it means to be both Jewish and German.

By including the voices of two contemporary German Jewish writers, Esther Dischereit and Rafael Seligmann, we round out this volume with the insights of those who, by virtue of their literary texts, shape the public opinion of their readers, with emphatic pleas for critique. The contributions by Dischereit and Seligmann place the reemergence of Jewish culture squarely in the realm of public imagination. They describe the genesis of their literary texts and the initial dismissal by some German publishers and some Jewish critics of their texts because they presented "Jewish" figures or issues in a differentiated fashion. Their experience suggests that Jewish identity is seen as isolated from other forms of identity, a topic Jeffrey Peck takes up in his call for increased understanding of the difference between white Jews and other residents (or citizens) of Germany, who, because of their skin color, are targeted for attack by rightist skinheads. Our readings of contemporary Jewish literature in Germany explore the relations between gender and Jewish identity in contemporary writing by Jews, who, for the most part, live in Germany. Sander L. Gilman focuses on the significance of circumcision for defining not only male Jewish identity but on a metaphorical level, Jewish identity *per se.* Karen Remmler traces the textual moves that en-gender memory in the works of three contemporary Jewish women writers, Barbara Honigmann, Esther Dischereit, and Irene Dische. Her contribution suggests that the representation of Jewish identity through the body requires not just a recognition of gender differences but also of other elements of identity, such as remembrance and family ties. Both Gilman and Remmler accentuate the gender differences that very much constitute the experiences that are represented in texts by contemporary Jewish writers but that have been tangential to the discussion of Jewish identity in Germany itself.

The complexity of Jewish German identity can be judged just by contemporary attitudes of Jews, even (or especially) the Jews new in Germany. A survey released in March of 1993 by the Salomon Ludwig Steinheim Institute in Duisberg, an institute devoted to the study of Jews in German culture, showed that Russian Jews who had recently settled in Germany were found to be overwhelmingly content with their choice. Only 13 percent would advise against settling in Germany. Still, at least 40 percent noted that they had been discriminated against because they were Jewish and 29 percent observed that they lost German friends when their religion was acknowledged. The overwhelming majority, some 90 percent, felt themselves at risk from the antiforeigner and anti-Semitic acts and rhetoric of the past year. Here the heightened visibility of an identifiable minority—identifiable not only because of their Jewish identity, which has to be announced, but because of their visibility as "foreigners" (through language, clothes, social conventions)—reflects the complexity of the German response to the Russian Jews.

The attitudes toward Jews and Israel in Germany were explored by an extensive opinion poll held by the newsmagazine *Der Spiegel* in 1992. (It was paralleled by a study of attitudes toward Germany and the Germans in Israel, as if there were no Jewish Diaspora in Germany to ask.) These figures were not very different from the 1988 study by the Allenbach Opinion Poll concerning West German attitudes toward Jews. The conclusion was startling if expected: every eighth German held anti-Semitic attitudes. Indeed, a majority—60 percent—of all Germans felt that anti-Semitism would remain at its present level and 18 percent felt that it would increase. And, not surprisingly, 77 percent of Germans who expressed anti-Semitic feelings also expressed negative feelings about the Sinti and Roma. 44 percent felt that "racial purity" was vital to the Germans. These figures indicate that the "Jewish problem" is now perceived to be part of the "foreigner problem." And yet the special status of the Jews in post-Shoah Germany (a status quite different from that of the Sinti and Roma) draws such a conclusion into question. "Jews" and "foreigners" are overlapping but certainly not interchangeable categories.

The *Spiegel* poll clearly assumed that "German" and "Jew" were mutually exclusive, that the center of Jewishness in German experience lay outside of the country, in Israel, and that no Germans were in fact also Jews. The category "Jews in Germany" vanished except as the fantasy of "Germans" about "Jews." Thus the very study that documented the attitudes of Germans towards the idea of the Jew replicated the real Jew's invisibility in Germany.

If it is important to criticize such a construction of "German" separate from "Jew," the question remains, who or what is a Jew in Germany? For the traditional and legal definition of the "Jew" as someone who belongs to the established state-defined religious structure and pays taxes for its support is not sufficient. Indeed, the undermining of "religious" definitions of the Jew in Germany (and recently in the United States) by those who ask whether a strictly religious definition does not exclude many individuals who desire to be understood as Jews (but wish to or must stand beyond religious authority) is well underway. The nineteenth-century "German of the Mosaic Persuasion" gave way after the Shoah to the image of the "Jew in Germany." This latter was bound, however, to older notions of Judaism as solely a religion, in opposition to the Nazi view of Jewishness as a purely racial category. Today, secularized Jews, liberal Jews, neo-Orthodox Jews, cultural Jews, Jews whose parentage puts them beyond the pale of religious definition, all claim the title "Jew." In this case, the Jewish Diaspora has become more and more "normal," looking like the Jewish Diaspora in other Western cultures. And yet the special history of the Jews in Germany marks this normalization as fraught with tensions on all sides. The negative attitude of "Germans" toward "Jews" is measured in the aggressivity of the anti-Semites, and their actions evoke memories of the Shoah for all Jews in Germany.

Ironically, the demand by many Jews that they be heard on their own terms contrasts with the current shift in emphasis in some intellectual circles to depict Germans as sufferers for whom the recognition of their victim status is overdue, such as in the recent surge of films depicting the deaths of German soldiers at Stalingrad. The demand by some Germans that the soldiers' remains be given a proper burial on site in the surroundings of the former city of Stalingrad represents a desire for overcoming missed mourning. The obsession with the scenes of burial runs parallel to an explosion in events commemorating the victims of the Shoah. The dubious conflation of the very different experiences has, as yet, not been fully analyzed. Consequently, the reemergence of Jewish culture in Germany must be seen within the contexts of unification and of many "German" German's redefinition of what Germanness means to them. The essays presented here by no means converge to a consensus about the possibility of a vital Jewish culture in Germany. Rather they begin a dialogue among scholars and writers that will hopefully encourage others to continue the dialogue and to take concrete action against a return to heightened racial and cultural conflict.

As this volume goes to press, the situation in Germany appears to be worsening. As the human rights guaranteed by the German constitution are reduced and the attacks by right-wing youths against foreigners continue, we must ask ourselves, as Peck does in his contribution: How do we carry this dialogue from the halls of universities and the pages of books to the halls of the German parliament and to the streets of Mölln, Hünxe, Rostock, and Solingen, not to mention Frankfurt, Hamburg, Berlin, and Dresden?

Note

1. The conference was held at Cornell University on March 6–7, 1993. It was organized and coordinated by Sander L. Gilman under the auspices of the Institute for European Studies and was sponsored by that Institute, and by the German Academic Exchange Service, the Goethe House, the Department of German Studies at Cornell University, and the Institute for German Cultural Studies.

PART ONE

Jewish Life in Germany

1. The Contemporary German Fascination for Things Jewish: Toward a Minor Jewish Culture

Jack Zipes

Given the outbreak of violent xenophobia and virulent anti-Semitism in Germany during the past several years, it would seem almost inconceivable that there could also be signs of a Jewish culture that is once again firmly entrenched in Germany, and that Germans are exhibiting a fascination for all things Jewish. Yet as Ian Buruma reported last summer in the *New York Review of Books*, there can be no doubt about it:

> If West German consumerism was reflected in such things as the *Freßwelle*, literally the wave of gluttony, and the *Sexwelle*, which speaks for itself, *Betroffenheit* has resulted of late in a wave of interest in Jewish matters, especially in Berlin, and most especially among young people. The sections on Judaica in German book shops are expanding all the time. In one average week of watching German television, I saw a program on historical Jewish communities in Europe, two programs on aspects of the Holocaust, a report on Jews returning to Germany, and several documentaries about Jewish artists and intellectuals. The biggest exhibition in Berlin this year was on the history of Jewish culture, accompanied by a festival of old Yiddish films.[1]

Buruma argues that the booming German interest in things Jewish is connected to the provincialism and guilt feelings of the Germans. Jews represent both cosmopolitanism and victimization, and depending on their particular reasons, Germans seek to identify with them to transcend their provincial mind-sets and their leftover guilt for the Holocaust. Though there may be some truth to Buruma's assertions, he makes it appear that the German fascination for Jews is entirely new and that Jews in Germany are somewhat passive with respect to this vogue, as if the Germans were digging up Jews in a wave of commodified nostalgia.

The fact is that this is not the first time that Germans have demonstrated great interest in Jewish culture and self-recrimination vis-à-vis the Holocaust. There have been periodic waves of demonstrable German concern and interest as early as 1961 during the year of the Eichmann trial, in 1967 during the Seven Day War, and in 1979 during the national telecast of the American film *Holocaust* to name but a few examples. What is perhaps different today—and what Buruma does not discuss—is that German Jews themselves are stimulating this interest and defining themselves in a way that they had not done in the immediate postwar years. Moreover, Buruma's perspective on how Germans relate to Jews is very much reminiscent of the traditional German approach to the "Jewish Question" in Germany: Jews are defined and seen through a German lens and placed in a German context. Yet Jews have themselves developed an alluring if not fertile "minor" culture of their own in Germany that enables them to view themselves in a much different light than do Germans (and Buruma for that matter) and to unsettle the major German culture in a way that enriches it.

Perhaps there's the reason for the German attraction and fascination.

But I am not really interested in why Germans are attracted to things Jewish. Rather, I want to focus on the resurgence of Jewish culture in Germany as a "minor" culture that has compelled the attention of Germans during the past fifteen years and altered their views of Jewishness and themselves and perhaps has laid the groundwork for a different kind of relationship, not dominated by guilt and certainly opposed to the anti-Semitism and xenophobia exhibited by a small minority of Germans today. By no means do I want to minimize the present danger of the radical right in Germany that threatens Jewish culture or the fear expressed by many Jews living in Germany, who may eventually emigrate; but I do believe that there has been a remarkable shift and re-emergence of Jewish culture in Germany during the past ten years that has to be taken into account if one wants to talk about the fascination of Germans for things Jewish.

In order to provide background for my remarks about the significance of Jewish culture, I want to briefly summarize some of the more recent German Jewish cultural developments with an emphasis on the last four years. Then I want to explore the usefulness of Gilles Deleuze and Félix Guattari's notion of a "minor literature" for grasping the impact of Jewish culture as a minor culture in Germany. Finally, I propose to examine several works by Jews as examples of Jewish minor culture that reveal an insistent demand by Jews to define their problematical role in Germany. Here I shall focus on novels by Rafael Seligmann, Esther Dischereit, and Barbara Hongimann; a collection of short stories by Katja Behrens; George Tabori's play *Weisman und Rotgesicht* (1991); Sally Perel's autobiographical book, *Ich war Hitlerjunge Salomon* (1992); and the film *Europa, Europa,* based on Perel's autobiography.

Recent Cultural Developments

Up until the showing of the American television film *Holocaust* in 1979, German Jews had not made their presence felt in either West or East Germany. This is not to say that Jewish culture did not exist. (In fact, I shall argue that Jewish culture was never destroyed in Germany even during the Nazi period.) But there had been an unspoken understanding among Jews and between Jews and Germans that it would be best to keep silent and blend in with the rest of the population, not to arouse attention. Moreover, for many of the Jews in Germany, the German language was not their native tongue. Germany was their adopted country, generally not by choice, and therefore, it was difficult for Jews to express their needs and assume that they would be understood, since they did not understand the German culture and lived in fear of the Germans, who were, in their minds, potential

Nazis. Only in emergencies were Jews expected to speak out and then mainly through the official channel of the Central Council of Jews. Even here Jews were expected to speak about political problems or about the Holocaust. No one expected or asked Jews to play a cultural role in Germany, and especially not the way they had played this role during the 1920s.

Consequently, when it came to the Jewish contribution to German culture in the postwar years, most of the attention in the public sphere was paid to dead Jews.[2] All those numerous publications, radio shows, and television programs about German Jews concerned the great gap caused by the destruction of Jewish culture during the Nazi period. It seemed that the deader the Jews, the more Germans could exhibit their interest in Jewish culture. Living Jews tended to be ignored. Of course there were exceptions when poets such as Paul Celan, Nelly Sachs, and Hilde Domin were discussed, but they did not live in Germany and were like relics. Nor was Peter Weiss really considered German or Jewish. Writers such as Manès Sperber, Jakov Lind, Wolfgang Hildesheimer, and Edgar Hilsenrath were also outsiders. From 1945–80, it appeared that there was no such thing as a true German Jewish culture any more. Germans paid homage to dead Jews, émigrés, outsiders, or exceptions.

All this began to change in 1980, when younger Jews in Germany began to speak out on different political and cultural fronts. In my opinion, the catalyst was the television film *Holocaust*, which created an immense but brief moment of national trauma, confrontation with the Nazi past, and new questions about Jews and anti-Semitism. But more important with regard to the formation of Jewish culture, this event coincided with the coming of age of two generations of Jews born after 1945 who began asserting themselves in public and raising questions about their identities as Jews and Germans.[3] Two important works mark a new Jewish consciousness and the onset of a more vigorous appearance of Jewish culture in Germany: *Fremd im eigenen Land* (1979), edited by Henryk M. Broder and Michel Lang and *Dies ist nicht mein Land—Eine Jüdin verläßt die Bundesrepublik* (1980), by Lea Fleischmann. Ironically, although these books dealt with the alienation that numerous Jews felt in Germany and their rejection of Germany, they also represented a commitment to Germany—a declaration that there were *live* Jews in Germany who wanted to be known for who they were and what they were doing. Concurrently with the rise of Jewish consciousness in the public sphere, there was also a noticeable if not profound growth of German nationalism and reassessment of the Nazi past during the 1980s.

If we look back at the decade 1980–90 with a focus on the cultural and political relations between Germans and Jews, it is clear that the rise of German nationalism and Jewish consciousness are very much related, and that Germans and Jews have never been as active and concerned in the post-Auschwitz era to identify themselves via the other as they have been during this decade. The key events for Jews in Germany have been the Israeli invasion of Lebanon, the Fassbinder scandal, the Bitburg affair, the *Historiker-Debatte*, the collapse of the Berlin Wall in 1989, the unification of Germany in March 1990, and the increase of anti-Semitism during the 1980s and the early 1990s. Whether religious or secular, Jews have become more and more visible during this decade in their endeavors to enunciate for themselves who they are, where they are, and how they position themselves in regard to all the debates in Germany. In this regard, as the hero in Rafael Seligmann's novel *Die jiddische Mamme* discovers and announces to his own dismay, Jews in Germany are very much German Jews: their cultural productivity and identities are stamped deeply by how they relate to Germany, and how Germans relate to themselves and the rest of the world.

Jews are very much alive in Germany as German Jews, and their cultural contribution to Germany during the last five years indicates that they are not about to abandon their commitment to Germany, even if they live in fear. In fact, most of their efforts are intended to direct Germans' attention, despite the xenophobia, to the fact that Jews are part of Germany's present history. To accomplish this, they are active in numerous cultural domains. For instance, there has been a noticeable upsurge in the number of novels and stories published by Jewish writers during the last five years. Among the more important works are: *Amanda herzlos* (1992) by Jurek Becker, *Wenn ich einmal reich und tot bin* (1990) by

Maxim Biller, *Joëmis Tisch* (1988) and *Merryn* (1992) by Esther Dischereit, *Eine Liebe aus nichts* (1991) by Barbara Honigmann, and *Rubinsteins Versteigerung* (1989) and *Die jiddische Mamme* (1990) by Rafael Seligmann. Two young poets have also made names for themselves: Matthias Hermann (*72 Buchstaben*, 1989) and Helena Janeczek (*Ins Freie*, 1989). Jurek Becker adapted his 1986 novel *Bronsteins Kinder* for the screen, and the film appeared during the summer of 1992. Perhaps the most important Jewish film in the last two years was *Hitlerjunge Salomon,* also called *Europa, Europa* (1991), that caused an international controversy because it was not considered sufficiently "German" by the German Export Film Union to be nominated for an Oscar. Other less controversial films were such telecasts as *Hier wollen wir leben* (1989) by Bernd Günzel and *Juden in Deutschland* (1989) by Jürgen Martin Müller, documentaries that depict how Jews currently endeavor to integrate themselves in Germany while dealing with anti-Semitism and the Nazi past. Theater productions by Jewish playwrights are less concerned with documentation than with problems of identity and stigmatization. Here George Tabori's recent dramas, *Weisman und Rotgesicht* (1990) and *Goldberg-Variationen* (1991), as well as the Dutch playwright Judith Herzberg's *Leas Hochzeit* (1991), have commanded critical attention.

However, it is not only through literature, film, and theater that Jews have made their mark on German culture. Throughout the newly expanded German nation, Jews and Germans have created monuments and plaques that are intended to remind Germans that Jews are part of German history, and that German history calls for assuming responsibility for the Holocaust.[4] There are also new Jewish gathering places for Jews and Germans such as restaurants and bookstores in Munich and Berlin specializing in Judaica. The Jüdischer Verlag at Suhrkamp, Bleicher, Fourier, Dvorah, and other publishing houses have made major efforts to sponsor books on Jewish themes and to support Jewish authors. Journals and magazines such as *Babylon* and *Semittimes* have provided outlets for scholarly studies and critical journalism. Most of the major Jewish congregations have established active Jewish cultural programs, and the Jewish museums in Frankfurt and Berlin have been responsible for some of the more important exhibits dealing with Jewish themes during the last five years. Two of the most important ones were in Berlin: "Jüdische Lebenswelten"[5] held at the Martin-Gropius-Bau from January 12 to April 26, 1992, and "Geschlossene Vorstellung. Der jüdische Kulturbund in Deutschland 1933–1941,"[6] held at the Akademie der Künste from January 27 to April 26, 1992. In addition to the exhibits there have been significant conferences such as the "Jüdische Identität im Spiegel der Literatur vor und nach Auschwitz" held at the Evangelische Akademie Hofgeismar from November 18 to 20, 1988,[7] and "Junge Juden in Deutschland" held in Munich from June 15 to 17, 1992.[8] Chairs for Jewish studies and literature have been established at universities in Aachen and Berlin, and in light of the increase of anti-Semitism and the interest in Jewish matters, Jewish critics such as Ralph Giordano, Henryk Broder, Micha Brumlik, Dan Diner, and others continue to publish books that deal with the questionable aspects of German nationalism and philo-Semitism that have a great bearing on how Jews determine their relationship to Germany.

Given all the recent cultural productivity by German Jews and the interest shown by Germans in things Jewish, how can one define this relationship? Do Jews operate on the margins of German culture? Do Germans like to relate to Jews and keep Jews in Germany because they are their alibis to the rest of the world and testify that Germans are no longer anti-Semitic? There is that significant German expression *Alibijude*, the "alibi Jew" who serves philo-Semitically to legitimate the government despite its feeble endeavors to deal with anti-Semitism and racism. Some critics like Frank Stern and Henryk Broder believe that the "good days" of German philo-Semitism are past and that a new era of overt anti-Semitism has returned to Germany. Whatever the case may be, the cultural role of Jews in Germany has yet to be clearly defined.

The Jewish Minor Culture

In their book, *Kafka: Toward a Minor Literature*, Deleuze and Guattari argue that "a minor literature doesn't come from a minor language; it is rather that which a minority constructs within a major language."[9] There are three characteristics of a minor literature: (1) the deterritorialization of language; (2) the connection of the individual to a political immediacy; and (3) the collective assemblage of enunciation. By deterritorialization of language they mean the impossibility of a minority such as the Jews to write in the language of the masses because they are cut off from them. Excluded from the majority, the minority invents an artificial or deterritorialized language for unusual and minor uses. Deterritorialization is thus a line of flight from the unity of the dominant language or culture enabling the formation of what Deleuze and Guattari call rhizomes or multiplicities. The line of flight or deterritorialization determines the political aspect of the minor literature that must operate within a cramped space. Whereas major literature can assume social understanding and acceptance by the majority of people in a particular nation, the minor literature cannot connect automatically to the social milieu and takes flight, raising questions that call for links to commerce, economics, bureaucracy, and the law. In this regard, the individual concern of minor literature assumes a collective value. As Deleuze and Guattari explain:

> Precisely because talent isn't abundant in a minor literature, there are no possibilities for an individuated enunciation that would belong to this or that 'master' and that could be separated from a collective enunciation. Indeed, scarcity of talent is in fact beneficial and allows the conception of something other than a literature of masters; what each author says individually already constitutes a common action, and what he or she says or does is necessarily political, even if others aren't in agreement. The political domain has contaminated every statement [*énoncé*]. . . . It is literature that produces an active solidarity in spite of skepticism; and if the writer is in the margins or completely outside his or her fragile community, this situation allows the writer all the more the possibility to express another possible community and to forge the means for another consciousness and another sensibility.[10]

What makes Jews in Germany definable as German Jews is their cultivation and use of minor literature and language to distinguish themselves as other than Germans and to express the possibility for other kinds of community. From the beginning, that is from the Middle Ages, or from that other historical demarcation, from the Shoah, Jews in Germany have lived in a language that is not their own. They have lived encircled and inscribed by values, norms, and laws that have not been of their own making, and Jewish culture as a minor culture has been compelled to be the unmaking of German culture. Unmaking as deterritorialization, and deterritorialization as minor culture—hence the Jewish threat, a real threat, always a threat to the dominant German culture.

Yet this Jewish threat is not one of destruction but one of enrichment, transformation, and creation, as is every threat posed to the constants of the majority by a minority. The unmaking or deterritorializing of a major culture is an unsettling creative act, for it involves tearing down hierarchies, questioning power, and producing greater possibilities for understanding and communication that speak to the needs of different groups within the major culture. Minority culture by its very situation contains seeds of revolution, but it is not necessarily revolutionary.

Nor is it minor literature alone that must be examined to understand the manner in which a minority inscribes and defines itself within the majority culture. Rather, we must expand Deleuze and Guattari's notions and investigate the minor, minority, or minoritarian culture itself as a whole, not as a homogeneous whole, but as an assemblage of transformative forces that seeks to question, undo, disassemble the training that gives people habits and makes them obey laws. The minority culture does not and cannot totally undermine the majority culture. However, it does draw lines from beneath the majority culture and redraws lines that enunciate and articulate the disparate needs of the minority. Here it is important to bear in mind the sociohistorical context of each minority culture to understand its specificity, for there is a danger that one might fall into a "postmodernist trap" of universalizing all minorities through abstraction. Therefore, in studying such a minority culture as Jewish culture in Germany, it is important to see how it historically reacts against German culture and also keeps alive the utopian component of culture in general. Deleuze has stated that culture endows consciousness with memory opposed to the faculty of forgetting. This memory enables humans to recall words and promises, especially commitments made to the future. "This is precisely the selective object of culture: forming a man capable of promising and thus making use of the future, a free and powerful man. Only such a man is active; he acts his reactions, everything in him is active or acted. The faculty of promising is the effect of culture as the activity of man on man; the man who can promise is the product of culture as species activity."[11]

It is especially through the acting of reactions that Jews have defined Jewish minority culture in Germany. As an example, let us briefly regard the situation of Jewish minority culture in Germany after 1945. In the formative years, 1945–65, most Jews who decided to remain or settle in Germany did not speak German as their native tongue, but German was to be their common language, if they were to be accepted by the majority. At home, among themselves, they spoke Yiddish, Hebrew, Polish, Russian, Hungarian, and so on, and if they spoke German it was to become German as a minoritarian. What distinguished them as "German" Jews was the fact that they as the persecuted voluntarily made their home in the country of their persecutors. And even if it was not decidedly voluntary, the question they asked themselves and the question that was asked by others including their children was: How could they live and speak German in the country of their executioners? Jewish culture in Germany after 1945 became distinguished from other Jewish minority cultures in the world by a question mark, reacting to the dominant German culture with a stutter, and reacting to the world outside, but also to the promise of culture, with a stammer.

But the question mark and stutter alone were not the decisive factor for Jews in Germany. The Jews had first to be reterritorialized so that they could deterritorialize and reconceptualize what it meant to be Jewish in Germany in order to be anarchic agents. That is, they had to form congregations, establish connections among themselves, stake out their territory within the major culture or have it staked out for them, so they could function as a minority. The Jews had to draw lines between themselves, the religious and the secular; the Eastern European Jews (mainly Polish, Hungarian, Czech, and Russian), the Iranian Jews, the Israelis, and of course the "authentic German"

Jews; the radicals, conservatives, and the liberals. As the Central Council of Jews gradually assumed the role of official mouthpiece for the registered Jews in Germany, mainly those Jews organized in congregations, Jewish minor culture continued to stamp itself within as a question mark—What are we doing here in Germany as Jews?—but it also raised other questions within the major German culture: Why wasn't the Nazi past being confronted in all its aspects? Why did anti-Semitism and racism still exist in Germany? How could Germans be proud of being German? Why was there such authoritarianism in Germany? How was the German language used to maintain authoritarianism? In short, the Jewish minority culture asked, "Was heißt deutsch?" What does it mean to be German?

Yet the existence of the Jewish minority culture and its development was not a destabilizing element in Germany; it was used to legitimate the majority culture because the official Jewish agencies respected the boundaries of decorum and entered into compromises that compelled many Jews to be compromised, whether they liked it or not. A minority is not the direct opposite of the majority; it is not defined by its official function. It is not defined by the outside. It cannot be discussed in binary terms. As Deleuze and Guattari explain:

> Minorities, of course, are objectively definable states, states of language, ethnicity, or sex with their own ghetto territorialities, but they must also be thought of as seeds, crystals of becoming whose value is to trigger uncontrollable movements and deterritorializations of the mean or majority. . . . There is a universal figure of minoritarian consciousness as the becoming of everybody, and that becoming is creation. One does not attain it by acquiring the majority. The figure to which we are referring is continuous variation, as an amplitude that continually oversteps the representative threshold of the majoritarian standard, by excess or default. In erecting the figure of a universal minoritarian consciousness, one addresses powers [*puissances*] of becoming that belong to a different realm from that of Power [*Pouvoir*] and Domination. Continuous variation constitutes the becoming-minoritarian of everybody, as opposed to the majoritarian Fact of Nobody. Becoming-minoritarian as the universal figure of consciousness is called autonomy. It is certainly not by using a minor language as a dialect, by regionalizing or ghettoizing, that one becomes revolutionary; rather, by using a number of minority elements, by connecting, conjugating them, one invents a specific, unforeseen, autonomous becoming.[12]

Jewish minority culture had first to form its own ghetto territories before a "becoming-minoritarian as the universal figure of consciousness" could be developed, particularly among members of the first and second generation of Jews born in Germany. But, let there be no mistake, Jewish minority culture, even when it has become rigid and stratified, has always functioned as a rhizome. Deleuze and Guattari use this term to explain a radical system. A rhizome is a burrow, or a multiplicity, that "ceaselessly establishes connections between semiotic chains, organizations of power, and circumstances relative to the arts, sciences, and social struggles."[13] Jews in Germany have over several centuries established a rhizomatic culture that has spread, not from a single root but from the unfolding of multiplicities, or rather by subtracting the unique from the multiple that leads to the formation of a rhizome or multiplicity. The rhizome flourishes by burrowing into the major culture, and through itself as burrow, it provides shelter, supply, movement, evasion, and breakout for its members. I am speaking now of the rhizome as minority culture, as Jewish minority culture in Germany. The rhizomorphic development of Jewish culture has not been thoroughly studied, but I want to suggest that Deleuze and Guattari point a way toward grasping what has transpired in Jewish culture during the last fifty years in Germany in their analysis of the rhizome. Again, a revealing quote:

> A rhizome may be broken, shattered at a given spot, but it will start up again on one of its old lines, or on new lines. You can never get rid of ants because they form an animal rhizome that can rebound time and again after most of it has been destroyed. Every rhizome contains lines of segmentarity according to which it is stratified, territorialized, organized, signified, attributed, etc., as well as lines of deterritorialization down which it constantly flees. There is a rupture in the rhizome whenever segmentary lines explode into a line of flight, but the line of flight is part of the rhizome. These lines always tie back into one another.[14]

In the case of Jewish minority culture in Germany we can trace the lines of segmentarity and deterritorialization since 1945 by focusing on the formation of the Central Council of Jews and the congregations. We could also focus efforts of German Jewish émigrés who returned to make cultural contributions to Germany. Or we might focus on how East European Jews assimilated while trying to retain their Jewish identity. It does not matter where we start because each rhizomatic line of a minority culture will lead back into each other, make connections, and ultimately call for the becoming-minoritarian of everyone. However, historically, it is crucial to understand why, more than ever, Jewish writers are now making a more pronounced effort to use minority or minoritarian elements in their works to forge a German Jewish culture that seeks to maintain its autonomy and be a provocative force while trying to keep alive human beings whose consciousness opposes forgetting and who intervene in daily life to prevent the foreclosure of possibilities to become their own kinds of Jews within the realm of German culture and culture in general.

Case Studies of Recent German Jewish Cultural Works

Writing in the German language, writing for a German audience, writing in a German sociopolitical context, a Jewish minoritarian always writes as a German Jew. To be sure, the writing has its rhizomatic elements that distinguish it from the majority German literature, but let us not be distracted by the protests of Jews in Germany who argue morally and ontologically that they are Jews and not Germans and do not want to be associated with Germans, whether as hyphenated German-Jews or unhyphenated German Jews. Rafael Seligmann, the provocative novelist, has summed up the present dilemma of German Jews this way:

> Today, 46 years after the end of the war, one must finally decide where one has his/her identity. This is the question which stirs up most of the Jews here. I question their identity as self-chosen exiles. These people are Jews who imagine things. They profit from the Holocaust and have lost their God. Most of them define themselves through reference to the Holocaust. In place of God anti-Semitism becomes a replacement. That is terribly sad. I won't let the sentence "I am a German Jew" be divided. Besides I feel that I am a better German than Mr. Schönhuber.[15]

Indeed, it is the problematic nature of German Jewish identity that distinguishes the Jewish culture in Germany from American Jewish culture, or Israeli Jewish culture. The deep, cutting question for all German Jews is how and why they continue to live in the land of their murderers. This question, however, has not prevented them from making connections among themselves and to the majority German culture, and it is actually the most productive component of the minority Jewish culture in Germany, for it gives rise to what Deleuze and Guattari call "nomad thought," which "does not immure itself in the edifice of an ordered interiority; it moves freely in an element of exteriority. It does not repose on identity; it rides difference. It does not respect the artificial division between the three domains of representation, subject, concept, and being; it replaces restrictive analogy with a conductivity that knows no bounds."[16]

Nomadic thought explodes the oneness of identity but not in a destructive manner. Rather, it breaks down barriers so that the mind and body can wander and create their own space and margins, forcing others to redefine themselves. It is the potential for re-formation and re-arrangement that makes nomadic thought so exciting and adventurous. Through such movement heterogeneous elements can come together in a new way, undermining traditional hierarchical power relations, suggesting modes of behavior, and respecting the multiplicity of elements.

Nomadic thought is engendered by nomadic experience and, in turn, produces different kinds of nomadic writing. Not all Jewish writing is nomadic, nor is all Jewish writing minoritarian. This distinction is important to bear in mind if one wants to do justice to the categories of Deleuze and Guattari, who seek to uncover and elaborate the revolutionary potential of minor literature and the strategies developed by minoritarian writers such as Kafka. However, if one abides too strictly by the notions of subversion and revolution developed by Deleuze and Guattari, then there are very few minority writers whom one might call minoritarian. And certainly, as a whole, Jewish culture in Germany is not minoritarian in a revolutionary sense. Therefore, it is necessary to qualify and modify Deleuze and Guattari's categories in order to grasp the significance of Jewish culture as a minor culture in Germany. In particular, the deterritorializing of German Jewish writers, artists, and intellectuals exhibits two dominant strains of nomadic activity: (1) the playful, provocative rearrangement of majority cultural constants that is not radical in its questioning but suggests readjustment; (2) the anarchic intervention in the majority culture that is self-reflective, and exhibits an emancipatory urgency by speaking for change in the name of oppressed others without an announced telos. Obviously, the deterritorializing line that one can trace in German Jewish cultural artifacts will vary depending on the position the individual writer/artist assumes vis-à-vis German culture and Jewish culture. However, by virtue of Jewish experience and culture in Germany, there is a strong tendency for most Jewish writers to adopt some kind of a nomadic attitude toward the majority German culture, and this nomadic aspect has become more and more pronounced and discernible during the past ten years. It assumes a minoritarian reaction with different degrees of deterritorializing play and radical expression, and I should now like to depict some of the *different* products of nomadic Jewish writing in Germany today that may in part account for the German fascination for things Jewish.

Among the prose fiction writers, Rafael Seligmann has been the most prominent during the last five years. His two novels, *Rubinsteins Versteigerung* (1989) and *Die jiddische Mamme* (1990), as well as his collection of essays about Germans, Jews, and Israelis, *Mit beschränkter Hoffnung* (1991), concern the predicament of young Jews, forced to live in what their parents call "Naziland" and unable to establish deep ties to Israel. For instance, *Die jiddische Mamme* is written in the first person by the forty-year-old Samy Goldmann, whose Israeli wife has just left him. Goldmann recapitulates the major incidents of his life that led his wife to abandon him, and it becomes apparent that he has felt like a pawn in his mother Bella's hands. From his viewpoint, his mother has constantly interfered in his relations with other women. After fleeing both his mother and his gentile girlfriend Karin in Munich, Samy goes to Israel, where he has one affair after another. However, he cannot escape his mother, who eventually arranges a marriage with Sara, a Sephardic Jew, who had consistently promised that she never had any intention of marrying him. Try as he might, there is nothing Samy can do against the united forces of his mother, aunt, and Israeli girlfriend. Ironically, after he returns to Munich with Sara and has children with her, she deserts him, and Samy is left feeling like a Diaspora Jew.

What is interesting about Seligmann's novel is the sense of wandering that he conveys that sends his protagonist on a trajectory that exposes his own self-destructive bond to his mother and the manipulation of German-Jewish/Israeli symbiotic forces that keep him in an infantile dependent state. Samy's promiscuous adventures with women and his flights back and forth between Germany and Israel derive from an ambivalent desire to attain a secure identity as Jew and to break the bonds to his overbearing Jewish mother, who wants to define his life for him. Ironically, Samy is abandoned at a point when he should be most settled and defined. But Seligmann suggests that there never will be a time when a German Jew can be settled. Moreover, if Seligmann exposes social and familial manipulation, then it is not so much German as it is Jewish. Similar to many of the protagonists in the works of Saul Bellow, Bernard Malamud, and Phillip Roth, Samy is a dangling Jew, whose quest for certitude and affirmation as a Jew will never be resolved. As he describes his first traumatic childhood experience with his mother, it appears that he will lie lost in darkness.

Whether Seligmann's novel is an accurate or profound depiction of the plight of German Jews is, for my analysis, a moot point. What is significant is the unsettling nature of *both* of Seligmann's novels, that is, the provocative narrative strategies he develops, for he challenges both Jews and Germans to reflect upon the manner in which they have tried to contain Jewish identity. In doing this he touches on the key motifs of Jewish nomadic writing: lost in darkness, wandering, searching, dangling, distressing, surviving at the margins.

These motifs are readily identifiable in the works of Katja Behrens, Esther Dischereit, and Barbara Honigmann. In her remarkable short story, "Nach innen ausgewandert," Behrens also employs a first-person narrator who describes her bewildering and disturbing experiences during her childhood when her mother and grandmother "collaborated" to deny their Jewishness for fear that the narrator as young girl would be harmed. Yet this denial, based on deep anxiety, sets the stage for the continual isolation of three generations of Jewish women who will remain stigmatized throughout their lives. Behrens reveals through the autobiographical narrative how the narrator is gradually alienated from both the German society and her own mother and grandmother. The only place and space to which she can move is within herself. And still the final scene of the story reflects a certain defiance on the part of the grandmother, who refuses to be branded by the Germans. Such refusal is at the basis of the reminiscence of the narrator, who seeks to reconstruct her identity by recalling how and why she went through such a stigmatized childhood.

Behrens's narrator appears as if she can reassemble herself paradoxically as that which she is not. In other words, her Jewish identity is *not* what Germans believe it is, nor is it what her mother and grandmother have tried to keep from her. It is formed through the narrative itself that challenges the expectations and categories of the reader. Such a strategy is also used by Esther Dischereit in her novel *Merryn* (1992), where she pursues it to its utmost limits. Constituted by complex and at times obscure fragments, Dischereit's narrative depicts the flight of a sixteen-year-old girl who wanders in France and Germany and takes jobs in a bar and printing company. Along the way she is continually confronted by men who exploit her and women who have been abused. Eventually she arrives in Berlin, where her grandparents had been sent to a concentration camp, and this place symbolically represents a cruel destination if not destiny, though it is not clear what will happen to Merryn. Torn apart by the indifference and brutality that she has experienced and witnessed, she writes: "The world is made up of small, prickly black hedgehogs who have tucked in their heads and tails for most of their lives. What good does it do to be humanitarian? Anything humanitarian suffers, cannot stop suffering. And yet the realm of the world is an open sea that is only waiting for reconnaissance and holds the answer in itself. Who wants to be boatswain? The answer; wouldn't it tear the questioner into the abyss of the black gullet? Thus we are left to splash about superficially on the banks. . . . and to smother a questioner in the roar of the surf" (115–16).

For Dischereit, the landscape for a young Jewish girl is bleak. There is no family, no community, no love. Left to her own, she is a survivor who, similar to Behrens's protagonist, has no place to go but to withdraw into herself.

The destination of Barbara Honigmann's narrator in *Eine Liebe aus nichts* (1991) is Paris, where she hopes to begin a new life. However, when her father dies and she has to return to Weimar for the burial, she too is compelled to realize that there is little hope for her future. The death causes the narrator to reflect upon her parents' lives, and how they as Jews had returned to East Germany after the war with the hope that they would contribute to a new beginning, only to be disillusioned. She finds no fulfillment in her theater work in East Germany, and her life appears to be nothing but an extension of their disillusionment, since her prospects in Paris are not very good. On her way back to Paris after her father's burial, she stops in Berlin to visit familiar sites, and she comments:

> In the final hours before my train departed, I went to the places where nobody lives any longer, to the house where I had lived with my mother before she returned to Bulgaria, and to the house where I had visited my father who was living at that time with the actress. She still lives there. But just like in Paris the entire present was wiped away, and even my memory, so it seemed to me, could not really bring back the places. Suddenly, as I stood before the houses, the departing and returning and friendship and the different places of the world no longer made any sense to me, as if they all dissolved or soared into the air when I approached them, and actually you cannot know whether they are evaporating or whether you yourself are fleeing. (104–5)

Honigmann leaves her narrator on a train, in darkness, on her way back to Paris. She refuses to remain in Germany, even though there is nothing of promise awaiting in Paris. Both her parents are dead, and she is homeless. The only concrete souvenir that she carries with her is her father's diary which he had brought with him to Germany after the war, and she changes the dates of the diary so that she can use it to record her new beginnings in Paris.

It would appear that the diary might signify a hopeful end of the narrative, but Honigmann's lapidary images and stoic style are more suggestive of capsulation. Like the writings of Seligmann, Behrens, and Dischereit, she uses the first-person narrative to ward off readers, to assert her difference, to draw lines. It is interesting that all four writers do not allow their protagonists to integrate themselves into German society. They are outsiders, whose "nomadic" thought processes lead them toward confrontation because they cannot accept the limits placed on their movements and desire to know the power relations that have in part formed the parameters of their lives as Jews. In this respect, to know themselves as Jews becomes a revolutionary act of refusal.

In a different genre, namely in dramatic form, George Tabori has been performing revolutionary acts of refusal for the past twenty-five years in German and Austrian theaters. Born in Hungary in 1914, Tabori emigrated to England and then the United States in the 1940s. He first made a name for himself with *Cannibals* (1969), a controversial and macabre play about a concentration camp, performed in New York and Hamburg. Since the 1970s he has produced and directed his plays mainly in Austria and Germany, and he continually raises the question of what it means to be a Jew faced with the possibility of extermination around the next corner. Like Kafka, Tabori's answer to murder, cruelty, bigotry, and torture is humor, the Jewish humor so aptly described by Freud in his book about jokes and their relation to the unconscious. As Wolf Biermann has remarked, "Tabori has the hang of it with his Anglo-Saxon self-irony and a wicked sarcasm that, however, never crosses the deadly boundary into cynicism. We laugh prophylactically about ourselves so that no one and especially no misanthrope can mock our suffering and hurt. Yes, ours, for I, too, belonged to the desperate clowns who tear open their ribcages and at the same time arm their hearts with laughter. The stance of the Jewish joke teller does not only protect oneself from pathetic self-pity—it brings, as Hölderlin once stated, serenity itself into suffering."[17] With his "Jewish" humor and his Central European background, Tabori is a unique minoritarian dramatist in Germany, for he does not write his plays in German or in Hungarian but in English. His wife,

Ursula Grötzmacher-Tabori, translates his plays into German, and they are rarely produced in English. Tabori is immersed in German and Austrian culture, but he uses the German language to emphasize his marginal if not alien position: "And I love this language, those beautiful sighs and that dry croaking, all the dialects, especially those banned from the stage. That is, the daily, uncultivated palaver just as much as the murmuring of spring in *The Magic Mountain,* or Kafka's and Heine's moaning on their death-beds. The list is endless, and I love this language even though I have never mastered it, and that is good for the foreigner who wants to remain foreign because he can protect his third ear this way, so that he can take the words literally with the curiosity of the foreigner and can thus continually rummage about in the intestines of the language."[18]

Despite his "alien state," or his life-style as a stranger/foreigner, Tabori is not oblivious to the recent rise of anti-Semitism and xenophobia in Austria and Germany, and it may well be one of the major reasons his last several plays have dealt with issues directly related to Jewish identity and suffering. One of his most innovative dramas, *Weisman und Rotgesicht: Ein jüdischer Western* (1990), was originally written as a short story in America during the 1960s, and he did not adapt it for the stage until he felt compelled by the times to do so, as if it were a necessity and an emergency to deal with the problem of Jewish identity in a different way.[19]

Weisman und Rotgesicht is indeed different. The drama centers on Arnold Weisman and his mongoloid daughter Ruth. They are driving from California to New York City with the ashes of Weisman's wife in an urn. Her last wish was that they be spread on Riverside Drive. Somewhere in New Mexico Weisman gets lost and stops the car in the middle of the desert. A ruthless hunter comes upon them and steals the car. Forlorn and desperate, Weisman and Ruth now encounter an Indian on a mule. The Indian has apparently come to this spot to kill himself and tries to get rid of Weisman and Ruth by giving them the animal. However, once they all become engaged in a conversation about their sufferings, Weisman challenges the Indian to a verbal duel to decide who has suffered the most, with Ruth as referee.

The duel, which approaches the limits of humor, reveals how absurd is the competition about who has suffered most, while it simultaneously dismantles and exposes the cruel stereotypes of majority cultures.

Weisman: Beaten by my father, my mother,
by my brothers, teachers and rabbi,
by 3000 young blacks with bicycle chains
and a left hook by Bella.
Rotgesicht: Electro-shocked in the Klu [sic] Klux Klan clinic.
Weisman: Doesn't exist.
Rotgesicht: Exceptional case.
Ruth: Your point. Two to nothing.
Weisman: Widower.
Rotgesicht: Divorced.
Weisman: Batterer.
Rotgesicht: Drug addict.
Weisman: Almost always alone.
Rotgesicht: Always too lonely.
Weisman: Unloved.
Rotgesicht: Loved too much.
Weisman: What do you really know about the capricious unpredictability of the male sex.
Rotgesicht: Everything. Unfortunately. Exactly.
Weisman: Touché.
Ruth: Three to nothing, three breakballs.
Rotgesicht: Uncle lynched in Disneyland.
Weisman: I find your copper humor chilling.
Rotgesicht: You know what you can do with your snow-white piety.
Weisman: Aunt burned to death in Treblinka.
Rotgesicht: Open hunting season. Jews are no longer a protected species.
Weisman: It's all starting up again.
Rotgesicht: You can't make a full evening out of being a Yid anymore.[20]

At the end of the duel, it appears that the Indian will win, but then Weisman confesses how mean he has been in his life and how he had actually tried to murder Ruth at one point. The Indian concedes that Weisman deserves to win as the old man suffers a heart attack. Ruth spreads the ashes from the urn over him and covers him with rocks. Then the Indian rides off with her toward Santa Fe on his mule, but before he does this he introduces himself to her as Geegee Goldberg while she announces her name as Turteltaube. As they ride away, the sun rises.

This play is indeed a *Jewish* western, an extended ironic joke that undercuts negative stereotypes of all minorities. Instead of a lonesome hero riding off into the sunset and leaving a woman behind him, Tabori presents an Indian riding off on a mule with a mongoloid Jewish woman, and the sun is rising. Nor are they heading into the unknown horizon but toward Santa Fe, a city where "mixed breeds" might possibly have a chance of living together. In German and for German audiences, this type of Jewish play can only alienate audience expectations accustomed to Karl May and American westerns and also philo-Semitic versions of Jews and revised idealized notions of Indians. The play that leads to a verbal duel between two minority figures refereed by a handicapped Jewish woman is a rude awakening. Nobody, according to Tabori, has a monopoly on suffering, and yet it does become clear that members of minority groups are enmeshed and crippled by stereotypes created through the power controlled by the majority, symbolized by the hunter, who is behind the scene of all the action. Indians and Jews are hunted if not haunted figures, and they are compelled to take their frustrations out on one another.

There are many parallels that one can draw with the conflict in this play: Jews and blacks in the States, or blacks and Koreans; Jews and Turks in Germany; Jews and Arabs in the Middle East. The victims squabble among themselves while the victimizers remain invisible. The resolution that Tabori offers, though hilarious, is meant to be taken seriously: a *verbal* duel so that both sides can expose themselves and realize how ridiculous it is to quarrel with one another. Hilarity becomes a nomadic means of questioning majority culture and of reversing identities so that understanding between different groups can be generated.

To a certain extent, this is also the case in the film *Europa, Europa*, although the hilarity of the reversal of identities is downplayed. Based on the autobiography, *Ich war Hitlerjunge Salomon*, by Sally Perel, the question of Jewish and German identity is not only posed in a most perplexing manner by the film, but the film's own "German" or "Jewish" identity became the center of an international scandal in 1991. Produced by a German Jew, Artur Brauner, and a French Jew, Margaret Menegoz, *Europa, Europa* was written and directed by a Polish Jew, Agnieszka Holland, and the language and actors were mainly German. Due to the alleged "international" composition of the film, the German Export Film Union decided not to enter *Europa, Europa* in the competition for an Academy Award because it did not conform to the national content rule of the United States Academy of Motion Picture Arts and Sciences. Whatever the true motives of the German Export Film Union were—and I shall return to the significance of this scandal later—it is clear that the film itself is minoritarian in conception, contents, style, and production.

Holland, the director of *Bitter Harvest*, a remarkable film about anti-Semitism in Poland during World War II and the brutal abuse of power by a Polish peasant, focuses her attention in *Europa, Europa* on the power relations that determined Jewish and German identity through the fascist period in Germany. The plot of the film follows Perel's autobiography fairly closely: Perel, born in Peine near Hannover in 1925, flees with his family to Lodz in 1935 to avoid the Nazis. However, after the German invasion of Poland in 1939, Perel and his older brother are sent to Russia by his parents. After he becomes separated from his brother, he spends some time in a communist school near the Polish border and learns Russian. However, in 1941 Perel is captured by the Germans and declares himself to be a *Volksdeutscher* to avoid execution. His ruse works. In fact, it works too well, and he is eventually sent to a special school for Hitler Youth in Braunschweig, where he assumes the identity of Josef Peters, nicknamed Jupp, survives the war by showing that he can live up to Aryan expectations, and eventually leaves Germany for Israel, where he can resume being a Jew.

There are many comic and absurd situations in Perel's life, but, unlike Tabori, Holland as director shies away from emphasizing the humor in the grotesque and bizarre adventures of Sally Perel. There is nothing of the picaresque in her protagonist. Rather, he is more the perplexed survivor who wants to be the obedient Jewish son, for his parents cast him and his brother away with the commands "Geht in Frieden!" and "Ihr sollt leben!"[21] The question Holland then asks is: What is the price Sally must pay if he is to live? To keep his Jewish self alive, he must become the perfect German. This is the paradox that frames the film, and Holland chooses a documentary narrative technique to avoid any moral or psychological exploration. Though her protagonist questions himself and tries to understand what he is doing and why, these questions do not explain or rationalize his actions. Rather, they are the naive and candid questions that Perel raises in his autobiography without great self-reflection.

In his autobiography, Perel takes great pains to forgive Germans who caused him great pain. He exhibits compassion and understanding and recalls recent visits to soldiers with whom he served and to former teachers. There is, however, no sentimentality, nor does he resort to melodrama or point his finger with pathos at the Germans. Perel had kept his secret life to himself for forty years, and his narrative takes the form of a confession that does not demand forgiveness but seeks relief. It is this contemplative confessional attitude that Holland captures by depicting the episodes that lead to the reversal of identities as questions of survival. Holland focuses on the stories within the major framework so that each narrative sequence ends with the question: What would you have done in this situation? Consequently, each one of her stories confronts viewers with possibilities and choices, compelling them to ask what determines German and Jewish identity.

In many respects, Perel, both in the film and in his autobiography, belongs to a long tradition of operated Jews. As Holland shows, Perel is operated on by forces beyond his control to try to make his body conform to Aryan specifications. From the initial circumcision scene, where Sally is approvingly operated on by Jews, through the scene where he tries painfully to restore his foreskin, to the end of the film when the off-camera narrator informs us that Perel has not hesitated to circumcise his son in Israel, the Jew's body as a site of operations to demarcate what purity and beauty should be according to the majority German Aryan model is the major topical image for Holland. Perel's face in Israel at the end thus becomes a provocation to all things German, but also to all things Jewish. Therefore, it is no surprise that the film as scandal caused a scandal.

The national content rule of the U.S. Academy of Motion Picture Arts and Sciences stipulates that nationals should be the primary contributors to the artistic aspects of a film and that the film must be funded by the same national group. In the case of *Europa, Europa,* Holland's Polish nationality and the German-French production team disqualified the film as German in the opinion of the German Export Film Union. Whereas the reception of the film in the United States was generally positive, the critics in Germany were divided and also distracted by the controversial decision of the German Film Export Union. Some charged that the film was artistically mediocre, voyeuristic, and incredible, while others argued that the film was indeed of artistic merit but that it did not fit the Germans' concept of what a German should be and what the past should look like. This debate about the film's nationalism and artistic merits cannot be and has not been resolved. What is significant is the controversy itself, for it was engendered by Jewish minoritarian culture in Germany.

Europa, Europa is a cinematic representation by Jews of what it has meant to be Jewish in Germany, and perhaps, what it means to be Jewish today. To feel the threat of extermination, to become anonymous, to operate on one's body, to live in fear of being discovered as a Jew—these were and are constitutive elements of Jewish identity, and as they are brought out in the film, they are distinguished by their nomadic quality that annoyingly will not go away in Germany. Perhaps this is fundamentally why the film and the book, *Ich war Hitlerjunge Salomon,* drew so much attention in Germany and perhaps why Jewish culture as a minor culture fascinates Germans.

We are left with the question, however, whether there really is such a thing as a Jewish minor culture in the sense that Deleuze and Guattari use the word "minor." In *A Thousand Plateaus,* they maintain at one point:

> There is a Jewish specificity, immediately affirmed in a semiotic system. This semiotic, however, is no less mixed than any other. On the one hand, it is intimately related to the countersigning regime of the nomads (the Hebrews had a nomadic past, a continuing relationship with the nomadic numerical

> organization that inspired them, and their own particular becoming-nomad; their line of deterritorialization owed much to the military line of nomadic destruction). On the other hand, it has an essential relation to the signifying semiotic itself, for which the Hebrews and their God would always be nostalgic: reestablish an imperial society and integrate with it, enthrone a king like everybody else (Samuel), rebuild a temple that would finally be solid (David and Solomon, Zachariah), erect the spiral of the Tower of Babel and find the face of God again; not just bring the wandering to a halt, but overcome the diaspora, which itself exists only as a function of an ideal regathering. (122–23)

Applied to the present situation of Jews in Germany today, Deleuze and Guattari's notion of a Jewish specificity that is constituted by a mixed semiotic can be useful in understanding the cultural forces among Jews that lend them their identity. Since 1945 Jews in Germany have maintained the nomadic impulses of Jewish culture in opposing despotism, totalitarianism, authoritarianism, and stigmatization, while they have simultaneously sought to regain a sense of community through their own resurrection as Jews, whether they be religious, secular, or zionist, by distinguishing themselves from Germans. The heterogeneous elements of becoming-Jewish in Germany have contributed to a minor culture, an assemblage, that has become a taboo for Germans and that accounts for the specificity of German Jewish culture. Jews in Germany have assembled themselves amorphously and defy Germans to define them. That is, they have refused to allow Germans to define them and, therefore, want to signify nothing as a taboo. It is this signifying nothing as a taboo which signifies becoming-Jewish that compels Germans and Jews continually to confront the past, to confront the myth of the German Jewish symbiosis, and to deal with the hegemonic formation of present-day German culture that makes Jews into a *fascinum.*

A *fascinum* is a spell or enchantment that is perilous because one can become enveloped by the *fascinum* and rendered unable to resist it. To be drawn to a Jewish minoritarian culture is thus self-effacement for a German, who is identified with the power of the majority culture, and this attraction can be both exhilarating and threatening. For Jews, their own *fascinum* in Germany involves the taboo against living in Germany as a Jew and making something culturally German out of becoming Jewish in Germany.

The recent Jewish writing in Germany that I have briefly analyzed represents a *minoritarian* impulse of Jewish culture, only one of its many impulses, that emphasizes the signifying nothing as taboo. Almost all the writers—Seligmann, Tabori, Perlmann, Holland—had to learn German as a foreign language, and part of being Jewish in Germany is learning German to alienate oneself from both Jewish and German culture. Therefore, one of the trajectories of deterritorialization that can be found in Jewish writing in Germany is a movement toward simultaneous undefinition and definition of what it means to be Jewish in a different-sounding and -meaning German. It was the unique sound and meaning of Kafka's Jewish writing in Prague that drew Deleuze and Guattari to conceive and explore their notions of minor literature. Certainly, not all Jews writing in Germany today are Kafkas, or like Kafka. But Germany for Jews is like Kafka's trial and castle, and in their search for justice and God, they have certainly left traces of what can be considered a Jewish minor culture marked by and marking the indomitable force of German culture.

Notes

1. The Ways of Survival," *New York Review of Books* 39 (16 July 1992): 11. See also "Juden und Deutsche," *Spiegel Spezial* 2 (August 1992). This special issue of *Der Spiegel* contains numerous interesting articles, reports, and polls about Jews and Germans and is yet another sign of the *German* fascination in things Jewish and how, through the very title, the Germans distance themselves from Jews as Germans.
2. Cf. Sander L. Gilman, "Jewish Writers in Contemporary Germany: The Dead Author Speaks," *Inscribing the Other* (Lincoln: University of Nebraska, 1991), 249–78.
3. I have discussed this at length in "The Vicissitudes of Being Jewish in West Germany," in *Germans and Jews since the Holocaust: The Changing Situation in West Germany* (New York: Holmes & Meier, 1986), 27–49.
4. See James E. Young, "The Counter-Monument: Memory against Itself in Germany Today," *Critical Inquiry* 18 (Winter 1992): 267–96.
5. Cf. Andreas Nachama and Gereon Sievernich, eds. *Jüdische Lebenswelten. jüdisches Denken und Glauben, Leben und Arbeiten in den Kulturen der Welt* (Berliner Festspiele: Argon, 1992). This was the "Wegweiser durch die Ausstellung."

6. Cf. Akademie der Künste, ed., *Geschlossene Vorstellung. Der Jüdische Kulturbund in Deutschland 1922–1941* (Berlin: Edition Hentrich, 1992).
7. Cf. Eveline Valtink, *Jüdische Identität im Spiegel der Literatur vor und nach Auschwitz* (Hofgeismar: Evangelische Akademie Hofgeismar, 1989).
8. Cf. Ellen Presser and Bernhard Schoßig, *Junge Juden in Deutschland* (Munich: Jugend- und Kulturzentrum der Israelitischen Kultusgemeinde München, 1991).
9. Minneapolis: University of Minnesota Press, 1986, p. 16.
10. Deleuze and Guattari, *Kafka*, 17.
11. *The Deleuze Reader*, ed. Constantin V. Boundas (New York: Columbia UP, 1993), 246.
12. *A Thousand Plateaus: Capitalism and Schizophrenia.*, trans. Brian Massumi (Minneapolis: University of Minnesota Press, 1987), 106.
13. *A Thousand Plateaus*, 7.
14. *A Thousand Plateaus*, 9.
15. "Warum ich nicht in Israel lebe," *Semittimes* 4 (August/September 1992): 8. See also his recent statements in, "Die Juden leben," *Der Spiegel* (16 November 1992): 75–79. He concludes this short piece by remarking, "Jews have been a part of the German society for a thousand years. It is high time that Jews as well as non-Jews finally accept this."
16. *A Thousand Plateaus*, xii.
17. "Kultur als Waffe," *Theater heute* 11 (1992): 23.
18. "'Liebe,' Büchnerpreis-Rede, gehalten am 10. Oktober 1992 in Darmstadt," *Theater heute* 11 (1992): 21.
19. Cf. the interview with Tabori by Ursula Voss and Peter von Becker, "Solche Begegnungen habe ich mein Leben lang gefürchtet und mir gewünscht," *Theater heute* 5 (1990): 16.
20. *Theater heute* 5 (1990): 23.
21. *Ich war Hitlerjunge Salomon* (Berlin: Nicolai, 1990), 14.

Bibliography

Primary Literature

Biller, Maxim. *Wenn ich einmal reich und tot bin.* Cologne: Kiepenheuer & Witsch, 1990.

Becker, Jurek. *Bronsteins Kinder.* Frankfurt/Main: Suhrkamp, 1986.

Behrens, Katja. *Jonas.* Pfaffenweiler: Pfaffenweiler Presse, 1981.

———. *Von einem Ort zum anderen.* Pfaffenweiler: Pfaffenweiler Presse, 1987.

Dischereit, Esther. *Joëmis Tisch. Eine jüdische Geschichte.* Frankfurt/Main: Suhrkamp, 1988.

———. *Merryn.* Frankfurt/Main: Suhrkamp, 1992.

Goldschmidt, Georges-Arthur. *Die Absonderung.* Zurich: Amman, 1991.

Hermann, Matthias. *72 Buchstaben.* Frankfurt/Main: Suhrkamp, 1989.
Honigmann, Barbara. *Roman von einem Kind: Sechs Erzählungen.* Frankfurt/Main: Luchterhand, 1976.
———. *Eine Liebe aus Nichts.* Berlin: Rowohlt, 1991.
Janeczek, Helena. *Ins Freie.* Frankfurt/Main: Suhrkamp, 1989.
Lindemann, Karin. *Wege heimwärts.* Gerlingen: Bleicher, 1990.
Seligmann, Rafael. *Rubinsteins Versteigerung.* Frankfurt/Main: Eichborn, 1989.
———. *Die jiddische Mamme.* Frankfurt/Main: Eichborn, 1990.
Spies, Gerty. *Im Staube gefunden.* Munich: Kaiser, 1987.
Tabori, George. "Weisman und Rotgesicht." Trans. by Ursula Grützmacher-Tabori. *Theater heute* 5 (1990): 19–24.
———. "Die Goldberg-Variationen." Trans. by Ursula Grützmacher-Tabori. *Theater heute* 6 (1991): 34–42.

Secondary Literature

Avidan, Igal. "Sally Perel erobert Deutschland. Interview mit Salomon Perel." *Semittimes* 4 (April/May 1992): 18–21.
Becker, Peter von. "Der wüste Westen." *Theater heute* 5 (1990): 9–13.
———. "Ball der springenden Herzen: Judith Herzbergs 'Leedvermaak/Leas Hochzeit.'" *Theater heute* 5 (1991): 26–29.
———. "Liebe und Lachen—nach Auschwitz." *Theater heute* 6 (1991): 28–31.
———. "Poesie und Politik der Gefühle. Über Judith Herzberg." *Theater heute* 11 (1990): 4–6.
Biermann, Wolf. "Kultur als Waffe." *Theater heute* 11 (1992): 22–23.
Biller, Maxim. *Die Tempojahre.* Munich: dtv, 1991.
Blasius, Dirk, and Dan Diner, eds. *Zerbrochene Geschichte: Leben und Selbstverständnis der Juden in Deutschland.* Frankfurt/Main: Fischer, 1991.
Boundas, Constantin V., ed. *The Deleuze Reader.* New York: Columbia University Press, 1993.
Broder, Henryk M. and Michel Lang, eds. *Fremd in eigenem Land.* Frankfurt/Main: Fischer, 1979.
Buruma, Ian. "The Ways of Survival." *The New York Review of Books* 39 (16 July 1992): 11–12.
Deleuze, Gilles and Félix Guattari. *Kafka: Toward a Minor Literature.* Trans. by Dana Polan. Minneapolis: University of Minnesota Press, 1986.
———. *A Thousand Plateaus: Capitalism and Schizophrenia.* Trans. by Brian Massumi. Minneapolis: University of Minnesota, 1987.
Diner, Dan. *Der Krieg der Erinnerungen und die Ordnung der Welt.* Berlin: Rotbuch, 1991.
Fleischmann, Lea. *Dies ist nicht mein Land: Eine Jüdin verläßt die Bundesrepublik.* Hamburg: Hofmann und Campe, 1980.
Gilbert, Jane. *Ich mußte mich vom Haß befreien. Eine Jüdin emigriert nach Deutschland.* Munich: Scherz, 1989.

Gilman, Sander L. *Inscribing the Other.* Lincoln: University of Nebraska Press, 1991.

Giordano, Ralph, ed. *"Wie kann diese Generation eigentlich noch atmen?" Briefe zu dem Buch: Die zweite Schuld oder Von der Last, Deutscher zu sein.* Munich: Knaur, 1992.

———, ed. *Deutschland und Israel: Solidarität in der Bewährung.* Gerlingen: Bleicher, 1992.

Höhfeld, Barbara. "Ein Film der Wunder." *Semittimes* 4 (April/May 1992): 69.

"Juden und Deutsche." *Spiegel Spezial* 2 (August 1992).

Kralicek, Wolfgang. "Die göttliche Komödie." *Theater heute* 8 (1991): 4–6.

Koch, Gertrud. "Corporate Identities: Zur Prosa von Dische, Biller und Seligmann." *Babylon* 7 (1990): 139–42.

Perel, Sally. *Ich war Hitlerjunge Salomon.* Berlin: Nicolai, 1992.

Nachama, Andreas, Julius H. Schoeps, and Edward van Voolen, eds. *Jüdische Lebenswelten. Essays.* Frankfurt/Main: Jüdischer Verlag, 1992.

Pierwoß, Klaus, ed. *Weisman und Rotgesicht. Programmheft 4.* Berlin: Maxim Gorki Theater, 1991.

Presser, Ellen, and Bernhard Schoßig, eds. *Junge Juden in Deutschland.* Munich: Jugend– und Kulturzentrum der Israelitischen Kultusgemeinde München, 1991.

Rabinbach, Anson and Jack Zipes, eds. *Germans and Jews since the Holocaust.* New York: Holmes & Meier, 1986.

Reich-Ranicki, Marcel. *Über Ruhestörer: Juden in der deutschen Literatur.* Stuttgart: Deutsche Verlags-Anstalt, 1989.

Seidl, Claudius. "Blamage mit Folgen: Über den Umgang mit dem Film 'Hitlerjunge Salomon.'" *Der Spiegel* 46 (26 January 1992): 177.

Seligmann, Rafael. *Mit beschränkter Hoffnung: Juden, Deutsche, Israelis.* Hamburg: Hoffmann und Campe, 1991.

———. "Warum ich nicht in Israel lebe." *Semittimes* 4 (August/September 1992): 8–10.

———. "Die Juden leben." *Der Spiegel* 46 (16 November 1992): 75–79.

Silbermann, Alphons and Herbert Sallen. *Juden in Westdeutschland. Selbstbild und Fremdbild einer Minorität.* Cologne: Verlag Wissenschaft und Politik, 1992.

Stern, Frank. "Jews in the Minds of Germans in the Postwar Period." Publication of the Robert A. and Sandra S. Borns Jewish Studies Program. Bloomington: Indiana University, 1993.

Tabori, George. "'Liebe.' Büchnerpreis-Rede, gehalten am 10. Oktober 1992 in Darmstadt." *Theater heute* 11 (1992): 21–22.

Valtink, Eveline. *Jüdische Identität im Spiegel der Literatur vor und nach Auschwitz.* Hofgeismar: Evangelische Akademie Hofgeismar, 1989.

Voss, Urusla and Peter von Becker. "'Solche Begegnungen habe ich mein Leben lang gefürchtet und mir gewünscht.' Ein Gespräch mit George Tabori." *Theater heute* 5 (1990): 16–18.

Wille, Franz. "Nathans Not." *Theater heute* 12 (1991): 2–3.

Young, James E. "The Counter-Monument: Memory against Itself in Germany Today." *Critical Inquiry* 18 (Winter 1992): 267–96.

Zipes, Jack. "The Vicissitudes of Being Jewish in West Germany." In *Germans and Jews since the Holocaust.* Ed. Anson Rabinbach and Jack Zipes. New York: Holmes & Meier, 1986.

Films

Bernd, Günther. *Hier wollen wir leben.* Munich: Aradt Film, 1989.

Hartwig, Thomas. *Nächstes Jahr in Jersualem?* Cologne: WDR International, 1986.

Holland, Anieszka. *Europa, Europa.* CCC Filmkunst, 1991.

Kawalerowicz, Jerzy. *Bronsteins Kinder.* 1992.

Müller, Jürgen. *Juden in Deutschland.* Munich: Bayrischer Rundfunk, 1989.

Ophels, Marcel. *November Tage.*

Raymon, Harry. *Sie waren unsere Nachbarn.* Munich: Eikon Film, 1987.

2. A Reemergence of German Jewry?

Y. Michal Bodemann

The idea is also ghastly—that the emigrants of today would form the new nucleus of a German Jewish culture rising from the ashes.[1]

Until two or three years ago, a textbook account of the history of postwar Jewry could be presented roughly as follows: before Nazism, over half a million Jews lived in Germany. About half of those managed to escape, a third were killed, and about 15,000 survived outside concentration camps—some in hiding, others in mixed marriages and (usually missing from the textbook account) still others were quietly protected by local Nazi potentates. Those Jews, mostly Eastern European, who survived and were liberated in the camps spent the following years as so-called displaced persons under Allied protection, on German territory. Most of these, probably over 200,000, had left the DP camps in Germany by the early fifties. Unintentionally, these camps had developed into Jewish cultural and religious centers in Germany, and even after most of the DPs had left Germany by the early 1950s, what remained of these centers influenced a new start of Jewish life in Germany. About 12,000 of these DPs remained in Germany, where they faced resentment and hostility, in the early years, from much of the surrounding population.

Forty years later, about 30,000 Jews were living in Germany—that is, Jews registered with the local communities. Most of these Jews are Eastern European, and only a small fraction are of

German Jewish origin. Documents on the grand history of two thousand years and of the traditions of the old German Jewry were to be preserved and cared for at the Leo Baeck Institute in New York. In the first years after the War, it was thought that Jewish life in Germany had come to an end, but it evolved again, despite the heterogeneity of the communities. Most of these were made up of immigrants who often came into conflict with the small German Jewish remnant that was still present there.

This textbook account, which like virtually all other contributions to the *Spiegel* special issue, omits any reference to the situation and number of Jews in East Germany, concludes with the observation by an unnamed rabbi, that the Jewish presence in Germany helps Germans to keep the memory alive. Indeed, a considerable number of Germans seem to be seeking a way to cope with feelings of guilt: "In this situation, the presence of a remnant of Israel in Germany assumes a very different perspective and meaning.... Never have I seen elsewhere such openness to Jewish thought, almost a longing for Jewish values, as today and here. In light of this development, and in the face of a newly rising anti-Semitism, Jews in Germany have a task and therefore a future here and a right to existence."[2] This is borne out by the role of the Jewish cultural centers and by the cultural and social life in the communities in which the awareness of the Holocaust, the remembrance of persecution and extermination, play a preeminent role. A further point of significance here is Germany's relationship to Israel: it is "a criterion of the condition of German-Jewish relations, a test for the possibilities of Jewish life on German soil and for the political maturity of Germans in the sense of humanism, tolerance and pluralist democracy."[3] So far, then, the textbook account that I have partly summarized, partly quoted and paraphrased, is the expert's sympathetic but dispassionate journey to German Jewry without many edges or questions—not unlike the average anthropologist's account of so many tribal groups living in the world today. It is taken from writings by the historian Wolfgang Benz, who heads the Institute for Studies of Anti-Semitism at the Technical University in Berlin; I call it a textbook account because it appears in this and similar versions in other writings by Benz and other authors, and such repeated use suggests consensus at the end of an era. This apparently definitive account, however, can no longer contain its questions and contradictions and must now be revised.

The question I would like to address here is this: In light of the deep transformations in the past three years in Germany and Europe, what is a likely scenario for the development of Jewish life in Germany in the future; in particular, is it conceivable that we will see a renaissance of German Jewish life, as the historian Sander Gilman has suggested? "The renaissance of Jewish life in Germany has already begun and in the near future it will blossom dramatically."[4] The question of a renaissance of German Jewry can be asked in two ways, and both of them shall be addressed here: first, the renaissance of German *Jewry*—Jewish life in Germany—and secondly, the renaissance of *German* Jewry—a Jewry that emphasizes its Germanness.

A Renaissance of Jewish Life in Germany?

Here, we first of all have to take a second look at the numbers. The textbook version still mentions that there are 30,000 Jews registered with Jewish communities in Germany. In light of the new Jewish immigration from the former Soviet Union, this figure is long since outdated, and moreover it is changing very quickly. The figure given by Ignatz Bubis in Israel at the beginning of 1993 was 38,000 Jews, that is, Jews registered with the Jewish communities.[5] Already one month later, Bubis had to revise the numbers again; he now spoke of 11,000 new members over the past years.[6] Using this figure, we would arrive at just over 40,000 Jews today. These quasi-official figures, as the previous official ones, include converts to Judaism, which today must be estimated in the many hundreds even though no data are available; and we may call the 38,000 or 40,000 Jews, following the suggestion of the American demographer Sidney Goldstein, the Jewish core group.[7] Since the German figures, however, unlike the figures for the United States, are based on formal synagogue membership, they exclude the proverbial German Jewish dentist and individuals of other high-income groups, whose spouses with an annual income of DM 500 are members while they themselves, with an income of DM 500,000 are not, in order avoid paying income-dependent high communal taxes. It excludes many secular Jews —for example expatriate Israelis and many others who have chosen not to register with the communities such as the *Jüdische Gruppe Berlin*, which is mostly left-wing and critical of Israeli policies towards Palestinians and German policies toward immigrants. A condition for admission to this group is that members consider themselves Jewish; they need not, however, be members of the *Jüdische Gemeinde*, or Jewish Community. Of the hundred or so people on the mailing list, about thirty to forty are not *Gemeinde* members, and its coordinating committee of five recently included two or three non-members.

The official *Gemeinde* figure mentioned above also excludes partly Jewish households and people of Jewish ancestry who do not identify themselves as Jews. To give one example of the magnitude of this: around 1990, before the new immigration, about five hundred Jews were registered with Jewish communities in East Germany; but from the number of pensions paid to "Opfer des Faschismus" (victims of fascism) of Jewish ancestry, we know that about four thousand individuals of Jewish ancestry live in the former GDR.

In light of all this: that many Jews are nonmembers or are only partly Jewish, I would estimate the total Jewish population in Germany today, including persons with at least two Jewish grandparents, at anywhere between 50,000 and 70,000; if we add to this figure non-Jews living in households with at least one Jew, and converts, which would still give an indication of possible Jewish milieux, we would probably reach the 100,000 mark. It is important to see therefore that the statistical data on Jews, as with most other ethnic groups elsewhere, are problematic: and this should also remind us again—as Jacob Katz has so nicely shown for an earlier Jewish case[8]—that ethnic boundaries are rarely sharply drawn but in continuous flux between one ethno-national group and the other.

Now, could the new influx of Jews from the former Soviet Union lead to a renewed flourishing of Jewish life in Germany? The dimensions of the influx are often based on wildly exaggerated figures. At present, the federal government distributes the Jewish immigrants throughout Germany by means of a quota that reflects the population size of the different *Länder* in question. This has brought Jews to places where there had been few Jews before: Stuttgart, for example. Since Baden-Württemberg is a populous *Land*, the community membership has almost doubled in the last three years, from 650 to 1,200. The oldtimers in this previously lingering community consider the newcomers as their "only hope," and the Stuttgart community with its Orthodox rabbi also welcomes the halachically non-Jewish relatives to all its activities without, however, wanting to convert them. Hamburg, on the other hand, already one of the larger communities in earlier times, with 1,344 members still in January 1990, had 380 additional members at the end of 1992, an increase of nearly a third. Here the administration of the community, to the chagrin of some on the community council, seems slow and reluctant to welcome the non-Jewish relatives of these new members.

In eastern Germany outside of Berlin, Jewish immigration has brought more drastic changes still. Leipzig, with a nominal and aging membership of 30, has doubled its membership to over 60; and even Chemnitz, with previously 10 Jews, has tripled its membership to 30. All these figures, however, are in constant flux. With some certainty we can state that the large majority of the new arrivals are convinced they did the right thing; only 12 to 15 percent would recommend immigration into a different country instead.[9] Forty-seven thousand applications for visas from the former Soviet Union have been or are being processed. Of these, the *Land* of Mecklenburg-Vorpommern has received a quota of 1,105 Jews—but only 155 actually entered Mecklenburg, and of these only 61 are actually resident there: where the others are is an open question, and even those actually present in Mecklenburg may also be members of a Jewish community elsewhere, for example in a community in the west, and therefore might be counted twice: neither the records of many *Gemeinden* nor those of the *Jüdische Zentralwohlfahrtsstelle* are very reliable. In Sachsen-Anhalt (Magdeburg) the situation is the reverse of that in Mecklenburg. This *Land* received a quota of 1,695 immigrants; of these, 530 entered one of the camps, but at least 900 are actually resident there. These figures, however, say very little about Jewish community membership because the individuals have received visas from German consular officials on the grounds of Jewish nationality in the former Soviet Union or because of Jewish ancestry—which is irrelevant in terms of *halacha.* Since an estimated 25 to 50 percent of the new immigrants are halachically not Jewish and a number of halachic Jews are not interested in taking out or maintaining membership in the Jewish community once they have to start paying for it, these relatively small figures have to be regarded with caution. On the other hand, however, the potential amount of migration is considerable: with the phenomenon of chain migration, and especially with further economic decline in the former Soviet Union, it can be expected that the current figures are only the beginning of a much larger Jewish immigration to Germany.

No matter how skeptically we may look at these figures, it is still apparent that there will indeed be a fundamental transformation of the Jewish community in Germany. The most apparent case here is that of Berlin. Before 1989, approximately one-half of its 6,000 Jews were of Soviet origin; they had come to Berlin since the mid-1970s. At present, the numbers have increased to over 9,000 Jews there, with many more outside the community who are halachically not Jewish and others who are but have not joined. While before 1989 some might still have wanted to overlook the important presence of Russian Jews, their presence in 1993 could no longer be ignored. In the electoral campaign for the new—and first post-Galinski—community council in March 1993, the pamphlets of the two contending groups were printed in both German and Russian; this is in clear contrast to the time when Heinz Galinski practically forbade the use of Russian in the Jewish Community Center. This bilingualism, however, has not yet taken hold of the official publications of this *Gemeinde,* such as its *Berlin Umschau,* the monthly bulletin, which is entirely in German, with at best an occasional flyer in Russian enclosed.

However, beyond mere numbers, a renaissance of Jewish life in Germany would require here as elsewhere at least three things. First of all, a repository of common cultural practices and memories; second, a degree of cohesive economic and social networks;

and third, a critical mass of individuals to form distinct Jewish milieux. This is not merely a question of numbers; it is also a question of the quality of intra-ethnic relations. While German Jewry would now count as a midsized Jewish diaspora community, until two or three years ago such a critical mass did not exist. The community was either simply too small or too heterogeneous and weak, otherwise there would have been the elaboration of such Jewish milieux and a fuller Jewish life as is found in other European diasporas. As far as the new arrivals are concerned—who after all are choosing to immigrate to Germany rather than Israel—we have to ask how people who often have had only the faintest ties to Judaism create a Jewish identity for themselves. A recent cursory analysis of a Russian newspaper for émigrés in Germany indicated that about 60 percent of its content concerned strictly Russian issues, 20 percent German themes, and only 20 percent with Jewish ones.[10] This is very different from one hundred years or so ago, when Eastern European Jews with a rich cultural Jewish heritage moved into Germany and North America. There is more cause for optimism on the second point. It has been observed that the Russian émigrés come with extremely strong family networks, which in turn might just become a vehicle for new Jewish values.[11]

What are some of the parameters of the identity of these immigrants, and how do they see their role in contrast to present-day German Jewry? In interviews conducted by Anita Kugler for *Die Tageszeitung*, one young Russian, asked why he had not emigrated to Israel, responded that with his knowledge of Yiddish, he feels much more at home in Germany than in Israel; for him, Hebrew is a foreign language. Another, in trouble with the authorities, confessed he "did not want to be anything more than a German Jew."[12] At the "Jüdische Kulturtage" (Jewish Cultural Festival) in Berlin in 1992, many hundreds of Russians packed the large hall of the *Gemeinde* for over three nights in order to hear a group from Moscow by the name of *Babylon*. While outwardly Jewish, there was little Jewish content in these dances or even in the music. Costumes portraying rabbis bore more resemblance to Russian Orthodox priests, and Jewish music such as the *Hatikvah* had an air of artificiality in contrast to the genuinely Russian pieces. As yet we have little testimony from the Russian immigrants, and no serious studies. One major document, however, is the book by Sonja Margolina, an émigré from Moscow: *Das Ende der Lügen.* This book is concerned with the role of Jews in the Russian Revolution: it asks whether Jews, although almost by necessity drawn to socialism, should not have been more restrained about their participation in the Revolution, and it attributes Soviet anti-Semitism in part to the Jews' active revolutionary role. Caught between nostalgia and resentment, Margolina plays down the severity of Russian anti-Semitism today and urges her co-nationals in Russia not to leave—her own reasons for leaving were strictly personal.

Margolina expresses a distaste for all organized Jewishness. With Isaak Deutscher, she insists that the role of the Jewish *Abtrünnige* (apostates) is itself a genuinely Jewish role (100). Moreover, she expresses contempt for organized Jewishness in Germany in particular, and for what she terms the industry of philo-Semitism. Here she also criticizes the central significance of the Holocaust for German Jewry today, and comes close to putting the Holocaust on an equal plane with the Stalinist exterminations: the ideas of Gorki, a friend of the Jews, of "biosocial hygiene" influenced Stalin in his liquidation of the kulaks, and "[t]he question is whether this history [i.e., Auschwitz] was indeed a completely different one" (71). She sees her own role, then, as that of a highly individualized free Jewish intellectual in Europe, beyond all nationalisms and tribal identities.

However, only a few Russian Jews in Germany today are intellectuals like Sonja Margolina. Many are professionals; others relish the joys of capitalism. What most of them have in common is that in contrast to present-day German Jewry, the Stalinist purges—not Auschwitz—are their primary trauma, and they are developing the patriotism of the immigrant, a phenomenon known all too well from North America: they are grateful for being able to start a new life in Germany. Some of this tone of gratitude (bitter memories notwithstanding) is expressed in a lyrical essay by a recent Jewish immigrant from Moscow in the *Frankfurter Jüdische Nachrichten.*[13] The author reminisces about her life in Moscow, remembers how for her as a little girl, "the word

'Germans' was synonymous with horror and death"—but how she came to realize later that not all Germans were bad, that among communists "there were genuine fascists as well," and that together with her aunt and uncle, innocent young Germans (even German soldiers) of the same age also died in a mad war of destruction. In Frankfurt, she writes, the memory of Katyn and of her hometown Minsk will be kept alive, with deep sadness; on the other hand, "everyday everything becomes more familiar to me. . . . [Frankfurt] has ceased to be a landscape running past the window, without associations and sympathies. This city is now my city." Younger Russian Jews agree, as in this statement in the Berlin Youth magazine *Ha-Ikar*: "Even though we have come into a country of which we were more afraid than of any other, we now have found affection for this new home. Germany has received us very well. I don't believe any other country could give us more. For all of us, conditions have been created which make us feel like citizens of this land."[14] Another writer asks "why chancellor Kohl always speaks of Jewish fellow citizens, and not of Germans of Jewish faith."[15]

It is my contention that an appropriate parallel to the new Russian Jewish influx is that of German Jewish émigrés to North America in the 1930s. For the most part, German Jews were estranged from Jewish traditions, and numerous anecdotes caricature the deeply German identity of these Jews. Especially in view of their rich heritage, I would argue that these Jews have contributed astonishingly little to Jewish life in North America and even in the second and third generations appear to be rather marginal to Jewish communal life. So too the Russian Jews in Germany. They are not a homogeneous group by any means of course, but the majority are far removed from Jewish traditions, and they are unlikely to contribute greatly to new flourishing Jewish life in Germany, certainly not in the generation of the immigrants. Nevertheless, the Central Council of Jews in Germany and its social service organization (*ZWST*) have spared no effort to integrate these Jews into the communities, helping them with jobs, apartments, and immigration. But the memories and cultural traditions of this group, even where they nominally identify as Jews, are far more Russian than Jewish, and the

Jewish organizations have apparently not yet realized that under the umbrella of the Jewish community a new Russian ethnic community in Jewish disguise has been taking shape in Germany. There will be some net benefit to Jewish life in Germany in the long run, and clearly an "invention of tradition" in some segments of these immigrants; but the lack of previous communal organization back home and their warden like dependency on the supermarket of services from the Jewish community are unlikely to generate autonomous Jewish identity.

A New German Jewish Identity?

I would now like to address the second question, that of a rebirth of a particularly German Jewish identity roughly equivalent to that in existence before 1933. Axel Azzola a professor of law and a legal counsel on immigration and citizenship issues to the *Zentralrat*, recently argued in an interview with *taz* journalist Anita Kugler that the Russian émigrés are young and to an altogether astonishing degree willing to assimilate. With these émigrés, there could begin to exist again, if not in this generation, then in the next, a German Jewry. And that brought Germany many advantages in the past.[16] Here we have to return once again to our textbook account of the history of German Jewry—more precisely, West German Jewry. This account states that there is hardly any continuity between prewar and postwar Jewries, and indeed it is unquestionable that the vast majority of present-day Jewry is religiously and culturally Eastern European, with only a small fraction of descendants of prewar German Jewish stock living there today. The Eastern European Jews who were stranded in Germany have shaped the character of the Jewish community. What I have called the "martyr-founders" of these communities[17] are, in their self-conception, Jews in Germany, not German Jews, and the memory of Auschwitz forms ultimately an unbridgeable divide between Germans and Jews—the coexistence of the two groups in Germany is what Dan Diner has aptly described as a "negative symbiosis."

What is rarely recognized, however, are the deep clashes in

values between the old German Jewish remnant and the Eastern European Jews in Germany in the immediate postwar era. Not only did the German Jews control most of the small, reconstituted Jewish communities; they also stood in bitter ideological opposition to Eastern Jewry. At a time when the full significance of the Holocaust had not yet hit home, many German Jews, particularly, it appears, those who had returned from Shanghai, expected a revival of the old German Jewish tradition, as loyal German citizens of a democratic Germany, like any other Germans—with just a minor difference.

In the struggle that ensued in virtually all communities, the anti-assimilationist faction of the former DPs won the upper hand; they broke the monopoly of power held by the German Jewish establishment. And for almost forty years, the idea of patriotic Jewish Germans seemed preposterous to most: the distance to Germany was based on their martyrdom, on Auschwitz; at best they could play a role as guardians of the new German democracy and as a continual reminder of the German past. In spite of all other differences in personality and style, such Jewish leaders as Werner Nachmann, Heinz Galinski, and presently Ignatz Bubis, have played that role—a role which was imposed upon them by the dominant political and social forces and constellations in Germany, and which they willingly assumed. I have described this phenomenon as "ideological labor."[18]

I suggest that with the transformation we are witnessing, specifically Jewish forms of ideological labor—Jews as the sculptors of Jewish *and* German memory and as the litmus test of German democracy—may well be soon a thing of the past, and there are signs suggesting that the old German Jewish "patriotic" tradition, which had been silenced for forty years, is beginning to rise again, with a new definition of the Jewish role, another *form* of ideological labor in Germany.

In this transformation, we see Auschwitz being pushed to the sidelines, replaced, perhaps, by a historical cult around the old German Jewry. This is exemplified in the work of Sonja Margolina: here, in contrast to Jewish identity as defined by the German Jewish leadership today, Auschwitz has been moved out of the center and is compared to the Stalinist persecutions.

Margolina dissociates herself from the political role assumed by today's Jewish leadership in Germany: she disdainfully calls them "professional Jews and professional philosemites" who force upon the assimilated Jews a Jewish nationality, and for whom she finds little more than contempt.[19]

A second example for the return of the "patriotic" Jewish tradition may be seen in "Jüdische Lebenswelten," the world's largest and most expensive Jewish exhibit ever, which opened in Berlin in January 1992. While this was conceived in the plural—Jewish life world*s*—one Jewish life world clearly stood at the center: that of German (if not Prussian) Jewry.[20] At first glance, this is understandable since the exhibit took place in Germany. However: (1) the visitor to the exhibit first had to pass through a section on German enlightenment Jewry before getting to the Jews of Greece, India, Israel or Poland; (2) in the exhibit, the Shoah was represented as a backdrop in one corner—understandably so because the theme was *life* worlds and not worlds of death—but it still poses questions as to the overall conception of the exhibit; and (3) the exhibit clearly ignored the prewar anti-assimilationist, orthodox faction of German Jewry. The extraordinary recent careers of historians of German Jewry, including the originators of the exhibit, only underscores this point.

All this is being lent support by an astonishing phenomenon entirely unique to Germany today which can only be called a Judaizing terrain, something like a semineutral territory, as Jacob Katz would say, on which otherwise deeply separated ethnic groups may meet.[21] While this Judaizing phenomenon may trace some of its genealogy to earlier forms of philo-Semitism, as a periphery in the Jewish ethos it transcends philo-Semitism by far. This Judaizing terrain is made up of converts to Judaism, of members of joint Jewish-German or Israeli-German associations, and of many "professional almost-Jews" outside and even inside the apparatuses of the Jewish organizations and *Gemeinden*.[22] It is important to see then that to a considerable degree, Jewish culture is being manufactured, Jewish history reconstructed, by these Judaizing milieux—by German experts on Jewish culture and religion. There can be no doubt, however, that they enact Jewish culture from within German biographies and from within German history; this has an important bearing on the type of Jewish culture that is actually being produced: a culture that is not lived, that draws heavily from the museum,[23] and that is still no less genuine for that. Michael Wolffsohn's contention of the Jewish concatenation of German identity—on the one hand, the accusation of the murder of Jews and of the murder of Christ; on the other, the new foundation of the Jewish and German states—are clearly one element in the ideological underpinnings of this Judaizing terrain.

My third example for a likely shift to a pronounced construction of German identity, finally, are the political views of Michael Wolffsohn, born in 1947, a professor of history at the German Military College (*Hochschule der Bundeswehr*) in Munich. Wolffsohn describes himself as "what since 1933 hardly exists anymore: a German-Jewish patriot."[24] He does not regret doing this because West Germany was, and the united Germany is going to be, a place very much worth living in, and his Jewish and his German consciousness are not mutually exclusive.

While his arguments cannot be considered here in full, I want to point out several important issues. As with Margolina, and as with "Jüdische Lebenswelten," the Holocaust is moved out of the center; Jewish history, Wolffsohn argues, should not be compressed into only a few years; the Holocaust is merely another part of a long tradition of persecution. As in the case of his mentor Ernst Nolte, from the side of the German Right in the *Historikerstreit*, Wolffsohn from the "patriotic" German-Jewish perspective therefore rejects the argument of the uniqueness of the Holocaust to which the German Jewish mainstream subscribes. Indeed, the political use of the "Auschwitz club" (*Auschwitz-Keule*) is tantamount to a defilement of the memory of the dead; he himself has not suffered and therefore could not be part of a community who have suffered. It is important to see that some younger Jewish intellectuals in Germany, such as Henryk Broder, Richard Chaim Schneider, and Rafael Seligmann are increasingly skeptical about this "Holocaust fixation."[25] Moreover, according to Wolffsohn, Auschwitz should be moved into the background because democracy in West Germany—and even more now in the united Germany—is a form of redemption; any allegations of the survival of Nazism especially in the early Federal Republic—Ralph Giordano's reproach to his German contemporaries of a "second guilt"—are therefore firmly rejected, and any survival of Nazism in the postwar era is firmly denied; the Western allies bear the burden of guilt as well. To save Jews, they should, and could, have done much more. Like Margolina again, Wolffsohn speaks with contempt of the Jewish leadership that influences the Auschwitz club in its own interests; he is contemptuous of organized Jewish life and has left the community. He admires such "individualistic" French Jews as André Glucksmann or Alfred Grosser who are only responsible to themselves, not to a Jewish collective.

Far more important than the writings by these outsiders in the younger generation of Jews in Germany is the reception they have received in the German media. Both Margolina and Wolffsohn have been fiercely attacked, almost in unison, by German Jewish publications—they have run up against a fundamental consensus among Jews in Germany that lasted for forty years. The title of Margolina's book, *Das Ende der Lügen* is also directed at the German Jewish establishment. At least as important as the attack by the Jewish mainstream is the enthusiastic reception Wolffsohn and Margolina have received from German conservatives. Both authors are being published by well-known conservative publishers, have received high distinctions or are paraded through talk shows on prime-time television—this includes Julius Schoeps, who, albeit a liberal and in a somewhat different form, is a proponent of this German Jewish tradition.

Earlier, Jews were the principal focus of suffering inflicted upon them by the Germans; now, the Jewish leadership along with German politicians are standing up against the new racist violence. Jews and the "good Germans" *together* are confronting images of persecution and murder of altogether different victims, no longer Jews—although the Jews are still very much a target; Jews are therefore beginning to lose their role as the principal victims in the Federal Republic.

I would suggest, then, that in the interplay between German society and politics on the one hand and the Jewish minority on the other, a new, provisional account of the Jewish role in Germany is being constructed. This account, however, might well become dominant and even provide the basis of a new form of Jewish ideological labor for the new, united Germany, in which Jews are no longer needed as the "litmus test of German democracy" but as a reminder of a glorious German and Jewish past. What we are therefore witnessing today is indeed a renaissance of German Jewry—but mostly on the terrain of the German public imagination. A reemergence of Jewish culture, unlikely anywhere in the world today, is therefore doubly improbable in the reemerging Germany.

Notes

1. Sonja Margolina, *Das Ende der Lügen* (Berlin: Siedler, 1992), 121.
2. *Spiegel Spezial* 2 (August 1992): 84.
3. Wolfgang Benz, "Sitzen auf gepackten Koffern. Juden im Nachkriegsdeutschland," *Spiegel Spezial* 2 (1992): 53.
4. *Spiegel Spezial* 2 (1992): 84.
5. A *Zentralrat* source, pers. comm.
6. *Frankfurter Allgemeine Zeitung*, 16 February 1993. Bubis spoke of 25,000 who "as Jews or as relatives of Jews had arrived in Germany from Eastern Europe, of whom 11,000 had become members."
7. See Sidney Goldstein, 1992, "Profile of American Jewry: Insights from the 1990 National Jewish Population Survey." *American Jewish Year Book*, (New York: American Jewish Committee, 1992). Goldstein defines as part of the Jewish core group (a) Jews by religion, (b) Jews by choice, and (c) secular Jews. Transposed into the German situation, individuals in all three groups would qualify, and in large part be, members of the Jewish communities; others are non-Jews in proximity to Jews, as (d) members of households with at least one Jew, (e) of Jewish parentage but of another religion, (f) children under 18 of (partial) Jewish descent raised in another religion, and (g) gentiles in households with at least one Jew.
8. Jacob Katz, 1973, *Out of the Ghetto: The Social Background of Jewish Emancipation 1770–1870* (Cambridge: Cambridge UP, 1973).
9. *Der Tagesspiegel*, 16 February 1993, reporting on a study by the Salomon-Ludwig-Steinheim Institut, 16 February 1993.
10. Anita Kugler, pers. comm.
11. See Steven J. Gold, *Refugee Communities: Soviet Jews and Vietnamese in the San Francisco Bay Area* (Berkeley: University of California, 1985), who found very strong networks among Russian Jews living in the United States.
12. *taz*, 28 March 1990.

13. Fanja Barannikowa, "Die Russen sind schon da. Oder: Wir kommen aus Russland. *Frankfurter Jüdische Nachrichten*, Winter 1992.
14. *Ha-Ikar. Zeitschrift des Jüdischen Jugendzentrums Berlin* 4 (Spring 1992), 7.
15. Ibid., 10.
16. *Taz*, 11 October 1990.
17. Y. Michal Bodemann, "Die Endzeit der Märtyrer-Gründer. An einer Epochenwende jüdischer Existenz in Deutschland," *Babylon* 8: 7–14.
18. Y. Michal Bodemann, "The State in the Construction of Ethnicity, and Ideological Labour: The Case of German Jewry," *Critical Sociology* 17.3: 35–46.
19. Margolina, 118.
20. This impression is borne out by the exhibition catalog and the critical essays that accompany it; see Andreas Nachama, Julius H. Schoeps and Edward van Voolen, (eds.), *Jüdische Lebenswelten.* (Berlin: Berliner Festspiele; Frankfurt/Main: Jüdischer Verlag, Suhrkamp, 1991).
21. See Katz, *Out of the Ghetto, passim.*
22. I offer a few examples. The two principal editors, one for fifteen, the other for almost forty years, of the major Jewish weekly in Germany were non-Jews. Numerous teachers in Jewish schools, professors in Jewish studies departments in the universities, Klezmer musicians, the heads of many major Jewish or Holocaust related cultural and research institutes, including the current director of Berlin's Institute for the Study of Anti-Semitism are non-Jews, and a not insignificant number of individuals in these roles are converts to Judaism. Without these people, the Jewish presence in public life would be considerably diminished.
23. Behind the "museumification" of Jewish culture and its popular appeal, we may of course see feelings of guilt and the desire to bring Jewish culture back to life. On the role of the museum today, see Andreas Huyssen, "Musealisierung und Postmoderne," in Frithjof Hager, ed., *Geschichte Denken. Ein Notizbuch für Leo Löwenthal* (Leipzig: Reclam, 1992), 183–93.
24. Michael Wolffsohn, 12.
25. For recent examples, see Rafael Seligmann, "Zeichen der Identitätskrise. Die Fixierung auf die Schoa verdrängt die Hersausforderungen der Gegenwart und Zukunft," *Allgemeine Jüdische Wochenzeitung*, 29 April 1993; see also Henryk Broder's attack against "Holocaust marketing," *Spiegel* 16 (1993).

3. Becoming Strangers: Jews in Germany's Five New Provinces

Robin Ostow

For Jews, as for other inhabitants of eastern Germany, the four decades of the German Democratic Republic began in the chaos of the postwar years. First and foremost was the geographic displacement of people. Altogether sixty million Europeans were uprooted as a result of the war, particularly through the policies of the German and Soviet governments.[1] Through the early postwar years millions of so-called displaced persons—including fourteen million German refugees from what had been Nazi Germany's eastern territories—were moving through Europe. Most were going from east to west, but some were moving from west to east. Among the Jewish population, for obvious reasons, this situation was even more extreme. Of the million Jews who survived the war in Europe, a mere 7,000 remained in the Soviet Occupied Zone.[2] Some of these Jews were locals who survived the war and stayed on.[3] A few Polish Jewish survivors settled in what became the GDR: they gravitated toward its eight Jewish communities. Jews relocating from west to east tended to be members of the German socialist elite, many of whom became creators and administrators of GDR culture. But they made their careers with the SED. Their commitment and identity were primarily socialist, and they kept their distance from the Jewish communities.[4] In other words, pre-GDR migratory currents generated by the Holocaust and the Cold War set the parameters of the composition and cleavages within the Jewish population as they did for the larger East German society.[5]

The early postwar years were also characterized in both the eastern and western zones of Germany by negotiations between the Jewish communities, the local authorities, and Allied military over rights to formerly Jewish property confiscated by the Nazis, subsidies for Jewish communal life, and social services for Jewish survivors and displaced persons. And Jewish demands for restitution became accompanied by considerable social tensions—including open or covert anti-Semitic agitation—at the local level.[6]

Within the Jewish communities, at the level of the membership as well as in the ranks of the functionaries, there was a complete rupture with the past. By 1943 all the prewar Jewish communities in Germany had been disbanded. Those Jewish leaders who survived the Final Solution—within the Third Reich or abroad—did not return to their former communities. Rather, it was new people coming into the old synagogues and administrative structures. Many of them spoke less German than Yiddish. These refugees from the East had been preoccupied with survival at an age when they might otherwise have been attending university.

The struggles of settling down and creating a new existence—demographically, institutionally, and socially—reached a climax with the anti-Jewish purges of late 1952 through early 1953. Following a sixty-page circular issued by the Central Committee of the SED accusing Jews of being agents of Zionism and American imperialism, many Jews were purged from positions of power in the state and party bureaucracies. The leaders of all the East German Jewish communities were interrogated and asked to sign statements which equated Zionism with fascism, denounced the American Joint Distribution Committee—which had been providing care packages and support to Jews throughout Germany—as an agent of American imperialism, and condemned the campaign for restitution payments as exploitation of the German people.[7] Over the winter the homes of almost all Jews were raided, identity cards were seized, and victims were ordered to stay close to home. The Berlin Jewish community split in two, and all Jewish institutions in the GDR were closed down, except for the cemeteries.

By the time the crisis subsided—with Stalin's death in March 1953—550 Jews had fled the German Democratic Republic, including all the leaders of its Jewish communities.[8] By mid-June 1953, however, there was an abrupt change in policy. Measures against Jews ceased, and the small remnants of the Jewish communities received large government grants to repair and renovate their synagogues. At the same time they were subjected to new leaders who were installed by and responsible to the state. Jewish artists and government officials who had lost their jobs were rehabilitated starting in 1956.

In other words, after this purge, which affected not only Jewish but also many non-Jewish institutions, the Jewish communities of East Berlin, Dresden, Leipzig, Erfurt, Halle, Schwerin, Magdeburg, and Karl-Marx-Stadt were integrated into the German Democratic Republic. This integration was a rather peculiar one from a postwar western perspective. It was carried out from above and with an iron hand. Jews in the GDR were defined as a group that (1) observed certain religious rituals, and (2) was persecuted by the "fascists." All national claims and all communication and/or identification with the state of Israel were suppressed. And Jewish culture became a rather low-profile, low-energy enterprise. Jewish life in the GDR remained a tense cohabitation of two groups—those with religious priorities and those with political ones. These groups maintained differing loyalties and experiences of history, and there was little love or trust between them.[9] The crisis of 1952–53 did not overcome this rift, but rather deepened it.

This integration of Jews in the GDR, complicated and tense beneath a smooth exterior, held for approximately three decades—the mid-1950s through the mid-1980s. Then it broke down, at first rather slowly. Jews from the political/cultural sphere started moving into the religious Jewish institutions.[10] And Jews of both religious and socialist orientations began to demand permission to visit Israel, with more and more success.[11]

By the late 1980s, the Honecker government had begun to negotiate trading ties to western countries—particularly the United States—as part of an effort to revive its moribund economy.

International Jewish organizations were perceived in the GDR as channels of communication and potential mobilizers of local Jewish support in western countries for trade with the East. The East German state then began to encourage Jewish life within its borders to mediate ties to the West and also to bolster its political legitimacy as an antifascist state, in the face of increasing popular impatience with its unwillingness to undertake serious political and economic reform. So, as the GDR went bankrupt, its Jewish communities—and Jewish initiatives outside the established communities as well—were awarded large sums of money to produce Jewish culture. Despite these measures, many Jews, as well as non-Jewish East Germans, began to leave the GDR for the West.

The collapse of the German Democratic Republic in 1989 brought a return of chaos to East Germany, including a renewal of many of the social dynamics and the reopening of major political issues of the late 1940s. Again an East-West migration of considerable dimensions has severely tested the absorptive capacities of Eastern Germany. In addition to the Roma and Sinti, the Bosnian refugees, and the asylum seekers from the Third World, thousands and perhaps tens of thousands of Soviet Jews have immigrated to the GDR/Germany since April 1990.[12] Most of them are being settled in eastern Germany where they represent the only hope for the rejuvenation and continuity of the tiny Jewish communities that were literally dying.[13] At the same time, the newcomers from the East tax the administrative powers and grate on the cultural sensibilities of the handful of older East German Jewish leaders who have taken on the responsibility of settling them in. Younger East German Jews who might otherwise provide leadership in this phase of transition are moving to western Germany or are preoccupied with attempting to secure their own existences.

Throughout the interregnum of 1990, multiparty talks took place involving the Central Council of Jews in Germany, the Conference on Jewish Material Claims against Germany, and the governments of Israel and the two Germanys regarding the amounts, scheduling, and recipients of GDR restitution payments. In the end, none were made, but the admission and integration of several thousand Soviet Jews was tacitly accepted as an alternative. Since 1989 negotiations have also been resumed over rights to formerly Jewish property in the five new *Länder.* And new agreements were worked out between the Central Council of Jews in Germany and the government in Bonn regulating pensions for East German Jewish victims of Nazism, who—unlike Jews in West Germany—were never compensated for lost property. At the same time, the Jewish communities that were formerly supported by the German Democratic Republic have been negotiating contracts for their maintenance with the new *Länder.*[14]

As in the late 1940s, this renegotiation of the maintenance and status of Jewish individuals, collectivities, and properties in eastern Germany has taken place against a background of increasing anti-Semitic incidents—desecration of Jewish cemeteries,[15] and the spray-painting of Nazi slogans and swastikas. In 1990, for the first time since the founding of the GDR, the Jewish communities in the East requested and were assigned police protection. In 1991 anti-Semitic agitation escalated to stabbing incidents involving Soviet Jewish victims in Brandenburg, Glauchau, and Rostock. In this case too, popular anti-Semitism is related to—though not identical with—competition between Jews and unemployed eastern Germans for the meager social resources locally available.

For the East German Jewish organizations, then, the rupture with their past existence is in many cases almost total. The East Berlin Jewish community—the largest in the GDR—was disbanded in January 1991, and its two hundred members were absorbed into what had been the West Berlin Jewish community of seven thousand. The Jewish community of Schwerin was also dissolved, and in the remaining Jewish communities the older members are dying, and the younger members are leaving. The new membership comes from the former Soviet Union.

Besides changing the membership and organization of what had been the Jewish communities of the GDR, the *Wende* and unification have brought the establishment of new Jewish institutions in eastern Germany. In September 1991 a Jewish community was founded in Potsdam, a city that had been institutionally *judenrein* for four decades. Its forty members are basically several families of Soviet immigrants. Its president is Theo Goldstein, an octogenarian and Brandenburg's only surviving German Jew. Despite generous promises from the Land Brandenburg, the Jewish community in Potsdam is functioning with great difficulty in three small rooms, totaling eighty square meters, with no adequate space or furnishings for prayer or social gatherings.

In former East Berlin two maverick Jewish institutions have opened. Both are recognized as corporate bodies by the city of Berlin, but they are seen as impostors by Berlin's established Jewish community and by the Central Council of Jews in Germany. *Adass Isroel*, a neo-Orthodox family enterprise, and the Jewish Cultural Association, a community service organization with a strictly kosher kitchen, provide Jewish religious, social, and cultural services—in German and Russian. Many members of the Jewish Cultural Association were not identified with Jewish life before the *Wende*. In the GDR they were active in the state prosecutor's office, the university, the media, and the foreign ministry. Now ultra-Orthodox rabbis from Israel lead them in Friday night prayers; the women have to pray in a separate room.

In other words, the reintegration of Jewish organizations in the eastern *Länder* represents a rupture with the former East German Jewish communities. The Jewish communities of eastern Germany now have mostly Russian members and operate under West German law. New agreements with Bonn and the eastern *Länder* regulate their property and financing, and the German police protect them against their newly anti-Semitic neighbors. Another new agent in the production of public representations of Jewish life in the East is the Israeli government, which recently opened a consulate in Berlin. The Israelis have become active in organizing Jewish cultural events and teacher and student exchanges between eastern Germany and Israel. The Jews of the former GDR are now "Ossies" in the Federal Republic; they are Jews in a population increasingly aware of its Germanness; and they have also become strangers in their own Jewish communities.

In the GDR many members of the Jewish communities organized their Jewishness as a series of private experiences within the walls of their homes and of community facilities that were often lovingly restored synagogues and halls located in courtyards with unobtrusive exteriors, invisible to the non-Jewish population. And in the GDR many relationships invested with value were organized in the private sphere.[16] Most of these people, though, were not producers of culture; and their lives and their Jewishness are less available to us today.[17]

If anything is to remain of a Jewish cultural tradition from the forty years of the GDR, it might be found in what was actually a prewar German Jewish institution, the *Bildungsbürgertum*,[18] the educated classes that produced and maintained a wide variety of intellectual and cultural enterprises. When Hitler came to power, many of these Jews emigrated. Some of them eventually "returned" to the GDR, where they became important in shaping the culture of the East German state. Of this older generation, many have died or grown old in recent years. One who has not, though, is Stefan Heym, who continues to be active in public life as a former citizen of the GDR and as a Jew.

The heritage of this first generation socialist cultural elite has, in many cases, passed to the children of the "Jewish Communists," children born between 1940 and 1955. Of these second-generation East German Jewish intellectuals—intellectuals in Gramsci's understanding of the word, that is, direct producers of culture, but also those active in shaping public discussion—Gregor Gysi is the most widely known. Other names in this category include writers Irene Runge, Wolfgang Herzberg, Barbara Honigmann, and Annette Leo; folk singer Jalda Rebling; film producer turned politician Konrad Weiss, and Anette Kahane, who was awarded the Theodor Heuss prize in 1990 for her leadership in integrating Soviet Jewish refugees and other foreign groups in East Germany.

Before 1989 these younger Jewish intellectuals worked—often freelance—in a state that generously supported cultural production. Since the collapse of the GDR, they live—as do their neighbors on the Prenzlauer Berg—partly engaged in free-lance projects, and partly employed in short-term, publicly financed, make-work positions—the well-known *ABM-Stellen* which often involve low-level social and cultural administration. As children of active communists, and as individuals who grew up with the socialist utopia, they had identified with the GDR and were bitterly disappointed by its contradictions and failures. And, unlike members of the GDR Jewish communities whose Jewishness remained a private affair, these intellectuals have produced and continue to produce their experiences of the GDR in the form of novels, biographies, cultural festivals, and new organizations—sometimes but not always with explicitly Jewish content.

In biographical works and interviews these people tend to construct their Jewishness first in connection with their parents' persecution by the "fascists." Jewishness is later seen as a factor in childhood experiences of family tensions and secrets in the 1950s, a time when their parents were likely to have been purged and later "rehabilitated." Narrated life histories of members of this generation in the 1960s and 1970s revolve around painful confrontations with the state. Sometime between 1979 and 1985 these intellectuals became more involved with their Jewish identities.

At a time when East German socialism seemed to offer less and less, and many non-Jewish GDR citizens were beginning to articulate, or in their words "discover," and to develop alternative—Christian, homosexual, Sorb, or punk—identities, these intellectuals began to explore their Jewishness. As a plurality of Western religious, cultural, and national traditions, Jewishness provided a rich heritage, including a mythical past, a set of exotic—for East Germany—symbols and rituals, and intellectual traditions for looking backward and forward, inward and outward. Most important, a Jewish identity provided a release from the ranks of an increasingly unpopular elite and a new status as a victim of socialist, of European, and of German history. One could observe and comment on the new era of transition in central Europe while keeping a dignified distance from the humiliation of the *Untergang*.

These East German Jewish intellectuals could, at certain levels, be compared to their West German counterparts—Dan Diner, Micha Brumlik, Gertrud Koch, Henryk Broder, and Maxim Biller. But the quality of their sensibilities is very different. West German Jewish intellectuals grew up in the Federal Republic as children of Holocaust survivors.[19] Raised by parents who defined themselves mainly as victims of German brutality, they lived with the myth of packed suitcases. Their existence in "Germany" was defined as temporary, contact with non-Jewish Germans was kept minimal and superficial, and, despite annual rituals of "Christian-Jewish Brotherhood," their relations with the West German state and its population were frankly hostile.[20] Jewish intellectuals who grew up in the GDR are for the most part not children of Holocaust survivors but rather "red diaper babies." They grew up in a Germany that was their home: the difficulty of leaving that "home" is a central concern in their writings.[21]

These different German Jewish biographies are reflected in the narrative forms and tones of East and West German Jewish writing. East German Jews tend to write romances and tragedies, genres which have heroes whose actions are informed with moral dimensions and whose struggles change the course of history.[22] Romances and tragedies are also about belonging. In romance, identity and integration are achieved through *engagement.* The tragic hero, by contrast, falls from the center of his or her society to its periphery. West German Jewish writers produce more satire, a genre which "takes for granted a world which is full of anomalies."[23] One of its central themes is, as Northrop Frye has observed, the disappearance of the heroic, and it "may often represent the collision between a selection of standards from experience and the feeling that experience is bigger than any set of beliefs about it."[24]

The German Jewish cultural enterprise in the East is currently moving in three directions simultaneously. Gregor Gysi and Irene Runge continue to work with the old state and party apparatus. But their attempts to be effective in a new political environment have led them into a postmodern aesthetic of shifting perspectives and open contradictions. Irene Runge leads a secularly defined Jewish Cultural Association with Israeli travel posters on the wall and a strictly kosher kitchen. Its 1991 Chanuka celebration featured music performed by children of former members of the Central Committee and blessings given by an ultra-Orthodox rabbi. Heinz Fink was invited and attended as an honorary Jew. In March of the same year, Gregor Gysi, as president of the PDS, led a delegation from his party on its first visit to Israel, and in July he met with Yassir Arafat in Tunis to demonstrate the solidarity of the PDS with the PLO.

At the other extreme are those East German Jews who maintain their moral purity by having rejected the GDR altogether. Writers Barbara Honigmann and Hans—more recently Chaim—Noll left East Germany in the mid-1980s. They now pursue intensely Jewish lives in non-German West European countries and write in German, as exiles. Living in France and Italy respectively relieves them of the discomfort of feeling torn between East German, unified German, and Israeli identities—all rather prickly—but it does not provide them a new home.

In between these extremes one finds East German Jews like Anette Kahane, Wolfgang Herzberg, Jalda Rebling, and Annette Leo. These intellectuals participated in the street demonstrations and the citizens' movement of autumn 1989. They are now involved in cultural projects that examine the careers and experiences of families—including their own—at the crossroads of Jewish socialist and German history. Their formulations of GDR Jewish culture undertake to exorcise the Stalinist evil and to locate and distill positive elements from the failed utopia, to conserve them for future generations, and to employ them as a standard for observing and judging the unified Germany.

What were the positive East German Jewish traditions, the heritage that might serve as an anchor as well as a compass in an era of transition and of devaluation of everything associated with the fallen regime? For Annette Leo, as for the recently deceased Helmut Eschwege (of the older generation), it is a mass of historical material that can now be analyzed and interpreted for public discussion in the newly unified Germany. For Jalda Rebling, a new East German Jewish culture was born on the Prenzlauer Berg in October 1989, when she and many of her Jewish and non-Jewish neighbors held a candlelight demonstration at the Gethsemane Church. The demonstrators were attacked and violently dispersed by the East German police on the evening of Yom Kippur, the Day of Atonement, the holiest and most somber day of the Jewish calendar. This event gave birth to what has become the Gethsemane Church community, a collection of neighborhood-based initiatives around multicultural, humanist, and ecological concerns. And performances of Yiddish music and poetry have become integral elements of the cultural events in Gethsemane. Anette Kahane's East German Jewish tradition took the form of initiatives to integrate foreigners in eastern Berlin in 1990 and has evolved into a work group which brings multicultural programs into eastern German schools.

At the center of the intellectual lives of former East German Jewish intellectuals, regardless of the direction of their Jewish agenda, is the confrontation with the German Communist experiment. Their Jewish identity is, by comparison, recent, derivative, and, in some cases, rather superficial. These Jews grew up in the villas of Pankow, and not—like their West German counterparts—in the shadows of Auschwitz. And the cultural production and the space they demand in national—and now regional—discourse are completely disproportional to their demographic strength.

What, then, are the prospects for the current eastern German Jewish cultural explosion? The project of saving, articulating and redefining Jewish life in the German Democratic Republic has attracted attention in eastern Germany and Berlin. But in western Germany it is barely noticed. The *Spiegel* special edition on Jews in Germany, published in Hamburg in September 1992, contains articles written in West Germany and Israel, but there is no mention at all of Jewish life and culture in the eastern *Länder*. The *New York Times Magazine* recently published a feature article on East German culture. The title: "A Nation of Readers Dumps Its Writers."[25] And the Soviet Jewish immigrants? What will happen when they learn German and begin to produce Russian Jewish interpretations of German history and society? Will they be grateful to Helmut Kohl for the privilege of immigrating to the wealthiest and most powerful state in Western Europe? Or will they remember that it was two former Stasi agents, Irene Runge of the East Berlin Jewish Community and Lothar de Maizière of the East German CDU, who opened the German border to them on April 18, 1990, and Helmut Kohl who closed it again on October 2?

Notes

1. Douglas Botting, *From the Ruins of the Reich: Germany 1945–1949* (New York: Crown, 1985), 149.
2. Jerry E. Thompson, "Jews, Zionism, and Israel: The Story of the Jews in the German Democratic Republic since 1945" (Ph.D. dissertation, Washington State University, 1978), 317. Thompson reported that in 1946, 3,480 persons were registered in the GDR Jewish communities (and 3,000 in 1952). I am assuming that an equal number of Jews lived in the GDR but did not join the Jewish communities. The category of those "racially persecuted" under Nazism, which usually presupposes some "Jewish blood," contains several thousand individuals.
3. Helmut Eschwege, "Die jüdische Bevölkerung der Jahre nach der Kapitulation Hitlerdeutschlands auf dem Gebiet der DDR bis zum Jahre 1953," in Siegfried Theodor Arndt, Helmut Eschwege, Peter Honigmann, and Lothar Mertens, *Juden in der DDR: Geschichte—Probleme—Perspektiven* (Cologne: E. J. Brill, 1988). Eschwege claims that most of these people left Germany or turned away from Judaism. Few of them joined the Jewish communities.
4. See Monika Richarz, "Jews in Today's Germanies," in *Leo Baeck Institute Year Book* 30 (London, 1985), 126–30.
5. Lutz Niethammer, "The Structuring and Restructuring of the German Working Classes after 1945 and after 1990." Unpublished paper presented at McMaster University, October 1992.
6. For a detailed description, see Thompson, "Jews, Zionism."
7. See Robin Ostow, *Jews in Contemporary East Germany: The Children of Moses in the Land of Marx* (London: Macmillan, 1989), chap. 1.
8. Thompson estimates the membership of the GDR's Jewish communities at 3,000 before the purge.
9. See Robin Ostow, "Helden und Antihelden. Zwei Typen jüdischer Identität in der DDR," *BIOS* 2 (1991), 191–204.
10. Robin Ostow, "Das neue nationale Bewußtsein der Juden der DDR," *Die DDR im vierzigsten Jahr: Geschichte, Situation, Perspektiven*, ed. Ilse Spittmann and Gisela Helwig, (Cologne: Edition Deutschland Archiv, Verlag Wissenschaft und Politik, 1989), 127–36.
11. It began to seem as though almost every Jew in the GDR visited Israel sometime between 1986 and 1990. Several reported watching the collapse of their state on Israeli television. See Robin Ostow, *Jom Kippur in Gethsemane* (forthcoming).
12. For a detailed account of this, see Robin Ostow, "German Democratic Republic," in *American Jewish Year Book 1992* (Philadelphia: Jewish Publication Society, 1992), 373–82, and Y. Michal Bodemann and Robin Ostow, "Germany," *American Jewish Year Book 1993* (Philadelphia: Jewish Publication Society, 1993), 282–300.

13. In 1989 the seven East German Jewish communities outside East Berlin numbered between five and forty-five members each.
14. For the details regarding all these issues, see *American Jewish Year Book 1992.*
15. For a discussion of racism and cemetery desecration, see Liisa Malkki, "National Geographic: The Rooting of Peoples and the Territorialization of National Identity among Scholars and Refugees," *Cultural Anthropology* 7,1 (February 1992), 24–44.
16. For a discussion of GDR society as a "*Nischengesellschaft,*" see Günter Gaus, *Wo Deutschland liegt: Eine Ortsbestimmung* (Hamburg: Hoffmann und Campe, 1983).
17. For some material on these people, see Jurek Becker's novels *Der Boxer* (Frankfurt/Main: Suhrkamp, 1976), and *Bronsteins Kinder* (Frankfurt/Main: Suhrkamp, 1986). See also Robin Ostow, "Das neue nationale Bewußtsein," and *Jews in Contemporary East Germany*; also Lutz Niethammer, Alexander von Plato, and Dorothee Wierling, *Die volkseigene Erfahrung. Zur Archäologie des Lebens in der Industrieprovinz der DDR* (Berlin: Rowohlt, 1991), 248–99.
18. See Y. Michal Bodemann, "Die Endzeit der Märtyrer-Gründer: An einer Epochenwende jüdischer Existenz in Deutschland," *Babylon* 8 (Feb. 1991), esp. 12–13.
19. There is now an extensive literature on "survivors' children." See Helen Epstein, *Children of the Holocaust* (New York: Putnam, 1979).
20. See Peter Sichrovsky, *Wir wissen nicht was Morgen wird, wir wissen wohl was gestern war: Junge Juden in Deutschland und Österreich* (Cologne: Kiepenheuer & Witsch, 1985).
21. See Hans Noll, *Der Abschied: Journal meiner Ausreise aus der DDR* (Hamburg: Hoffmann und Campe, 1985). Also Barbara Honigmann, *Eine Liebe aus nichts* (Berlin: Rowohlt, 1991); Monika Maron, *Stille Zeile Sechs* (Frankfurt/Main: Fischer, 1991); and Annette Leo, *Briefe Zwischen Kommen und Gehen* (Berlin: Basisdruck, 1991).
22. See Ostow, "Helden und Antihelden."
23. See Northrop Frye, *Anatomy of Criticism* (Princeton, N.J.: Princeton University Press, 1957), 226.
24. Ibid., 229.
25. *New York Times Magazine,* 10 January 1993: 23 and *passim.*

PART TWO

Contemporary Issues: Politics, Religion, and Immigration

4. What Is "Religion" among Jews in Contemporary Germany?

Marion Kaplan

Germany's Jews are 99 percent secular—so asserts a keen observer of Jewish life in Germany.[1] Thus an essay on religious life has to look beyond practicing Jews and to understand "religion" to include the idea—common to Jews in many modern, secular societies—of culture. In other words, "religion" here is interpreted broadly. This essay will look at synagogue life, religiosity, and spirituality only briefly, and go on to discuss Jewish "culture," by which I mean an intellectual interest in religion as well as "that complex whole which includes knowledge, belief, morals, law, custom, and any other habits acquired" by Jews in Germany today.[2] More precisely, when one looks at how Jews in Germany relate to their religion and traditions, one sees a great deal of activity—not a reemergence of culture with a big "C" as we might imagine Weimar in the 1920s or New York now—but of "culture" as anthropologists and social historians define it.

Signs of Decline, Signs of Hope

In the immediate postwar era, both the world Jewish community as well as most Jews in Germany assumed that Jews would forever abandon the land that had spawned Nazism.[3] Thus, from the moment of its inception, the new Jewish community in postwar

Germany was to have died out. Even as a small and very diverse group of Jews remained, they were at best ignored and at worst vilified by other Jews for continuing to live among their former murderers. From 1945 onward—and continuing in some Jewish quarters until today—a positive prognosis on the health and future of the Jewish community in Germany was, and is, unwelcome. Nevertheless, by the mid-1980s there were about 30,000 Jews officially registered with their communities in the Federal Republic—and unofficially as many as 50,000.[4] As we approach 1995, the fiftieth anniversary of the reestablishment of Jewish communities in Germany, it is time to admit that these communities have not only persevered, despite continuous predictions of their imminent demise, but are also in the process of physical renewal as younger members inherit positions of power from the older generation and as new immigrants increase the population of Jews.

Still, there are signs of weakness in contemporary Jewish life. The most obvious is in number. Even as the community grows significantly, it is a shadow of the 600,000 Jews of the pre-Nazi era and is small compared to most European Jewish communities today. Moreover, it is not concentrated in one or two places, as is the case in Belgium, for example, and, thus, for the most part, lacks the numbers necessary in any but the major cities to support a full-scale cultural—as opposed to religious—life. For the latter, one needs only ten "people" (read *men* in the German case); for the former, one needs a wide variety of talent and perspectives and a critical mass of supporters. Thus, size and content are related: if a particular community is small *and religious* it can survive, but since most are not religious, they will die out. A lively secular Jewish cultural life presumes a larger Jewish population.

The case of Bielefeld, an example of the decline of many small communities, may illustrate this issue. The community of Bielefeld consists of only fifty members. About twelve elderly men attend abbreviated Sabbath services only twice monthly. The women's group consists of seven elderly women. On the High Holidays, this small community joins with other tiny ones in order to fashion some kind of holiday services. These cities and towns offer no Jewish education or cultural activities and keep very low profiles.[5] It is hard to imagine how a revival could take place there, particularly since most new immigrants tend to prefer larger cities.

Another problem is the integration of young Jews, here defined as those between ages 18 and 25. A recent survey of youth in the former West Germany shows that they desire more contact with their Jewish Communities (*Jüdische Gemeinden*) rather than greater integration with non-Jews, but that they are dissatisfied with the Gemeinden as they stand. Many consider the structures of the Gemeinden to be archaic and "no place for young people." Moreover, many young Jews lack basic knowledge about their religion and, hence, about their roots.[6]

The problem of the "Einheitsgemeinde"—a single official Jewish community per city that represents all Jews, and, therefore, ostensibly, all diversity within one area—makes alternative projects difficult to sustain. German authorities find it easier to deal with one official Gemeinde that receives all government financial and political support. That Gemeinde, in turn, is reluctant to share benefits with what it perceives as outsiders or illegitimate claimants to public funding. In effect in Germany only since the end of World War II, this political structure tends to stifle, rather than encourage, change and growth.[7] At the present time, the official Gemeinden represent the older generation, although younger Jews have begun to make their appearance even in the Gemeinde leadership as well.[8] The official Gemeinden also represent more conservative political alternatives than some Jews advocate. The resolution of this vexing issue will either promote or destroy pluralism, and, hence, vitality in the Jewish communities in Germany.

Moreover, intermarriage statistics—as high as 70 percent—continue to concern Jewish community leaders, as does the indifference of many Jews to religion in a traditional sense and to other issues affecting them as Jews. The vast heterogeneity of the Jewish community, including Jews from Eastern Europe, Israel, Iran, and prewar Germany, also makes communication, not to mention integration into a unified community, difficult.

Still, there are signs of hope. Most important, since the Wall came down, population has grown rapidly.[9] The influx of Russian

Jews—which began before the Wall's demise but has increased ever since—has added life and energy to the aging Jewish communities in many cities of united Germany. And, since the influx of ex-Soviet Jews will continue, even if at a slower pace,[10] these immigrants will ultimately assure the success or failure of a Jewish revival in Germany. As one scholar has noted, "In ten years, there will be a new German-Jewish community here, mostly consisting of people of Russian descent."[11]

Some communities have made tremendous efforts to integrate the ex-Soviets. Here but one example, since others are scattered below. In Düsseldorf, the community has grown one-third in one year. In January 1992 it had 2000, members, including 400 mostly young Russians. A year earlier there had been 1504 members of whom almost 50 percent were over the age of 60. Düsseldorf integrated proportionately more Russians than some Jewish communities in larger cities[12] precisely in order to enliven and revitalize its community. In January 1992 the community reported that the Russians were energetically involved in language and religious education and active in community endeavors.[13] The crucial issue here is whether the Russians will remain loyal to the Jewish communities once their immediate social welfare and social integration needs are satisfied. I would argue that the prognosis is good.

Other signs of vitality, to be discussed below, include the burgeoning organizations outside the official Gemeinden, such as the *Jüdische Gruppen*, the *Kulturverein* (Cultural Association) in East Berlin, and private study/prayer groups. These groups are indications of a political and cultural split growing since the 1970s within the Jewish community with younger, second-generation Jews in the forefront. Often the *Gruppen*, their journals, and the political and cultural events they sponsor result from their disappointment with the activities of the Gemeinden. This younger generation set up its own organizations when individuals no longer felt represented by what they saw as authoritarian or patriarchal leadership patterns in the official Gemeinden. This "small, critical and vocal group . . . was bent on distinguishing itself from the older Jews, their own conservative Jewish peers, and most Germans."[14] They offer a more intellectual discourse about Jewish problems, searching for Jewish identity beyond what Dan Diner has called the "negative symbiosis" of Germans and Jews after Auschwitz.

Keeping the above issues in mind, I would like to focus on the past few years, since the Wall came down. This kind of contemporary history can only be an indication of trends, since events evolve and change so quickly. For reasons of their separate histories, I have divided the paper into "west" and "east." Although these divisions officially ceased to exist for Germany since October 1990 and for the Jewish community since January 1991, they continue to linger on in many quarters both culturally and emotionally.

West German Jewry

Cultural Judaism

Although most of Germany's Jews are not religious, it does not follow that the over seventy official Gemeinden in the new Germany are languishing.[15] In fact, in the large cities it is quite the opposite if one takes institutions as a measure. Not only are there synagogues but youth centers, social welfare bureaus, sports clubs, and cultural events. Some communities have set up their own kindergartens, Berlin and Frankfurt boast their own Volkshochschulen, and there is even a Jewish institution of higher education, or Hochschule für Jüdische Studien, founded in 1979 in Heidelberg. There are also local Gemeinde newsletters, independent organizational newsletters (e.g., WIZO), a national newspaper, the *Allgemeine Jüdische Wochenzeitung*, and two Jewish bookstores (in Munich and Berlin).

In Frankfurt, for example, the community maintains two kindergartens, a primary school, and a Volkshochschule. A recent contract with the city will provide a generous yearly subsidy to the community to enhance its programs, including the building of 230 apartments for Gemeinde members, the care of the elderly, and programs for addicted and unemployed youth.[16] A group of about fifty Jewish doctors, calling themselves the Maimonides

Society after the famous medieval Jewish doctor and philosopher, was founded in 1990. It focuses on issues of Jewish medical ethics but is also interested in scholarly exchanges with Israeli doctors, in learning about the history of Jewish doctors during the Nazi period, and in continuing education, for example, on AIDS. Promising continuity into the next generation, about 28 percent of the Frankfurt community's over 5,000 members are under the age of 30,[17] as are about one-third of its elected representatives.[18]

Religiosity—here meaning participation in synagogue services or religious ritual at home—is not of primary interest. In Frankfurt's recent election for the board of directors of the Jewish Community (*Gemeinderat,* June 1992), the "establishment" slate offered an eight-point program of which only two points could be translated as "religious" in any traditional sense: maintenance of culture and Jewish tradition and a continuation of Jewish education from kindergarten through adult education. The other points emphasized the battle against anti-Semitism, solidarity with Israel, as well as various kinds of social welfare activities (surely a traditional Jewish *mitzvah* but not a means of furthering Jewish knowledge and religiosity). To underscore my point, the new head of the Jewish community in Germany (*Zentralrat der Juden in Deutschland*) and longtime leader of the Frankfurt Jewish community, Ignatz Bubis, recently went to the Sachsenhausen concentration camp memorial site to protest an anti-Semitic event there. He went on the Sabbath.[19] At a meeting (December 1992) of the Jewish community in Frankfurt, to which an unusually large number of people came,[20] only a small handful of Orthodox Jews criticized him for desecrating the Sabbath; for the rest, his protest was more important than his disregard of the Sabbath. When later criticized for this transgression on a public television program by another Jew, he retorted that the Zentralrat was the political representative of Jews in Germany, for religion one called upon the rabbis.[21]

A careful examination of the Community's newsletter of the last three years provides evidence of secular, cultural interests: the newsletter, a hefty, glossy magazine of between forty and sixty pages, focuses on Jewish culture and history (including commemorations of the Nazi genocide against the Jews and Jewish life in

Germany before and during the Nazi era), on Jewish organizations and social welfare issues, and on Israeli politics and society. Editorials concern politics, whether attacks on foreigners, anti-Semitism, rightist extremism, or the Gulf War. Only occasionally, the Community's rabbi writes an article on the meaning of a holiday or on such topics as "should girls light the Sabbath candles?"[22] Bubis himself notes that the main problem the communities face is the "turning away from tradition, the increase in marriages with non-Jews or with indifferent Jews."[23]

Are there any signs of increasing religiosity? On the surface it appears so, but I think the signals are ambiguous, showing an increased interest in religion, not necessarily an increased religiosity. For example, Frankfurt's Jüdische Volkshochschule, started in 1988, can itself be seen as the result of an awakening of interest in Jewish topics. It presents a mix of intellectual and cultural topics, for example, courses on Yiddish humor, Jewish life in America, and famous Jewish writers. It also offers courses with deeper religious implications: in 1991, these included Jewish festivals and holidays, the kosher kitchen, and the World of the Prophets.[24] In 1992 the courses with greater religious content included: Texts from the Talmud; The Work of Gershom Scholem on Sabbatai Zwi; Hebrew; Rabbis of the 19th and 20th Centuries; and, again, Jewish Festivals and Holidays and the Kosher Kitchen. If we are willing to see this as an indication (rather than a "trend" for which even the most reckless of us might want a few more semesters to compare), then over half of the courses in 1992, compared to about one-quarter of the courses in 1991, have material that could enhance religiosity.[25] The director of the school believes that students *are* demanding courses with more religious themes.[26] The school has even started to provide an expanded lecture series on religious topics in order to fortify its course offerings, hiring lecturers from the Hochschule für Jüdische Studien in Heidelberg.

What does this really tell us? On the one hand, despite the director's assertions, we cannot learn very much about increasing religiosity among Jews, since the courses that I list above as relatively "religious" are also taken by non religious Jews and by non-Jews. There has always been interest in Judaism among non-Jews in Germany, where most books about Jewish life are bought by non-Jews. In fact, in 1990, Heinz Galinski, the former head of the Jewish community of Berlin and of Germany who died July 1992, noted that "it is above all, non-Jews (*unsere nichtjüdische Umwelt*) that come to the Gemeinde House."[27] On the other hand, the influx of Jews from the Soviet Union, who know very little of their Jewish heritage, also plays a role in the new offerings.[28] Immigrant Russians in particular may be taking these courses to increase their religious knowledge and this could lead to a possible development of religious practice among some of them. Since the course offerings cannot serve as a clear sign of religious interest, the only conclusion one can venture with certainty is that the flourishing enrollment of the Volkshochschule[29] documents a strong interest in Jewish culture and tradition.

Similar cultural motivations may cause parents to send their children to the Jewish day school in Frankfurt. In the United States, people send their children to Jewish day schools primarily for religious reasons. This is the case in Amsterdam and Budapest as well. But in Frankfurt, the majority of parents who send their children there are secular and have more practical and, one could say, political or cultural reasons. It offers long hours in the early years, compared to the German schools which end in midday forcing parents to cope with a variety of child-care arrangements. The children at the school are bi- and trilingual (frequently the children of immigrants), thus a bright and educated peer group. And, importantly, the school provides a Jewish identity in the face of a German environment that is sometimes hostile and often perceived as fraught. The children learn about and celebrate customs and holidays that they would miss in a German school and in an overwhelmingly Christian context. It is not uncommon, therefore, to find children coming home and asking their entirely secular parents to light Sabbath candles and perform other religious rituals, to their parents' surprise and consternation.[30]

The Jewish Community in Berlin is similar to Frankfurt's in supporting a wide variety of educational and social institutions, including schools (a Jewish Gymnasium opened in August 1993), old-age homes, and many services for Russian immigrants.[31] It attempts to provide Jewish environments for children through day care and youth groups as well as vacations for Jewish children and teens. Teens can even attend Purim disco parties.[32] Recent plans include expanding cultural offerings, schools, old age facilities, the Volkshochschule and day care to the eastern parts of the city.[33] Information sheets for October and December 1992, printed in German and Russian, offered a multiplicity of courses including Hebrew lessons, discussions on Jewish themes, arts and crafts classes, video club, guitar club, folk dancing, discotheque, chess club, checkers circle, basics of computer use, aerobics, and a "health" sports group.[34] Also in Berlin, a group of Jewish doctors and psychologists has met for several years at the Jewish community center.[35] Finally, similar to Frankfurt, the Berlin community commemorates important anniversaries of Nazi persecutions (e. g., the November pogrom) and uses these occasions for public education as well. Berlin fosters a variety of lectures, courses, and clubs (from WIZO and four B'nai B'rith lodges to a singles group and an organization of children of survivors). Moreover, similar to Frankfurt, the Jüdische Volkshochschule in Berlin had added more courses on religion in late 1992, noting that the "demand in this field has grown very large in recent times."[36]

Just as a plethora of cultural offerings does not necessarily indicate increasing religiosity, even an increase in actual religious practice cannot be taken at face value. Are we seeing the revival of religiosity or an interest—intellectual and/or emotional—in Jewish culture and tradition by people who have no further spiritual interest and whose synagogue attendance is nonexistent? One example may suffice: In Koblenz, the Gemeinde sponsored Passover, Hanukkah and Purim events. The community used to consist of about sixty families; now it has over one-hundred (due to the Russian immigrants). The Gemeinde's attempt to increase the size of the community has been successful. More and more people now come to these religious/cultural events, but not to services.[37]

In several discussions I had with Jews in Germany, both active and inactive in official community events, this cultural Judaism became even clearer. Jewish events, such as the celebration of holidays, take place privately, in the extended friendship/kin circle. These circles are getting bigger. First, there are now three generations of Jews in Germany, and Jews are also making concerted efforts to reach out to each other. These two phenomena are partly related. When Jewish parents try to give their young children a sense of what it means to be Jewish within the family, they need to reach out to other families to make holidays more festive. Several people expressed a real sense of optimism about the Jewish community as such and traditional communal/familial practice but did not believe that synagogue attendance would be enhanced.

Similar tendencies towards cultural Judaism are apparent in some cities, where large enough numbers of Jews live to support activities outside of the Gemeinde and, sometimes, in defiance of it. These alternatives to the Gemeinde, calling themselves "Jüdische Gruppen" and originally made up of Jews born after the war, are looking for a form of Jewish identity with which they can feel comfortable. While the "sitting on packed suitcases" identity of their parents does not quite suit them (although it may reappear in times of crisis—such as now),[38] they could not adopt a religious identity either. Most feel estranged from religious practice or are atheists. Many have intermarried. Many of these people are intellectuals and are left-leaning politically, and they see the strong identification that Jews in Germany feel toward Israel as a form of "substitute identity" (*Ersatzidentität*)[39] which they do not share to the same extent. Most importantly, all suffered from what Micha Brumlik has called a "post-Shoah identity" (which they share with all Jews in Germany).[40] The result of this dilemma, besides the inevitable confusion, seems to be a desire to find a cultural answer to their "Jewish problem." A culture-based identity could be a counterweight to an entirely negative, Shoah-based identity and would, at the same time, absorb the Shoah. Since the official Gemeinden seemed inhospitable to their needs, these younger Jews formed their own groups, creating an informal split in the Jewish community.

This split is reinforced by religious and political differences as well. As already mentioned, these Jews are estranged from the way in which the Gemeinde defines Jewishness. Moreover, many in the groups are angered by the politics of the older generation of Jews (and their successors) whom they accuse of being socially and politically conservative. In the heat of the disagreements, more pessimistic observers see a growing gap in the Jewish community. From a distance, one could in fact see a necessary and important spark of vitality.

These Jüdische Gruppen started first in Frankfurt (in the late 1970s) and Berlin (1982).[41] They meet to discuss Jewish culture and politics. More recently (in the last five years), they have sprung up in Cologne, Hamburg, Munich, and Düsseldorf, growing in size yearly. For a while now, many New Left Jewish groups have formed in Germany. One thing ties these groups together: independence from the established Jewish communities in their cities.[42]

Cologne can provide an example of how such a group functions. Begun informally in 1987, it has grown to about eighty members and now meets regularly on Friday evenings.[43] It formalized its organization as the Jüdisches Forum Köln e.V. in January 1991, holding its first general assembly the following month. The Forum does not want to be seen as an alternative to the synagogue but as an addition, and, indeed, there is a crossover between the groups, with individuals visiting cultural and religious events in both places. Still, many of its members would not be accepted in the official Gemeinde because of their mixed parentage.[44]

Focusing on Jewish literature and philosophy, Jewish customs, and tradition, The Forum intends to enhance the self-understanding of Jews.[45] The members, most of whom are between the ages of 30 and 55, eat a potluck meal together. Some light the Sabbath candles and say prayers over bread and wine.[46] They then listen to a lecture or discuss a topic of Jewish interest.[47] This can include speakers to the left of the traditional spectrum when the topic turns to politics or Israel.[48] The group has celebrated Passover together and made Hanukkah and Purim parties for its children. Family and friendship networks can be cultivated at these occasions. Some members of this same group celebrated the High Holidays on their own, outside the community. As of July 1990, in Hamburg, too, a group of about fifty paying members (and a larger group of sympathizers) meets regularly for the Sabbath. The Hamburg group accepts people rejected by the regular Gemeinde—for example, children of mixed marriages whose fathers are Jews. It has set up a school ("Religionsschule") for forty children. Of late, the Berlin association (calling itself Jüdische Gruppe Berlin) sponsored its own "Culture Days" (November 1992) to coincide with those sponsored for the past seven years by the official community. It also founded a Jewish Round Table along with the Kulturverein of East Berlin and the Orthodox Adass Isroel, both of which I will discuss below. The official Berlin community boycotts the round table.[49] Members of these groups have also been instrumental in the founding of several journals (*Babylon, Semit, Nudnick*) which present religious, political, and cultural alternatives to those propagated by the official Gemeinden and the Zentralrat der Juden in Deutschland.

Religious Stagnation, Religious Revival

Jewish religion as traditionally practiced, including synagogue observance, serious Jewish learning, and the maintenance of home ritual, including *kashrut*, is far from the norm for the vast majority of Jews in Germany. "From a religious perspective," one observer noted in 1985, "Germany since 1945 is a desert. . . . Most Jews have only a kindergarten-level Jewish education."[50] All agree that Jews in Germany are "Dreitagesjuden," attending synagogue three days a year—on the High Holidays—if at all.

Berlin community leaders are unhappy but tolerant about the lack of synagogue attendance. A recent editorial in the Gemeinde newsletter noted that during the High Holidays many young people stood *outside* the synagogue. It concluded: "We are happy about all people who seek the proximity of other Jews during the High Holidays; thus even the presence of many young people in the courtyard, outside of the actual sanctuary, must be valued positively."[51] Behind these words, however, is the acknowledgment that "the future of Judaism (*Judentum*) in Germany will not depend on how large the numbers (of Jews) are, but whether we succeed in securing Jewish identity."[52] The evidence here—from the perspective of the Berlin Gemeinde, for example—is not particularly encouraging. Its leaders do not note a large number of active Russian participants in religious or cultural events.[53] Rabbi Ernst M. Stein, of the western Berlin Pestalozzistraße Synagogue, who has officiated in Berlin for over ten years, describes this dilemma in the following manner: "The problem . . . is that the Gemeinde does not know how to function as a Jewish Gemeinde—in contrast to a Jewish organization. . . . It is a good organization. . . . It has to learn how to be a Gemeinde—a *kehillah.*"[54]

Dr. Julius Carlebach, rector of the Hochschule für Jüdische Studien in Heidelberg,[55] sums up the situation as follows: "The main problem of Jews in Germany is that they want to be Jews, but not Jewish [daß sie zwar Juden sein wollen, aber nicht jüdisch]. And, how that should progress, I don't know."[56] Why this is the case has been debated. Some argue that we live in a secular age in which people no longer find solace and inspiration in religion, while others point to the worldwide revival in religion and to the fall of communism as a possible impetus for a return to Judaism. While some note the small number of Jews and the limits of the Einheitsgemeinden, others argue that the few Jews in Germany or the Einheitsgemeinden are no excuse for the lack of religiosity: there were even fewer Jews at the height of Jewish learning in medieval Germany and smaller postwar Jewish communities in Holland and Switzerland have developed pluralistic Gemeinden.[57] Some suggest that most Jews simply don't care what kind of Gemeinde they have. Most convincing to me are those who contend that a tiny number of Orthodox Jews has inordinate power in the communities and has successfully pushed the communities too far to the right, producing tension between Orthodox and Reform Jews and estranging the majority who seek a more moderate version of Jewish practice. (Most synagogues in Germany, although stemming from the German reform movement of the mid-nineteenth century, differ significantly from the American Conservative movement. They do not have mixed seating, do not allow women in minyans, or hire women rabbis, and are, thus, far closer to Orthodoxy than in the United States. There are no Reform synagogues as we know them in the United States and the broad spectrum of Jewish life, from ultra-Orthodox to Reconstructionist or Chavurah alternatives, is simply not available.) Since most Jews are not observant, the argument goes, they do not feel they have an articulate claim to Judaism or to redefining the religious framework. Moreover there is a sense of inferiority, a lack of self-confidence, a feeling that the Orthodox are "legitimate" and that other Jews (particularly those who know nothing—even if they do care) have no right to assert their preferences and no ability to learn on their own.[58] And, of course, the Orthodox concur in this assessment. Hence, the less observant Jews allow the Orthodox to play an extremely powerful role, skewing the Gemeinde toward a version of Judaism that shuns more modern rituals or attitudes that can be found, for example, in North America or England. The result is the common expression: "The Gemeinde is Orthodox, only the membership isn't."

Movements toward religious, that is spiritual, change are few and far between, but they do exist. In Düsseldorf, for example, an American Orthodox man had set up an improvised Yeshiva in his home. He had several Russian Talmud students "learning" with him.[59] The alternative group in Cologne mentioned above, generally secular in its interests, held High Holiday services (1991 and 1992) in a small village synagogue in Stommeln near Cologne.[60] The group felt the need for religious expression but not in the manner in which the Cologne Gemeinde would have proceeded.[61] In Berlin, a woman rabbinical student from the Jewish Theological Seminary in New York has helped to start a Rosh Chodesh group of about fifteen women.[62] (It had met three times by mid-December 1992.) She will be in Berlin for a short time, but group members are optimistic that they will continue on their own.

Why such a group? One member explained that she had been brought up in a Jewish home in which holidays were celebrated as family events rather than spiritual ones. As a result, she felt a lack of knowledge about Judaism. As a Jew in Germany, she was constantly asked questions about her religion which she could not answer. But she was not joining this group to answer others. Rather, she had come to the point where she wanted to engage in this quest herself.[63] Other Jews, too, seem to be taking this approach, and some might go even further. The rabbinical student wrote that she had "met people who might be prepared to try a private egalitarian minyan, the emphasis is on *private*, for inside the community they simply do not dare raise such an issue."[64] My own feeling is that unless reforms set in, especially with regard to women,[65] the synagogues will lose the small chance they might now have to attract the new, Russian Jews, some of whom might be willing to join with their families, but most of whom would find the idea of women "upstairs" hopelessly alien.[66] On this point, some Jews in Germany already disagree with me, arguing that Russian Jews find the synagogue itself hopelessly alien, not the separation of the sexes.[67]

Observers close to the scene contend that synagogues and rabbis are not the ones who will bring more Jews into the fold. In fact, they do not seem interested in outreach. New visitors to sabbath services often feel ignored or treated suspiciously and, conversely, those who regularly attend such services feel annoyed at being treated like an "exhibit in a museum."[68] When people want to join the Gemeinde, they must provide proof of their claim to be Jews. Many do not have such proof since their parents' documents were destroyed or lost during the war. The Gemeinde insists on this because of situations in which German Christians claimed to be Jews. Even with proof, some rabbis demand a year of Jewish education before accepting the new members.[69]

Outreach is also hindered because rabbis are generally itinerant (there aren't enough to be stationary except in the big cities), and the ones who do have synagogues stick to their tried and true ways.[70] Finally, since rabbis are far less independent than in the United States, beholden to the Gemeinde leadership, any outreach or change could be stifled by the latter as well as by a small but loyal and very conservative congregation.[71] The case of Rabbi Neuman, treated below, attests, in part, to this phenomenon.

Judaism Is More Than Religiosity, Anyway

The new, though admittedly limited, interest in religion that I have described may be part of a new Jewish self-assertion vis-à-vis non-Jewish Germans, one that affirms Jewish cultural and political values. Just as racism and anti-Semitism in Germany are increasing, Jews and Jewish events are more visible and numerous than ever before. Critics are quick to attribute this abundance of Jewish culture to a perverse interest by Germans. According to Henryk Broder, there is an inverse correlation between the number of Jews who live in Germany and interest in their culture by Germans.[72] I think this is too simple. Jews, too, are hungry for

Jewish culture.

A few examples may suggest the extent and variety of organizations and events that have developed in a very short time, some for Jews and non-Jews, others for Jews alone. In 1992, the exhibition "Patterns of Jewish Life" in Berlin attracted over 350,000 visitors and another 115,000 people attended the thirty theater and forty concert events associated with the exhibition.[73] An association of Yiddish film enthusiasts formed as a result of the films which accompanied the exhibit and plan to popularize Yiddish films in Germany.[74] On November 9, 1992, the foundation for a new Jewish museum was laid in Berlin (to replace the three rooms set aside for Jewish topics in the Berlin Museum in the 1980s), and other Jewish museums are sprouting in smaller towns as well. In the fall of 1992, the first Jewish feminist foundation, the "Stiftung zur Förderung jüdischer Frauen in Wissenschaft und Kunst" opened its doors in Berlin. Supported by private donations from the children and grandchildren of Germans who profited from "Aryanization," this foundation will subsidize the work of Jewish women scholars and artists in Germany. On a more political level, some Jewish doctors and psychologists in Berlin have demanded (November 1992) that non-Jewish medical professionals do something about racism and anti-foreigner hostility ("Wir, die jüdischen Ärzte und Psychologen, fordern jeden auf, sich seiner Verantwortung zu stellen").[75]

In Frankfurt, a Jewish museum was founded in 1988. Its various programs and exhibitions attract wide publicity and many visitors.[76] A Musica Judaica e.V. was founded in January 1989 to play "music of relevance to Jewish culture or with Jewish themes" and to make this music better-known to the public through performances, lectures, and publications.[77] The city of Frankfurt is planning the Fritz Bauer Institute, a "Holocaust Documentation Center" focusing on the history of the genocide and its effect on postwar society.[78]

Within the feminist movement Jewish women have spoken out about their invisibility and Jewish lesbians formed their own secular "Schabbeskreis" with non-Jewish women in the late 1980s. Although the latter dissolved, a "Rundbrief für jüdische Lesben und Feministinnen" recently offered its third issue,[79] and a successor organization, Women against Racism and Anti-Semitism, unites Jewish and non-Jewish women in a political working group. Moreover, L'Chaim, an organization of lesbian and gay Jews, meets to pursue its own interests as well as to raise consciousness about Jews and anti-Semitism in the feminist, lesbian, and gay communities.[80] A book in progress, tentatively entitled "Jewish Women in Berlin," has further served to create a network among Jewish women,[81] and an offshoot of a multicultural feminist project funded by the Berlin senate offers a forum in which Jewish feminists celebrate Jewish holidays such as Hanukkah and Passover.

Many individuals from the Jewish community speak out on racism and anti-Semitism on radio programs, give newspaper interviews, and join discussions at universities (*Podiumsdiskussionen*) but refuse television interviews, fearing for their own safety. Ignatz Bubis has tirelessly spoken out against extremism and strongly criticized the government for having linked hostility toward foreigners with the asylum laws. It was he, not the leading German politicians, who received the longest round of applause after his spontaneous outburst against those who sought to disrupt the antiracist demonstration of November 8, 1992, in Berlin.[82] It remains to be seen whether Jewish organizations will take as high a profile fighting racism as has Bubis. So far, the most publicized action was when *French* Jews went to Rostock in October 1992 to protest the deportation of Roma.[83]

Finally, since unification, Jews have even created a few public places in which they can feel comfortable as Jews. Oranienburger Straße, where the newly renovated synagogue stands, offers cafes, a fashionable kosher restaurant where one can read Jewish newspapers and listen to Israeli music, and theater. Close by another kosher cafe, snack bar, and shop with kosher food and ritual objects are run by Adass Isroel (below). As a result, the Jewish community is seen as playing an important role in Berlin life once again. Night life on Oranienburger Straße is an attraction that brings people from all over Berlin. This may be one of the few places, in fact, where east and west actually mix.[84]

Jews in the Ex-GDR

By 1988 there were approximately 4,000 East Germans of Jewish descent and only about 380 registered Jews in the eight Jewish communities of the GDR. Half of these lived in East Berlin, where the Gemeinde of approximately 180 consisted of about 100 people over the age of 65.[85] A decline in overall numbers showed no sign of slowing. Performance of religious obligations, like maintenance of the cemeteries and the synagogues, would have been impossible for such small communities without the help provided by an ambivalent state. State subsidies, out of all proportion to the population of Jews, provided for the upkeep of cemeteries, monuments and memorial places and the reconstruction and upkeep of synagogues.[86] State youth organizations, as well as private volunteer and church groups, assisted the Jewish community in the physical maintenance of cemeteries.[87] The GDR's major contribution, the reconstruction of the "New Synagogue" on Oranienburger Strasse, will be both a religious community and an international institution for the study of Jewish culture and history, housing a museum and an archive.[88] It is expected that, upon completion, this center will enhance the state of Jewish learning in what is now called the "new *Länder*," and perhaps the state of religiosity as well. This at least was the hope when the New Synagogue was consecrated. Jewish leaders saw it as one of the steps needed to attempt a "vital future for Jewish life" in Berlin.[89]

Few Jews and a weak Jewish infrastructure made Jewish religious and cultural life meager and frequently dependent on Christian support. Religious services were held regularly on the Sabbath in Berlin and on holidays in Dresden, Leipzig, and Erfurt. There has been no permanent rabbi in the east since the death of Dr. Martin Riesenburger in 1965, although sometimes cantors from Hungary would enhance the services of the Gemeinden in Berlin, Dresden, and Leipzig.[90] In Leipzig and Dresden, a choir of Christian women joined the service, adding to its appeal, according to Helmut Eschwege, an historian and citizen of the former GDR. The state subsidized the synagogue choir of over forty in Leipzig.[91] Berlin had a kosher butcher who came regularly from Budapest.

There were few opportunities for Jews to learn much about their religion and culture. Starting in the mid-1970s groups from a Christian organization, Begegnung mit dem Judentum, and individual priests began to hold talks regarding Jewish history. "For Jews in the communities outside Berlin, the talks given by Begegnung mit dem Judentum offered the only opportunity to become acquainted with their history, culture, and religion."[92] Jewish children also had little or no exposure to Judaism. Although a summer camp for Jewish children set up by the Verband der jüdischen Gemeinden *der DDR* had functioned for thirty years, it had not been able to impart much knowledge about Judaism. This educational element was made possible in 1989 when the Zentralrat der Juden in Deutschland sent an Israeli teacher to the camp.[93] Since 1989, the camp included telling children about Judaism and teaching them Jewish and Hebrew songs as well as the Hebrew language.

The East Berlin Community had one recent experience with a rabbi. In the fall of 1987, Rabbi Isaac Neuman, an American rabbi born in Germany, began to officiate in East Berlin. Originally there were high hopes when he accepted this post. The state provided him with an apartment, housekeeper, and an automobile with a driver. The community welcomed him enthusiastically. Soon, however, tensions arose between the rabbi and community leaders. It seems that the community leadership had no intention of rocking the boat vis-à-vis the government, hence the rabbi's open championing of Israel was often a source of conflict. The rabbi, experienced in university towns in the United States, attempted some outreach. An observer reported: "Several—perhaps dozens—of younger, uncommitted Jews in the GDR seem to be intrigued by the prospect of joining the community. Getting them involved in the community's activities would not only enhance their individual lives, but also refurbish Judaism in the country. Some active Jews, however, were less enthusiastic. Community leaders in East Berlin express no interest in organizational commitments that may attract new members whose fundamental faith is questionable."[94] Moreover, the rabbi tried to introduce Reform services, also attempting to bring women into the main seating section. This caused a furor among the traditionalists. He was also perceived by some to be "here for the West Germans and for Israeli television," that is, to be too Zionist, too overwhelming, and too concerned with his congregation's media image in the West.[95] When he resigned in May 1988, both sides seemed to breathe a sigh of relief. Disappointed in his expectations for a Jewish revival, the rabbi concluded that it was "too little and too late."[96] The religious community remained tiny (about two-hundred members and far fewer active participants).[97]

Until unification, the most serious problem of the Jewish community of the East was its declining numbers. Older members had joined for religious reasons, with secular Jews keeping their distance.[98] Members' children often remained within the community and were joined by young people whose parents had broken away from the communities in the past. This solidarity was not necessarily religious: Eschwege felt that "anti-Israel propaganda of the mass media certainly played a significant part."[99]

Since unification, with an increase in the number of Russians as well as an indication that some young Jews, like young Christians, are renewing their interest in religion, there is the possibility of a religious or cultural awakening. The community is thus composed of both religious and non religious Jews. The latter attend synagogue on some occasions, wrote Eschwege, "either out of a sense of solidarity with the parental home or because they feel the ties of a common history."[100] For them, he continued, Israel and/or Jewish history and culture often substitute for religion.

Beyond the official Gemeinde institutions, the examples of the Kulturverein and of Adass Isroel may serve as indications of other options open to the community. In the mid-1980s, a group of about fifty Jews from outside the official community came together for the first time upon invitation by the Gemeinde. This group, called "Wir für Uns," continued to meet, celebrating holidays together, although only few individuals (about 15 percent) actually joined the official Community. "The narrowly religious orientation and strict admissions procedures were deterrents."[101] What developed was "an interested Jewish public around the Jewish Community"[102] that attended its cultural events. In several ways similar to its western counterparts, the alternative Jüdische Gruppen, Wir für Uns consisted largely of writers, intellectuals, and artists, most of whom had strong feelings about being Jews but were either not religious or atheists. For many of them, Wir für Uns was their Jewish "coming out," as one member described it. (Some were communists who did not join the Jewish religious community out of principle.) A good number would also not be considered halachically Jewish and would therefore not have been accepted in the Gemeinde.[103] These Berliners of Jewish or partly Jewish ancestry were mostly between the ages of 25 and 50, that is, similar in age to the generation that has set up alternative groups in the West. Ultimately this group may have numbered between 150 and 250 East Berliners, thus possibly outnumbering the Gemeinde in East Berlin. The Jüdischer Kulturverein grew from this largely secular group.

The Kulturverein was founded in January 1990 by those who remained apart from the official East Berlin Gemeinde and refused to be swallowed up by the 6,000 West Berlin Jews and their "West German arrogance."[104] It sought a sense of "what it meant to be Jewish"[105] and stood open to all self-identified Jews with a secular, leftist identity. It intended to "bring together all GDR citizens of Jewish ancestry [*Herkunft*] and their next of kin regardless of their world view [*Weltanschauung*] and in memory of the millions of Jewish martyrs. The club will focus on Jewish history and the spread of knowledge about Jewish history and culture and, as a result of its efforts, strives to preserve Judaism and Jewish life."[106] Its newsletter stated: "It does not matter to us how much someone knows about Judaism or where they come from. We are tolerant. Without any ado Jewish immigrants and their families are welcome. . . . [We consider ourselves] left, conversational . . . intellectual, ready to help, curious and able to learn."[107] Unlike the groups it resembles in the West to whom Russians come in small numbers, the Kulturverein is quite popular among immigrants from the former USSR. Work with Jews from the former Soviet Union is a priority. The organization provides conversations between Soviet- and German-born Jews to encourage interaction;[108] it offers German conversation circles to help the former Soviets improve their new language skills; it supports the Friedländer School to help former Soviet Jews learn German (an eight-month course is now recognized by employment offices); its members act as unofficial intermediaries between the former Soviets and the Berlin bureaucracy; and it sponsors a Russian-language edition of its newsletter.

While the official Gemeinde has far greater means at its disposal, and hence can care for many more ex-Soviet Jews, the Kulturverein reaches out to those whose Jewish identity is closer to its own. The ex-Soviets have come with very complicated backgrounds. One example may suffice. One man has a Jewish mother and a Russian father. He feels deeply rooted in Russian culture. By nationality he is Russian, by Jewish law he is Jewish. In Lithuania, he was considered a Russian, and he is in Berlin only because he could claim to be a Jew. His wife and child, however, are not considered Jews by the Gemeinde. On his membership card in the Gemeinde there is a big "N" (for not Jewish) in front of their names.[109] The Kulturverein, on the other hand, welcomes precisely such families.[110]

The Kulturverein is spurned by those who see Judaism as a commitment to a synagogue community and hence see the Kulturverein as competing with the synagogues. The Kulturverein welcomes everyone, thereby recognizing a split in the community between those accepted as Jews by the synagogues and those whose Jewish heritage/lineage (from mixed marriages in particular) is subject to question. Some fear that because the Kulturverein does not define Jewishness in purely religious categories, it breaks with previous German-Jewish traditions which defined Judaism as a faith and raises the specter of seeing Jews as a "national minority,"[111] which some Hungarian Jews are actually demanding.[112] This could play into the hands of those Germans who also see Jews as a different nationality, hence not "German." Also, some steer clear of the Kulturverein because many of its members were either children of communists, were themselves once close to the SED, or are still in the PDS.[113] The Kulturverein offers a meeting place for East Berlin Jews who "mourn the utopia of a just state." According to one regular visitor, "They have lost their political and state identities and are discovering their Jewish one."[114] Here we see Jewishness as an alternative to politics or a cover-up for politics in contrast to the western alternative groups whose organizations are also an extension of politics. While one can recognize the loaded political context in which the Kulturverein was founded and continues to operate, it nevertheless attempts, successfully for the moment, to recreate a form of Jewish life.

What does Jewish life consist of at the Kulturverein?[115] In terms of strictly religious devotion, the Kulturverein only informs its members about the newspapers that list synagogue services. Yet there is a surprising amount of religious activity and religious interest. On Rosh Hashanah, they invited members to meet after services to eat apples and honey together.[116] Purim presented an opportunity for exchanging ideas about the Story of Esther and eating Hamantaschen. In 1991 the Verein sponsored its first Hanukkah dance. An ultra-Orthodox rabbi in Jerusalem places weekly calls to one of the Kulturverein organizers, Dr. Irene Runge, to explain the portion of the Torah that is designated for the Sabbath. He sees this as a *mitzvah* and is neither paid for the service nor reimbursed for the phone calls. Then, on Friday evenings, the rabbi's interpretations are shared in German and Russian with Kulturverein members, who observe the Sabbath by lighting candles in their meeting room.[117] The Kulturverein also arranges access to rabbis for further education. These rabbis are visitors from Jerusalem and from the west. In particular, rabbis come from the ultra-Orthodox Chabad sect in London; they serve free of charge and see this as a mission. Their participation raises the obvious question of what kind of Judaism these leftists are encouraging—that excludes their female leaders and makes women pray separately? Strange bedfellows. Cost is a crucial factor in accepting the aid of the ultra-Orthodox, since the Kulturverein can not afford its own rabbis. But, Runge, a journalist, sociologist and indefatigable organizer, also argues, "We have to know the real rules before we make our own." She believes, "We need religious people [*die Frommen*] in order to learn. We may run dry, but not the Orthodox."[118] Like some of her western counterparts, Runge's statement gives the impression of a feeling of inferiority vis-à-vis the "legitimate" Orthodox and a lack of confidence that Jews can function without tutelage of this kind.

When a visiting rabbi is available, the Kulturverein invites members to discussions (after regular Saturday morning services in other synagogues) about the portion of the Torah that was just read,[119] and Orthodox rabbis lead the Passover Seders and Hanukkah celebrations. Since the membership is often uneducated in Jewish traditions, German transcriptions of Hebrew or Yiddish songs make celebrations easier.[120] The newsletter offers short explanations of various holidays or traditions, explaining basic religious terminology such as the concept "erev."[121] It is not unusual for the newsletter to remind men to wear a head covering if they visit a synagogue service. Moreover, the Kulturverein playfully mixes some holidays. It invited members to a "Weihnukka" afternoon where, in good German-Jewish tradition, Hanukkah was celebrated with Christmas *Stollen* and coffee. As can be seen with the mixture of Orthodox (*Chabad*) rabbis and Christmas *Stollen*, the Verein will "adopt parts of the tradition as it sees fit." ("Wir werden im Kulturverein auf unsere Weise an diese Tradition anknüpfen.")[122]

To promote Jewish culture, the Kulturverein has offered a broad variety of lectures by visiting scholars and Jewish spokespeople, all of whom appear without honoraria. The Verein has also sponsored Jewish and Israeli dance classes, a music group, a theater group (which performed *The Dybbuk*), an Isaac Babel evening, evenings of Yiddish, Hebrew, and Russian songs, readings by Jewish authors, and films on Jewish topics. It is also trying to increase its lending library of Jewish periodicals and books on Jewish themes. Of further interest to some members is research on the genocide against the Jews. The newspaper has made a call for survivors' testimonies.[123] Discussions about children who survived[124] and readings by authors who survived take place. Further, the Verein organizes vacations for Jewish children in a Jewish summer camp.[125] Lectures and films focusing on Israel offer participants a variety of options for relating to the state of Israel. In other words, since many ex-GDR and ex-Soviet citizens have heard nothing but anti-Zionist views, the Verein attempts to introduce them to the pros and cons of the "actual existing" state of Israel.

The Verein has had mixed relations with other Jewish organizations. Discussions and cooperation with other "outsider" groups takes place, but it seems to be ignored by the official community. When asked in a "letter to the editor" (*Leserbrief*) about how the Jewish "establishment" relates to the Kulturverein, its editors answered coyly: "We assume that they value us because we are Jews who work for other Jews, and assume that because of time constraints [*aus Zeitgründen*] they have not been able to share these feelings with us yet."[126] There is bitterness, because the *Verein* believes its attempts to attract funding from the city are blocked by the official community.[127]

In sum, and most importantly it seems to me, the Kulturverein offers a place for Jews who feel alienated from or are rejected by the Gemeinde. Its meetings and club rooms provide a home for a growing numbers of secular Jews. Along with the Jüdische Gruppe and the new ex-Soviet immigrants, it constitutes a growing segment of the Jewish population of Berlin.

One further case deserves brief mention: the former Orthodox community Adass Isroel, founded in 1869, was reestablished in the late 1980s by Mario Offenberg, the son and grandson of former members of the community. His lawyer, Lothar de Maizière, who was briefly prime minister of the GDR, was able to get the former property of Adass in Berlin returned to its representative, Offenberg. The community has few members, but Offenberg was able to receive a large subsidy from the state when de Maizière was in office. A bitter controversy has ensued regarding the congregation's legitimacy as well as the pluralism Adass represents, a threat to the Einheitsgemeinde. Ironically, it is the Orthodox Adass which today stands for pluralism within Judaism, demanding that German[128]—and Jewish—authorities recognize the variety of Jewish synagogues, organizations, and clubs that already exist and may be founded in the future.[129] Adass attempts to increase the number of Orthodox Jews and to teach new Russian immigrants Orthodox customs. Besides regular services and a lecture series, it has established a small Talmud Torah, seminars about Judaism and Jewish history, a kosher cafe, a kosher store and snack bar, and Hebrew classes (twenty-three students in 1990). It has also continued to restore its old cemetery (a project begun by the ex-GDR) and built a small chapel there. Having renovated the synagogue, Adass is presently reconstructing a mikva.[130] About seventy people attended last year's Passover Seder, which—like the Seder of the atheist Kulturverein—was supported by the Chabad

Center in London.[131] Clearly, the Lubavitch have found receptive audiences in the new Germany.

What can we expect from Jewish life in the new *Länder*?[132] My sense is that we will not see a religious revival, but that a cultural revival is occurring at this very moment. Lest one expect too much, however, we must keep in mind that Judaism is not the main concern on the minds of Jews of the former GDR. In many ways, they share more with Christians of the ex-GDR than with Jews from the West. They share the hopes and fears of other Germans in the East with regard to the concrete situation of their lives:[133] fears for their jobs, loss of social security nets to which they had grown accustomed, and the general psychological and political pressures they face vis-à-vis the "Wessies." With regard to the last issue, the eastern Berlin community has been amalgamated with the western one, which means that financial decisions are made in the West, not a particularly happy situation. Whether greater contact with Israeli and Western Jewry will lead to more guest rabbis in the East or more exchange visits by children is yet to be seen.

"People are starting to feel Jewish again," states Leon Zelman of Vienna's Jewish Welcome Service. Young East European Jews come there to find out what it means to be Jewish.[134] The new freedom in Eastern Europe, along with increasing anti-Semitism and emigration to Israel, has raised Jewish consciousness there. In Hungary, there are about 80,000 Jews, mostly in Budapest, where they make up five percent of the city's population. But one need not have resided behind the so-called Iron Curtain in order to experience the renewal of Jewish life. In France, too, with its approximately 600,000 Jews, one can speak of a revitalization in the Jewish community and an increase in religiosity. In both countries, to varying degrees, a vigorous Jewish culture has developed, likely due to their large Jewish populations.

If one adds the approximately 40,000 Jews from the western and the approximately 4,000 Jews from the eastern sections of Germany together, one still has a small number—perhaps ultimately too small to support a renaissance of religious or secular Jewish culture.[135] Nevertheless, the last decade, particularly the years since the *Wende*, has seen the growth of a lively secular Jewish culture in the big cities.

What one observes developing in Germany is a broader definition of "Judaism" and a broader spectrum of cultural and secular groups than was known previously. Encouraged by the unification and frightened by the increase in anti-Semitism, Jews in Germany are turning to each other and developing new forms of Jewish expression, some religious but most secular. The challenge will be to maintain these varying forms of Judaism, to include the smaller cities and towns in them, and to involve the new Russian immigrants in Jewish life.

Notes

1. Interview with Cilly Kugelmann by Tobe Levin, 17 November 1992. Thanks to Tobe Levin for sharing the interview with me.
2. I would like to thank Maria Baader, Wendy Henry, Tobe Levin, and Lothar Mertens for providing source materials and much encouragement. Many thanks go also to Douglas Morris for his editorial advice and support. Any errors of fact or interpretation are, of course, my own. "Culture" is defined in this way by Edward B. Tylor, *Primitive Culture* (London, 1871), and is also used in much this manner by Frykman and Löfgren, *The Culture Builders* (New Brunswick, N.J., 1987). Mordechai Kaplan, rabbi, philosopher, and founder of the Reconstructionist Movement, also defined Judaism broadly in his book *Judaism as a Civilization*, and created the idea of the Jewish Center.
3. Micha Brumlik *et al.*, eds., *Jüdisches Leben in Deutschland seit 1945* (Frankfurt/Main, 1986). In particular, see the essay by Monika Richarz in this volume.
4. Monika Richarz, "Juden in der BRD und in der DDR seit 1945," in Brumlik, *Jüdisches Leben*, 22.
5. Daniel Wildmann, "Eine Gemeinde im Sterben," *Semit* February 1991, 75–76, 88. See also several of the communities surveyed by Michael Brenner in the *Allgemeine Jüdische Wochenzeitung* in January and February 1985.
6. Discussion of new survey by Alphons Silbermann and Herbert Sallen, *Juden in Westdeutschland. Selbstbild und Fremdbild einer Minorität* (Verlag Wissenschaft und Politik) in *Die Zeit*, 13 November 1992. Attitudes toward the *Gemeinde* can be found in an article on recent Jewish youth conference; see *Allgemeine Jüdische Wochenzeitung*, 26 November 1992.
7. Y. Michal Bodemann, "Jüdische kulturelle Vielfalt, oder Judentum der Funktionäre?" in *Semit* March 1991, 82–84.
8. In Cologne, for example, half of the Gemeinderat of twelve comes

from the younger generation. *Allgemeine Jüdische Wochenzeitung,* 1 February 1985.

9. Population, for example, has grown rapidly. Statistics for 1991 show the following figures for the largest *Gemeinden:* Berlin (both East and West), 9,394; Frankfurt, 5,322; Munich, 4,095; Cologne, 1,437; Hamburg, 1,393. Berlin added a record number in 1991: 2,659 new members. As of 1991, 33,630 Jews lived in Germany, including more men than women. Age groups most heavily represented include: thirty-one to forty, 5,498; forty-one to fifty, 4,809; sixty-one to seventy, 4,225. Source: *Zentrale Wohlfahrtsstelle der Juden in Deutschland e.V. Mitgliederstatistik* January 1992 in *Unabhängige Jüdische Stimme,* September 1992, 11. This journal was only into its second issue as of September 1992. It is the organ of the "Demokratische Liste," an alternative to the establishment list and the opposition within the representative body of the Berlin community.

   More recent statistics quoted by Ignatz Bubis in an interview were: roughly 40,000 Jews in Germany, up from about 28,500 in 1989 as a result of the Russian immigration (*Rheinischer Merkur,* 13 November 1992). Estimates go as high as 50,000 Jews, since many are not registered with the Jewish communities.
10. About 25,000 Soviet Jews have entrance permits to Germany (*New York Times,* 23 March 1992: A4).
11. *Washington Post,* 5 March 1992: Dl, D4, quoting Julius Schoeps. See also: *Frankfurter Allgemeine Zeitung,* 12 March 1993.
12. Cologne, with almost as large a community, took only 100 Russians, and Frankfurt with 5,000 members took 250. *Semit,* December 1991/January 1992, 71.
13. *Semit,* December 1991/January 1992, 71.
14. Jack Zipes, "The Vicissitudes of Being Jewish in West Germany," in Anson Rabinbach and Jack Zipes, eds., *German Jews since the Holocaust* (New York, 1986), 38.
15. The figure of 75 comes from the *Rheinischer Merkur,* 13 November 1992, 3.
16. *Stimme,* September 1992, 10
17. *Jüdische Gemeindezeitung Frankfurt,* October/December 1990, 6.
18. *Unabhängige Jüdische Stimme,* September 1992, 10.
19. This precedent was set years ago by Heinz Galinski in going to Auschwitz on the Sabbath to protest Reagan and Kohl's visit to Bitburg.
20. Five hundred people, or 10 percent of the community, attended, probably as a result of the increasing attacks on foreign residents and rising anti-Semitic incidents.
21. *Allgemeine Jüdische Wochenzeitung,* 19 November 1992.
22. *Jüdische Gemeindezeitung Frankfurt,* October/December 1990, 8.
23. *Rheinischer Merkur,* 13 November 1992, 3.
24. Program, spring 1991 and fall 1991—six out of twenty-four offerings.

25. Six out of fourteen courses.
26. *Jüdische Gemeindezeitung Frankfurt*, September/October 1992, 24.
27. *Berlin-Umschau*, April 1990, 2.
28. The complete course offerings for spring 1991 included Jewish Festivals and Holidays; Israeli Literature; the Jewish Proletariat of Frankfurt; the Crusades; two Yiddish language courses; the Kosher Kitchen; Israel and the Gulf War; Russian Jews since 1914; Yiddish Humor; the World of the Prophets; Jewish-American Literature. In fall 1991, the school offered: Jewish Festivals and Holidays; the Kosher Kitchen; the Jew in Literature; Yiddish Humor; Yiddish Songs; the World of the Prophets; two Yiddish language courses; Anti-Semitism; Jewish Literati; Russian-Jewish Literature; Jewish Life in America. The fall 1992 offerings included: Jewish Festivals and Holidays; the Kosher Kitchen; Hebrew; Jewish Literati; the Rabbinical World; Dr. Esperanto; Gershom Scholem's Sabbatai Zwi; Yiddish; Modern Rabbis; Art and Judaism; Jewish Life in Germany; Jewish Expressionist Authors; Jewish Cemeteries in Frankfurt. These programs are available from the Jüdische Volkshochschule Frankfurt am Main.
29. The school presently runs fifteen courses for 220 students. *Jüdische Gemeindezeitung Frankfurt*, September/October 1992, 24.
30. Interview with Tobe Levin, whose child attends the Frankfurt school, December 1992. Similar issues seem to be involved in the Berlin day school: a longer day is attractive to parents, as is a smaller school in which the children get to know one another and are sheltered from anti-Semitic language or incidents. Class size remains 18 to 20, small by German public school standards. Although this year's sixth grade went to Israel, the children do not seem to learn Hebrew well. One pupil noted that "we learned more English in one year than Hebrew in five." *Stimme*, September 1992, 27.
31. "Nachrichten aus der Jüdischen Gemeinde," *Berlin-Umschau*, November 1992, 14. The gymnasium has 24 students; *Boston Globe*, 7 August 1993, 1.
32. *Berlin-Umschau*, March 1990, 5.
33. *Berlin-Umschau*, October 1992, 13.
34. Available from Jüdische Gemeinde zu Berlin.
35. For more information, contact Jüdische Ärzte und Psychologen in Berlin, Postfach 12 73 25, 1000 Berlin 12.
36. *Berlin-Umschau*, October 1992, 4.
37. On Koblenz: Marguerite Marcus, active in the Jewish community, discussion in December 1992.

    The Jewish Community of Halle (in the ex-GDR) held its first Seder in fifty years in March 1991. The Gemeinde rented a restaurant and invited Russian Jews to attend the Seder, giving it both a reason and the extra bodies it needed to make a festive occasion. *Mitteldeutsche Zeitung*

Halle, 3 March 1991, 7.

38. Unfortunately, since Rostock, the picture of the packed suitcase has reappeared. When Bubis appeared in Rostock as a result of the right-wing attacks on foreigners, the Vorsitzender des Innenausschusses der Bürgerschaft, Karlheinz Schmidt, asked him, "You are a German citizen of the Jewish faith? Your home is Israel. Is that right?" *Die Zeit,* 25 December 1992, 7. Moreover, while recent right-wing attacks have caused severe depression and increased anxiety among Jewish survivors of concentration camps, young Jews, too, have reacted by thinking about emigration once again. See *taz,* week of 10 December 1992, interview with psychologist Anath Sieff.
39. Anat Feinberg, "Wende, Umbruch, oder Krise? Anmerkungen zum jüdischen Leben in der Bundesrepublik," *Tribüne: Zeitschrift zum Verständnis des Judentums* 29. 114 (1990), 139.
40. Feinberg, "Wende," 139. Brumlik called it a "Nach-Shoah Identität."
41. Similar groups appeared outside of the FRG as well, in Zurich and Vienna in the early 1980s.
42. Jan Turner, "In der deutschen Diaspora tut sich was," *Semit,* February 1991, 74.
43. There were about forty members as of November 1990 and over eighty members as of spring 1992. As of January 1991, the group calls itself the Jüdisches Forum e.V. The group actually grew out of an earlier group that was formed as a result of the invasion of Lebanon in 1982.
44. Feinberg, "Wende," 144. She estimates that 40 percent are not halachically Jewish.
45. Turner, "Deutsche Diaspora," 74. Some members of the Cologne group describe the difficulty of having the Gemeinde accept a diverse cultural program to which unaffiliated Jews and interested non-Jews would come. Moreover, they insist there are many unaffiliated Jews who do not come to the Gemeinde because they don't feel represented by the aged, isolationist Gemeinde in Cologne (the Berlin and Frankfurt Gemeinde are old and patriarchal but not isolationist). Most initiative and energy that comes from outside is sabotaged by an elderly, fearful Gemeinde leadership. Even as younger people enter the leadership, problems still occur. Rafi Rotenberg and Anat Feinberg, "Von Solchen, die auszogen, Jüdische Kulturarbeit zu machen," *Semit,* March 1990, 56–58.
46. Feinberg, "Wende," 143.
47. Jüdischer Kulturverein newsletter of November 1990.
48. *Semit,* February/March 1992, 63, notes discussions with Israeli Mapam members.
49. Igal Avidan, "Wem Schenkte der Senate eine Ausstellung?" *SemitTimes: Das Deutsch-Jüdische Meinungs- und Zeitmagazin,* April/May 1992, 58.
50. Pnina Navè Levinson, quoting Yizhak Ahren in "Religiöse Richtungen

und Entwicklungen in den Gemeinden," in Micha Brumlik *et al.*, eds., *Jüdisches Leben in Deutschland seit 1945* (Frankfurt/Main, 1986), 141.

51. *Berlin-Umschau*, November 1992, 2.
52. *Berlin-Umschau*, October 1992, 14.
53. *Berlin-Umschau*, October 1992, 14.
54. *Berlin-Umschau*, February 1990, 8.
55. The Hochschule was founded by the Zentralrat der Juden in Deutschland in 1979. It offers a Masters degree (*Magister Artium*) in Jewish studies. About 20 percent of its students are Jewish. Many of them go on to work in Jewish community offices as social workers, youth leaders, and teachers. Those who want to go on to become rabbis must go out of the country for rabbinical schools and ordination. *Berlin-Umschau*, January 1990, 1, 6–7. *Die Zeit* claims that 20 of 125 students are Jewish, 25 December 1992, 8.
56. *Berlin-Umschau*, January 1990, 7.
57. Levinson, "Richtungen," 143.
58. Thanks to Daniel Levy (Cologne and New York) for this discussion. New York, January 1993.
59. Last quotation in letter from Monika Richarz, 12 February 1993. Yeshiva mentioned in letter from Monika Richarz, 25 October 1992, re Dr. Tuwia Kwasmann, now teaching Talmud at the university in Cologne.
60. About forty people attended the services in Stommeln in 1991. *Semit*, February/March 1992, 63.
61. Letter from Monika Richarz, 25 October 1992.
62. Discussion with Marguerite Marcus, December 1992.
63. *Ibid.* The woman rabbinical student has also necessitated some very minor changes in the Fränkelufer Synagogue, where she sits with the other women but is allowed to wear her Talit as long as it looks like a scarf under her jacket. She sometimes discusses the weekly readings of the Torah with members of the congregation during Kiddush, after the actual services are over.
64. Letter from Bea Wyler, 18 December 1992.
65. The issue of women seems to be raised only by a younger generation of critics—and male at that. See Y. Michal Bodemann, "Vielfalt," 83. At a Youth Congress in 1990, Micha Brumlik talked about the need for reform in the synagogue regarding women's position. "Galinski ist uns über: Jüdischer Jugendkongress 1990," *Semit*, January 1991, 39.
66. At the moment, about 70 percent of the 9,000-member Berlin Jewish Community is made up of recently arrived Jews from Eastern Europe, mostly from Russia. *Frankfurter Allgemeine Zeitung*, 24 November 1992, trans. in *The German Tribune*, 4 December 1992, 11, 14.
67. Letter from Bea Wyler, 18 December 1992.
68. Lothar Mertens, "Jüdische Gemeinden in der DDR: Zwischen Anpassung und politischer Instrumentalisierung," *Tribüne: Zeitschrift zum*

Verständnis des Judentums 28.111: 180. Although this is a description of the East German situation, similar feelings are prevalent in the West.

69. Susan Neiman, *Slow Fire: Jewish Notes from Berlin* (New York, 1992), 212.
70. Discussion with M. Marcus.
71. Instead of practicing outreach, the Gemeinden had to sift out the "real" Jews from the many who claimed Jewish identity for special privileges after the war. This attitude remains to this day, with strict adherence to Orthodox definitions of "who is a Jew." See Levinson, "Richtungen," 149.
72. *Spiegel* Spezial, February 1992 ("Juden und Deutsche"), 26.
73. *Der Tagesspiegel*, 26 April 1992, trans. in *The German Tribune*, 15 May 1992, 10.
74. *German Tribune*, 15 May 1992, 15.
75. Poster that was distributed in hospitals and clinics to attract the attention of non-Jewish medical personnel, November 1992. Thanks to Marguerite Marcus for giving me this material.
76. *Jüdische Gemeindezeitung Frankfurt*, August/September 1990, 62–63.
77. *Jüdische Gemeindezeitung Frankfurt*, October/December 1990, 13.
78. *Frankfurter Jüdische Nachrichten*, December 1992, 2.
79. Tobe Levin, speech to the Europäische Frauen Aktion conference, 3–7 December 1992, Berlin. Issue No. 3 was published on 15 May 1992. The newsletter has since been temporarily cancelled due to the illness of its editor.
80. L'Chaim was founded in 1990 in Amsterdam, where the second European Conference of Lesbian and Gay Jews met. The group intends to give its members the opportunity to "jointly live the Jewish tradition." Members of the group who are authors have given readings, and the group as a whole has also demanded citizenship rights for immigrants and open borders for refugees.
81. The book is being edited by Wendy Henry, Jessica Jacoby, and Gudlinde Lwanga.
82. *The European*, 12–15 November 1992, 12. The Zentralrat (with Bubis as signatory) and the Gewerkschaft Erziehung und Wissenschaft have also cooperated on anti-racist programs and flyers. (Joint Petition of the Zentralrat der Juden in Deutschland and the union Erziehung und Wissenschaft, Frankfurt/Main, 9 December 1992.)
83. The Frankfurt Gemeinde newsletter also runs editorials against right-wing extremism. In Berlin, during the official Gemeinde commemoration (1992) of the November pogrom, the Gemeinde chair, Jerzy Kanal, criticized government policies to an auditorium full of Berlin officials: "If Article 16 is questioned today as a result of pressure from the mob [*Pöbel*], then this is more than an encouragement to further crimes; then this mob determines the politics of this country." In 1991 the Gemeinde had suggested the formation of a "Bündnis gegen

Ausländerfeindlichkeit," which was joined by major unions (DGB), the Berlin senate, and the Landesregierung of Brandenburg. The Gemeinde initiated a silent protest (*Schweigemarsch*) with these groups on 16 September 1992 against increasing racism in Germany. Flyer announcing *Schweigemarsch*, printed by Jüdische Gemeinde zu Berlin, September 1992. See also *Berlin-Umschau*, October 1992, 1. Some alternative Jewish groups have also formed alliances for demonstrations against racism, for example, on 9 November 1991, the *Jüdisches Forum* in Cologne joined six other organizations in a "Stop Rassismus" demonstration. *Semit*, February/March 1992, 63.

84. *Frankfurter Allgemeine Zeitung*, 24 November 1992, trans. in *The German Tribune*, 4 December 1992, 11, 14.
85. Thanks to Lothar Mertens for sharing this information with me. In 1989 only 350 members were left. Lothar Mertens, "Jüdische Gemeinden in der DDR," *Tribüne*, 28.111 (1989), 171. See also: *Jerusalem Post*, 13 February 1990, 7.
86. Paul O'Doherty, "The GDR, Its Jews, and the USA," in *Politics and Society in Germany, Austria and Switzerland*, 4.2 (1992), 26. For a full discussion of the ambivalence of the GDR toward the Jewish community, see, Helmut Eschwege, "The Churches and the Jews in the German Democratic Republic," in *Leo Baeck Institute Year Book*, 1992, 497–513.
87. Richard L. Merritt, "Politics of Judaism in the GDR," *Studies in GDR Culture and Society* 9 (Papers from the Fourteenth New Hampshire Symposium on the German Democratic Republic, Lanham, 1989), 177–78. For example, the statistics indicate that the Jewish community in Magdeburg has twelve members to look after forty-two cemeteries in the surrounding province, the city of Erfurt has twelve members to care for thirty-five cemeteries in Thuringia, and four Jews in Mecklenburg have to look after three cemeteries. Without Aktion Sühnezeichen and the churches, this would be impossible. Eschwege, "Jews in the GDR," 505.
88. Merritt, "Politics of Judaism in the GDR."
89. *Die Welt*, 28 (6 September 6 1991), 2.
90. Mertens, "Jüdische Gemeinden," *Tribüne*, 180.
91. Eschwege, "Jews in the GDR," 500, 506. Today Leipzig has only sixty-three Jews, thirty of whom are immigrants from the ex-USSR. Most of the German members of the Gemeinde are over the age of sixty. *Die Zeit* 18 December 1992, 10.
92. *Ibid.*, 502.
93. *Ibid.*, 506.
94. Merritt, "Politics of Judaism in the GDR," 186.
95. Robin Ostow, *Jews in Contemporary East Germany: The Children of Moses in the Land of Marx* (New York, 1989), 152–53.
96. Mertens, "Jüdische Gemeinden," *Tribüne*, 180. For the rabbi's point of

view, his reasons for leaving, particularly his dislike of Dr. Kirchner and the Stasi, see Anita Kugler, "Ein Rabbi für die Staatssicherheit," *Semit*, February/March 1992, 49.

97. Dr. Peter Kirchner, the head of the East Berlin community, pointed out that about ten percent of the community attended prayer services (about twenty people), "which isn't bad compared to other communities." Ostow, *Jews*, 18.
98. Ostow, *Jews*, 16.
99. Eschwege, "Jews in the GDR," 501.
100. *Ibid.*, 510.
101. Robin Ostow, "German Democratic Republic," *American Jewish Year Book 1989*, 351.
102. *Ibid.*, 351.
103. *Jerusalem Post*, 12 December 1989, 7. "Coming out" quote by Konstantin Münz, *Wochenpost*, 14 January 1993, 6–7.
104. *Die Zeit*, 18 December 1992, 10.
105. *Jüdische Korrespondenz* (this is the new name of the *Kulturverein* newsletter), February 1992, 1.
106. "Er soll . . . der Zusammenschluss von in der DDR lebenden Bürgern jüdischer Herkunft und ihren Angehörigen unabhängig von ihrer Weltanschauung sein und ist dem Gedenken der Millionen jüdischer Opfer verpflichtet. Der Verein richtet seine Aufmerksamkeit auf die Geschichte der Juden und auf die Verbreitung des Wissens über jüdische Geschichte und Kultur und erstrebt mit seiner Tätigkeit die Bewahrung des Judentums und des jüdischen Lebens. . . ." Stefan Schreiner, "Zwischen Hoffnung und Furcht: Die jüdischen Gemeinden in der DDR nach der Wende," in Dieter Voigt and Lothar Mertens, eds., *Minderheiten in und Übersiedler aus der DDR* (Berlin, 1992), 195.
107. *Jüdische Korrespondenz* , February 1992, 1.
108. Jüdischer Kulturverein newsletter, June 1990. The first Soviet Jews arrived in East Berlin in April 1990. About 6,000 Soviets entered Germany between April 1990 and March 1991; about 4,000 of them came to Berlin. By the summer of 1991, about 11,000 more permits had been requested of the Soviet authorities. Irene Runge, *Vom Kommen und Bleiben: Osteuropäische jüdische Einwanderer in Berlin* (Berlin, 1993), 17.
109. *Ibid.*, 44.
110. One study of 500 immigrants from the former Soviet Union in a dormitory in Lichtenberg found only 15 percent who were Jewish by strict Jewish law. *Ibid.*, 52.
111. Schreiner, "Zwischen Hoffnung und Furcht," 196.
112. "Teuflisches Kind: Antisemitische Haßtiraden aus der Regierungspartie: Der Schriftsteller István Csurka beunruhigt die Juden des

Landes," *Der Spiegel*, 42 (1992), 24.
113. Schreiner, "Zwischen Hoffnung und Furcht," 196.
114. *Die Zeit*, 18 December 1992, 10.
115. An examination of its newsletter for the last two years gives some clues as to the interests of its members (over 100 as of February 1991 but with far larger attendance at its major events).
116. Jüdischer Kulturverein newsletter, 31 August 1990.
117. "Phoning the Faithful," *New York Times*, 16 January 1993, L9.
118. First quote from *Jerusalem Post*, 12 December 1989, 7. Second quote from *Stern*, 16 December 1992, 115 ("[Zum Lernen] Brauchen wir die Frommen. Denn wir versiegen. Die Orthodoxie nicht").
119. Jüdischer Kulturverein newsletter of November 1990.
120. *Jüdischer Korrespondenz*, April 1992, 4.
121. Jüdischer Kulturverein newsletter, February 1991.
122. *Jüdische Korrespondenz*, April 1992, 1.
123. Jüdischer Kulturverein newsletter, February 1990.
124. Jüdischer Kulturverein newsletter, November 90. The discussion was led by Dr. Judith Kestenberg (New York), a psychoanalyst who has worked with children who survived.
125. Irene Runge, *Vom Kommen und Bleiben*, 50.
126. Jüdischer Kulturverein newsletter, July 1991, 4.
127. *Jüdische Korrespondenz*, December 1991, 2.
128. The Berlin Senate, for example, does not recognize Adass. *Nachrichten von Adass Isroel*, April 1992, 7.
129. *Nachrichten von Adass Isroel*, September 1992, editorial entitled "Vielfalt," 15–17. See also Henryk M. Broder, "Tote Seelen in Berlin; oder Die Wundersame Wiederaufstehung der jüdischen Gemeinde *Adass Isroel* als Familienbetrieb—eine deutsch-jüdische Posse aus der Wendezeit," *Die Zeit* 4 (26 September, 1991), 52. For the GDR side of this affair, see Lothar Mertens, "Die SED und *Adass Isroel*," in *Tribune: Zeitschrift zum Verständnis des Judentums* 31.123 (1992).

For Adass's response to Broder, see: "*Adass Isroel* lebt," by Mario Offenberg in *Semit*, December/January 1992, 34–9. After listing the services that Adass provides, he pleads for many Gemeinden on the model of other countries, rather than forcing differing types of Jews into an *Einheits*gemeinde. (He argues there are five Gemeinden in Paris and Zurich, thirty-one in London, and hundreds in New York.)
130. *Nachrichten von Adass Isroel*, September/October 1990, 4,6,8; *Nachrichten von Adass Isroel*, September 1992, 15.
131. *Nachrichten von Adass Isroel*, September 1992, 2. In the summer of 1991 it supported a two-week summer camp where Jewish children from Germany and Eastern Europe learned Jewish customs and Hebrew. *Nachrichten von Adass Isroel*, September/October 1991, 12–3.
132. First of all, a consolidation has taken place. In united Germany,

Berlin combines both eastern and western Berlin communities (as of 1 January 1991) and the remaining seven communities are supposed to amalgamate into two (with Erfurt joining Hesse.) Eschwege, "Jews in the GDR," 512.

133. Schreiner, "Zwischen Hoffnung und Furcht," 189.

134. *Newsweek*, 7 May 1990, 37.

135. This was the point made by Ignatz Bubis in an interview on the Norddeutsche Rundfunk, radio interview, 2 January 1993: "With a community of 30,000 recently risen to 40,000, you cannot talk about a renaissance."

5. "What Could Be More Fruitful, More Healing, More Purifying?" Representations of Jews in the German Media after 1989

Katharina Ochse

After years of widespread disinterest, there is no doubt that the attention paid to contemporary things Jewish, especially in the western part of Germany, has grown tremendously since 1989. Considering the number of publications, exhibits, and the large focus on Jewish topics in the media, one could get the impression that the country had a few hundred thousand Jews and a blossoming German Jewish culture. The increased attention given Jews is remarkable when one takes into account the past disinterest and the size of the Jewish population: there are about 40,000 Jews. In a united Germany with approximately 80 million inhabitants, these Jews have become a mini-minority. The probability that a non-Jew would ever meet a Jew is very small. So why is there such an interest in Jewish subjects? An analysis of the media coverage can provide us with a partial answer to this question, shed light on the reasons for this interest in things Jewish, give us an idea of how the majority of (non-Jewish) Germans perceive the Jews, and at the same time offer insight into current Jewish self-representation. Examining the representation of Jews in the media in terms of Germany's historical and contemporary self-definition will help us to clarify what this trend reveals about Germany's attitude toward its history and its present.

"Liebe jüdische Mitbürger"[1]—"My dear Jewish fellow citizens"—with these words *Bundespräsident* Richard von Weizsäcker opened his Rosh Hashannah greeting in the *Allgemeine Jüdische Wochenzeitung*. The formula "jüdische Mitbürger," which is quite in vogue,[2] implies that Jews are not German citizens in the same sense as non-Jewish citizens. The form of von Weizsäcker's address itself leads to the question of how Jews are perceived in Germany. The answer to this question illuminates the current German conception of Self and Other.

A recent special edition of the news magazine *Der Spiegel* was entitled "Juden und Deutsche."[3] In the United States "Jews and Germans" is the standard formulation. However, whoever uses this terminology robs the Jews of their citizenship, as if they were not also Germans. To speak of "Jews and non-Jews" reduces the identity of those who aren't Jews to the compliment of "Jews." To speak of "Jews and Christians" outside of a religious context does not live up to the reality of today's largely secularized Germany, either, so this sort of terminology is found only in articles on interfaith meetings. It may be that the solution to this dilemma is to ask Jews how they refer to themselves, that is, how they would like to be referred to. But one would get various answers to this question. Some call themselves "Jews in Germany," others understand themselves to be "German Jews," while still others use the term "Jewish Germans."[4] Those who prefer the expression "Jews in Germany" or "German Jews" reject the label "Jewish German" as inappropriate. For the "Jewish Germans," the expression "Jew in Germany" is an exclusionary term. Ignatz Bubis, the new chairman of the Zentralrat der Juden in Deutschland (Central Council of Jews in Germany), relies on an old variation: "deutscher Staatsbürger jüdischen Glaubens"—a "German citizen of the Jewish faith."[5] By employing this self-description common during the Weimar Republic, he establishes a continuity with Jewish life before 1933. This perspective is not likely to find many adherents. It appears that the only common ground among Jews is not wanting to be referred to as Richard von Weizsäcker did: as "jüdische Mitbürger."[6]

The variety of formulations employed to describe the relation between the two groups corresponds to the various Jewish, or rather German, perception of Self and Other. The impossibility of grasping the relation between the two groups linguistically in a way that would be accepted by everybody is, in the deepest sense, an expression of the ongoing difficulty in understanding the relation.

According to the press reports of 1992/1993, two factors influence current Jewish life in Germany: an increasingly open anti-Semitism and a burgeoning interest in Jewish culture.

The Increase in Open Anti-Semitism

Desecration of Jewish cemeteries and memorials are not new in German history. New are attacks on concentration camps such as those that took place at Sachsenhausen and Ravensbrück. But in both cases the perpetrators remained anonymous. Recently, however, the anti-Semites no longer feel the necessity to hide behind anonymity. Basilius Streithofen, a monk and unofficial advisor to Helmut Kohl, declared that "the Jews exploit the German taxpayers."[7] And Franz-Dieter Schlagkamp, the mayor of Senheim, a small town on the Mosel River, wrote to Ignatz Bubis, calling him the "Oberjuden"—the "Head Jew"—and saying how glad he was that no Jews live in his town, as they always cause trouble.[8] Physical attacks on Jews have not yet been reported. There are above all two reasons for this: first, the Jewish population is very small; second, Jews are nearly invisible, aside from the ones who are known to the public at large. Those who want to identify Jews as Jews would have to go to a synagogue on the sabbath.[9] The vandalism of cemeteries and concentration camps, as well as openly anti-Semitic statements, again made the public aware of the potential threat Jews face in Germany. "Do the Jews in Germany Still Feel Safe?"[10] "Fear Amongst the Jews?"[11] "Images of Horror from the Nazi Period Return"[12]—such headlines again place Jews, as potential targets of anti-Semitism, forcefully into the consciousness of the public.

When asked for his assessment of the situation, Ignatz Bubis, the new chairman of the Zentralrat (who after being in office only five months has become a media star),[13] said that anti-

Semitism has not become stronger but has become "acceptable in polite society."[14] With his public political and journalistic fight against anti-Semitism and xenophobia, with his support for the retention of the individual right to asylum, and with his criticism of the inaction of politicians, Bubis has assumed an active role for the interests of the Jewish population—as well as the interests of foreigners living in Germany. He thereby unintentionally strengthens the image of Jews as "foreign guests." In a recent poll, only 43 percent of the population thought that Bubis was a German citizen (22 percent assumed he was "Israeli," 32 percent said they "don't know," and 2 percent thought he was neither German nor Israeli).[15]

In addition to Bubis, other Jews have spoken out against the current hatred and violence. The writer Ralph Giordano sent a telegram to Chancellor Kohl announcing that Jews would arm themselves if the state neglects to protect them.[16] Such statements have found great resonance in the press. Some Jews have made it very clear that they are not willing to become victims of German anti-Semitism once again. It is no coincidence that in 1993 the Jewish Community of Berlin remembered for the first time an act of resistance which had taken place in Berlin in 1943 in front of the Sozialverwaltung (social agency) of the Jewish Community in the Berliner Rosenstreet.[17] This action, as well as the protest launched against the presentation of Rainer Werner Faßbinder's play *Der Müll, die Stadt und der Tod*, are now recalled as important acts in building Jewish self-confidence in Germany.[18] The Jews' will for self-affirmation (*Selbstbehauptung*) and resistance seems to converge with the desire of the German media to present Jews as fighters rather than as defenseless victims.[19] This explains why the attack of a few "Jewish Italians" on an anti-Semitic right-wing group in Rome last summer[20] and the temporary occupation of the city hall in Rostock (19 October 1992) by a group of young French Jews were considered by some newspapers to be major news.

The media attention given to Jews who go on the offensive, as well as the media's caution in reporting about Jews who are involved in dubious activities[21] reveal that what is at stake here is specifically the established correlation of German Jews as victims and of non-Jewish Germans as aggressors. In 1992 *Der Spiegel* published parts of the book *Stella* by the Berlin-born American Jewish author Peter H. Wyden. It tells the story of the Jews who betrayed other Jews to the Gestapo after 1942 to save their own lives.[22] Wyden's motivation for writing the book was primarily a personal one: as a teenager he knew the woman whose name was chosen for the book's title. *Der Spiegel* claimed Wyden was breaking a "Holocaust research taboo," although a number of books on this topic had already appeared.[23] Seen within the contemporary political context, the presentation of this book runs the risk of relativizing the Germans' persecution of the Jews, and it hints at the Germans' desire to free themselves from the taint of the role of "victimizers."

Considering the recent anti-Semitic attacks and, above all, the memory of the historical experience of Jews in Germany, the extensive media coverage of Jews does not seem surprising. But this attention begs for an explanation if you compare it to the disinterest in those most affected by the increased hate, those who have to fear for their lives—Turks, Vietnamese, or Africans—people who in their appearance look markedly different from the German majority. Even after three Turks were killed in an attack on a Turkish family in the small town of Mölln, one can barely find interviews with Turks and other foreigners or articles that consider their perspective. While the police stand guard in front of every synagogue—and every *Amerika Haus*—they show up at the homes for asylum seekers only after they have been burned down.

The fixation on Jews as potential victims of German xenophobic attacks seems to be enmeshed in a refusal of non-Jewish Germans to confront reality. Fearing a repetition-compulsion, the non-Jewish German public stares spellbound at the victims of the Shoah and at their descendants, hoping they themselves can deal with the hatred. It is almost as if by fighting for their "fellow citizens'" rights, non-Jewish Germans could stop a recurrence of the past. In 1933 it was said: "The Jews are our misfortune." Now the motto appears to be: "The Jews are our salvation." Thus it is not at all surprising that the cry "Bubis for President!" was raised. It would be—according to the liberal weekly *Die Woche*—"not for the rest of the world, but for us! . . . What could be more fruitful, more healing, more purifying?"[24] This statement implies that the non-Jewish Germans perceive themselves as not fruitful, as sick or dirty—a self-perception which dovetails remarkably with the non-Jewish Germans' perception of Jews in the Nazi period. The anti-Semitic image of Jews has become a German self-image. Those who were once victims are expected to become therapists and political advisors. In the meantime non-Jewish Germans have once again become persecutors—especially of those who look different.

The expectations that Jews could be the saviors tells us more about the non-Jewish Germans than the Jewish population. Asking Jews how to deal with the hatred may be a comfortable way for non-Jewish Germans to avoid having to question themselves, and it is a sign of the political helplessness of those who favor tougher measures against right-wing extremists. Thus, statements by Jews about the current development are used for the moral legitimization of non-Jews' opinions.[25] This appropriation of political statements by Jews contrasts with the diminishing influence of the Jews' representatives. In vain the Zentralrat der Juden pressed to secure Germany's responsibility vis-à-vis Jews in the preamble of the *Grundgesetz* (the German constitution). And in vain Bubis spoke out against a change in the asylum law.

The Booming Interest in Jewish Culture

Concomitant with open anti-Semitism has been an enormously growing interest in Jewish culture. The annual "Jüdische Kulturtage" (Jewish Culture Festival) in Berlin, Cologne, Chemnitz, and Munich; exhibits, concerts, and readings; the opening of two Jewish bookstores, one in Berlin and one Munich, and of Jewish restaurants; the broadcast of *Jüdisches Kulturmagazin* (Jewish Cultural Magazine) on a television channel[26] as well as publications addressing Jewish subjects—all are taken by the media as a sign of a reemergence of Jewish culture.

In the first place, speaking and writing about Jewish culture proves nothing except that there is an interest in having such a culture. But does this German-Jewish culture really exist? In the field of literature, following Jurek Becker, Edgar Hilsenrath, and

Stefan Heym, a new generation of authors have made names for themselves as German-Jewish writers: Maxim Biller, Raphael Seligmann, Barbara Honigmann, and Esther Dischereit. They write, however, with the knowledge that the overwhelming majority of their readers are non-Jews.[27] Let us take a look at the list of publications of the newly founded Jüdischer Verlag (Jewish Publishing House, a subsidiary of the big Suhrkamp Verlag). Here we find above all translations, such as Gershom Scholem's *Sabbatai Zevi* or Abraham Sutzkever's *Griner Aquarium*, and reprints, such as the *Jüdisches Lexikon* from 1927. Other publications include books by American Jews, such as James E. Young's *Describing the Holocaust.* And what about the annual Jüdische Kulturtage? The 1992 program in Berlin presented the singer Chava Alberstein (from Israel), The Klezmatics (from the United States), as well as an exhibition of photographs of Eastern Europe's Jews taken by Ed Serrota (also from the United States). The situation of Jews in the former Soviet Union was the topic of a lecture held by Michael Gorelik from Russia.[28] No doubt, these are Jewish artists and intellectuals producing Jewish culture. They come from almost all over the world, but seldom from Germany. They sing and discuss in Hebrew, in English, in Russian, and in Yiddish—seldom in German. To be sure, there are signs of a Jewish culture in Germany—produced, however, by mostly non-German Jews for a mostly non-Jewish public.

Whether or not in the future there will be a German Jewish culture produced by Jews for Jews (and non-Jews), depends to a great extent upon the demographic development of the Jewish population. A lively, genuinely Jewish culture needs a greater Jewish community as a base. The future will tell whether the Jewish immigrants from the former Soviet Union, who, for the most part, know very little about Judaism—will assimilate with the Germans, or whether they will search for their roots and become involved in Jewish cultural activities.

Regardless of the fact that Jewish culture is produced mostly by non-German Jews for a non-Jewish public, the press speaks of a "German-Jewish coming-out,"[29] and even of a "new German-Jewish symbiosis."[30] Talking about a "German-Jewish coming out" (an English term used in Germany only in connection with gay men and lesbians) implies that German-Jewish culture had always existed, but was hidden. The second expression links the current phenomenon explicitly to a legend: the legend of the German-Jewish symbiosis during the Weimar Republic. As representatives of the "new symbiosis," one journalist named the historian Michael Wolffsohn, the author Rafael Seligmann, and the journalist Henryk M. Broder.[31] Wolffsohn would probably approve of this assessment, Rafael Seligmann kindly rejected the idea,[32] and Henryk M. Broder would likely make the man regret he ever wrote a word about a Jewish topic.

How should we explain this interest in what is presented as "Jewish culture"? According to Henryk M. Broder, "the interest in things Jewish is based on the formula: the scarcer the human supply, the greater the cultural demand."[33] This may sound comical, as do many of Broder's observations, yet it holds true—at least for the Turks. Their "human supply" is greater than that of Jews, and Germans' interest in them is limited to kebab. But for other minorities, including the Jews, Broder's interpretation falls short. The "human supply" in Germany of Sorbs (a Slavic minority living in the south of Berlin) as well as of Vietnamese is even scarcer than that of Jews, and so is the attention paid to them. Explanations based on the mechanisms of a market economy do not strike at the heart of the interest in what is presented as Jewish culture. Instead it is to be traced back to the non-Jewish Germans' need to break free from the victim/persecutor relationship in which they seem locked.

In the consciousness of the non-Jewish public, the Jews have almost exclusively been thought of as victims of the Shoah. The representation of Jews in this context evoked feelings of unease, if not guilt, feelings that do not foster curiosity. Consequently there is an enormous lack of knowledge about anything concerning Jews and Judaism other than the Holocaust, which does not necessarily mean that non-Jewish Germans know much about the Shoah. When asked how many Jews had lived in Germany before 1933, a visitor at the monumental exhibition "Jüdische Lebenswelten" (Jewish Life-Worlds)[34] in Berlin—ironically a communications professor at the Berliner Hochschule der Künste (the Berlin Academy of Arts)—answered "six million"—the number of the victims of the Shoah. The "Jüdische Lebenswelten" exhibit, the "Jüdische Kulturtage," and all the other events which present Jews within a cultural context seem to have the potential to be a bridge for non-Jewish Germans to previously unknown Jewish worlds, thus possibly opening a path for non-Jews to free themselves from their prejudices and get a more differentiated image of Jews. In spite of the considerable difference in historical precedents as well as goals, this process reminds one of the role that German culture played for Jews in the period of their emancipation.

However, there are three factors that make the current interest in things Jewish questionable. First, there is a tendency to give attention to "cultural products" by Jews solely because they are made by Jews, regardless of their quality or significance. Second, there is no reflection on the significance of Jewish culture for the Jews themselves. Third, there is no self-reflection about the reasons for the attention paid to Jews and their culture. The nonexistence of Jewish culture was a "visible" invisible sign of the Shoah. The representation of Jews only as victims of the Shoah has always inundated non-Jewish Germans with Germany's recent past, in which Germans were the perpetrators. The need to promote the image of the "cultural Jew," like the emphasis on the image of Jews as fighters, obviously stems from the Germans' unconscious desire to alter this self-perception.

In December 1992 an article appeared in the alternative *Tageszeitung* with the title, "How Yiddish Do We Germans Speak?" The author attempted to prove that countless words in German are of Yiddish origin. This holds certainly true—and not only for the word *meschugge* (crazy). But the tendency of the article was to invoke the impression that Germans, then, actually speak Yiddish, as though they were actually Jews themselves.

A converse assumption was offered in a letter to the editor of the *Süddeutsche Zeitung* by a member of the CSU (Christlich-soziale Union), the conservative party of Bavaria. The author supported the position of the Green Party and the PDS (Partei demokratischer Sozialismus, the follower of the former East German ruling party SED, Sozialistische Einheitspartei Deutschlands) that "the 100,000

Jews from the CIS [Community of Independent States] who have applied to immigrate to Germany should be admitted 'generously.'" Interestingly, he substantiated his opinion not historically or politically but culturally: "The Soviet Jews are almost all Ashkenazim, and thus, German Jews. . . . Their traditional language is Yiddish, a German dialect. . . . How could these Germans [!] not be welcome here?"[35] His rationale gives the impression that the immigration of Soviet Jews could help to abate the influence of the "foreign influx," a danger which is constantly referred to in the discussion about the asylum laws.

The (mis)appropriations brought to the surface within the political sphere can also be observed within a cultural context. The political dimension of the cultural appropriation revealed itself with unmistakable clarity in a discussion of the Jüdische Kulturtage in the *Berliner Tagesspiegel*, one of three major Berlin newspapers. In reference to the non-Jewish spectators it was stated that "in this country, it isn't primarily groups like 'Böse Onkelz' or 'Kraft durch Freude' [both neo-Nazi rock groups] that are a hit with our young people," but rather the "Klezmatics."[36] The author of this article recommended as "watchwords" for the German Jews: "Raus aus dem Abseits": "Stop being 'off-sides,' come away from the victim-mentality, say good-bye to the Holocaust fixation, and put an end to the Israel-orientation." It is time to speak of "Jewish Germans"—not of Jews in Germany. It is one thing when Jews seek out a new orientation, and quite another when non-Jewish Germans want to prescribe one for them.

Political as well as cultural appropriations are the flipside of exclusion: they demonstrate an inability to accept Jews as equally entitled Others. It is therefore not at all surprising that non-Jewish Germans pay little attention to the Jewish reaction to their interest in Jewish subjects.

The Significance of Jewish Culture for German Jews

In fact not only "Jewish culture" but also the attention non-Jewish Germans are paying to it has been almost completely ignored by the Jewish public. The few existing statements on this subject are almost completely skeptical. Avraham Ehrlich declared in *tachles*, a journal edited by the Jüdisches Forum in Cologne, that a "construction called 'Jewish Culture' does not exist."[37] For Richard Chaim Schneider, Jewish culture in Germany presents a "murky mixture of gefilte fish, a few words in Yiddish" and "an idiotic pride in Jewish Nobel Prize winners."[38] Y. Michal Bodemann rejects the possibility that what is currently presented in Germany as Jewish culture is likely to establish a "'positive' Jewish identity."[39] The Jewish publisher Peter Moses Krause criticized the Berlin Jewish Community's presentation of Jewish culture as an "inedible mixture of 'gefilte fish and Sachertorte.'"[40] Only Michael Brenner praises the great interest that non-Jewish Germans are showing in Jewish culture, pointing out at the same time that Jewish culture is above all presented to a non-Jewish public. In over four decades, he adds, the Jewish communities in Germany have not provided even "the minimal basis for a transmission of the basic knowledge about things Jewish and of Jewish culture."[41]

These skeptical evaluations do help one understand why the Jewish public, for its part, has said little about Jewish culture—but they do not explain why the Jewish public has kept almost silent about the non-Jewish Germans' attention to what is presented as Jewish culture. As though there were no Jüdischer Verlag, no Jüdischer Kulturverein, no Jüdische Kulturtage, as though the media had overlooked Bubis, and as though one were never able to watch a program dealing with a Jewish topic on television, people as diverse as Michael Wolffsohn, Rafael Seligmann, and Hanna Rheinz accused the German public of being interested only in dead Jews.[42] This complaint stands in tension both to the accusation that the Germans are repressing the Holocaust and to the booming interest in Jewish culture. It appears to be a reaction to the deepened identity crisis of younger Jews brought on by reunification[43] and is understandable as an intent to affirm the significance of the younger Jews in public life of post-Wall Germany.

For obvious reasons, having a Jewish identity in Germany after 1945 has always been difficult, and it did not become easier after 1989. Most of the non-Jewish Germans interpreted the fall of the Wall as a beginning of a new stage in German history, as a first step on the way to a normalization of the relationship between West and East Germans, but also between Germans and German Jews, though there has rarely been any explicit consideration of what is to be understood by "normalization." Among Jews living inside and outside of Germany, who interpreted the Wall to be a consequence of Auschwitz (and not of the Cold War), fears grew that Germany might completely repress the Shoah. As a consequence, it can be assumed that there is an increasing pressure of the older Jews whose identity is primarily shaped by Shoah upon younger German Jews to keep reminding the Germans of the past. These developments come at a time when younger German Jews no longer want to remain in the position of victims[44] and are intensively searching for a "positive identity." Distancing oneself from the expectations of one's parents is always difficult, all the more so if they have survived the Shoah, and still more so in times when open anti-Semitism confirms their fears.[45] In addition, giving up the identity-conception passed down by the older generation runs the risk of Jews losing the public's attention that the parents had worked so hard to hold.[46] Since accusing their own parents of being obsessed with dead Jews is taboo, the younger Jews turn against those whom it is more acceptable to criticize.

Torn between the desire to free themselves of the role of the victim and the longing for a "positive identity" while maintaining the public's attention, young Jews seem to be blind to the increased non-Jewish German interest in things Jewish—and the questionable role it plays in the national discourse.

With the fall of the Wall in 1989, Germans gained unity—and at least the non-Jewish Germans lost their most defining Other. Thus, with unification the question of German identity was again on the agenda. In searching for identity, it seems as if the non-Jewish western Germans in particular (re)discovered Jews as their (old) new defining Other. Being invisible Others—and speaking the same language—the German Jews appear to be an ideal screen onto which non-Jewish Germans can project their ambivalent self-images. In fostering the representation of Jews as fighters, the fear of a repetition of the past is banished. And by speaking so much about "a German-Jewish symbiosis" and "Jewish culture" that the public is likely to believe in its existence, an illusion is evoked: where in fact one lives in country with a few hundred thousand Jews.

Notes

1. "Grußwort des Bundespräsidenten," *Allgemeine Jüdische Wochenzeitung*, 29 September 1989, 1.
2. See "Fühlen sich Juden in Deutschland noch sicher?" *Bild am Sonntag*, 8 November 1992, and Jutta Rippegather, "Die Freude der Juden im Osten ist zwiespältig," *Frankfurter Rundschau*, 13 March 1990.
3. "Juden und Deutsche," *Spiegel Spezial*, February 1992. According to the *Neue Zeit*, the historian Julius H. Schoeps speaks of "Jews and Germans" as well. S. Klaus Rost, "Die Entfernung der Erinnerungen von Juden und Deutschen," *Neue Zeit*, 30 January 1992.
4. This expression is used by Andreas Nachama, the general secretary of the Berlin Jewish Community. See "Gegenseitige Verwundungen ertragen. Interview mit Andreas Nachama, dem Leiter der Jüdischen Kulturtage," *Die Tageszeitung*, 23 November 1992.
5. Giovanni di Lorenzo, "Ein Drahtseilakt in Deutschland. Der Vorsitzende des Zentralrats der Juden läßt sich vom Radikalismus nicht in der Hoffnung einer Bundesrepublik beirren, in der sich Juden zu Hause fühlen," *Süddeutsche Zeitung*, 19–20 December 1992.
6. See among others Julius H. Schoeps, "Die schwere Last des Exils. Berichte deutscher Juden über Vertreibung und Rückkehr—ein Lehrstück auch für die gegenwärtige Asyldebatte," *Die Zeit*, 11 October 1991. Based on a recent poll, the sociologist Alphons Silbermann came to the conclusion that a majority of the Jews in Germany continue to prefer their Central Council to be called *Zentralverein der Juden in Deutschland*, (Central Council of the Jews in Germany) and not *Zentralverein der deutschen Juden*, (Central Council of German Jews). See Alphons Silbermann and Herbert Sallen, *Juden in Westdeutschland. Selbstbild und Fremdbild einer Minderheit* (Cologne: Verlag Wissenschaft und Politik, 1992). Considering these results, it seems likely that a majority would favor the term "Jews in Germany" or "German Jews" and not "Jewish Germans."
7. Quoted by Sarah Silberstein: "Glückwunsch Bruder Basilius," *Die Woche*, 1 February 1993, 40.
8. See Michaela Schießl, "Der Youngster der Juden Deutschlands," *Die Tageszeitung*, 21 January 1993.
9. The invisibility of Jews in Germany makes it difficult for newspapers to illustrate articles about Jews. The solutions available seem to be either not to illustrate the articles, or to print a photo of the Western Wall, of American or Israeli Orthodox Jews, of a Jewish cemetery. See Richard

Chaim Schneider, "In der Haut der Eltern. Deutsche Vereinigung – Verlust der jüdischen Identität?" *Die Zeit*, 7 December 1990; Michael Wolffsohn, "Vertrauen in das neue Deutschland. Die Juden und die Wiedervereinigung," *Frankfurter Allgemeine Zeitung*, 8 November 1990; "Wie sie Deutschland erleben. Umfrage unter jüdischen Emigranten aus der Sowjetunion," *Der Tagesspiegel*, 16 February 1992.

10. "Fühlen Juden sich in Deutschland noch sicher?" *Bild am Sonntag*, 8 November 1992. Five out of seventeen Jews who were asked if they felt safe declared that they felt personally threatened, while the answers of the others indicated "apprehension."
11. "Furcht unter Juden?" *Der Tagesspiegel*, 4 November 1992.
12. Marianne Heuwagen, "Juden in Deutschland fühlen sich bedroht. Schreckensbilder aus der Nazizeit kehren wieder," *Süddeutsche Zeitung*, 31 October 1992
13. Every major newspaper has published either an article about Ignaz Bubis or an interview. See "'Der Antisemitismus braucht keine Juden um sich auszudrücken,' Vorsitzender des Zentralrats der Juden in Deutschland, über das Zögern des Staates bei der Verfolgung von Gewalttätern," *Frankfurter Rundschau*, 15 October 1992.
14. "'Antisemitismus ist salonfähig.' Spiegel-Gespräch mit dem Vorsitzenden des Zentralrats der Juden, Ignatz Bubis, über Rechtsradikalismus, *Der Spiegel* 51 (1992). His assessment is shared by the Jewish journalist and author Inge Deutschkron. See Heribert Ickerott, "'Ich weiß nicht, was ich in diesem Land noch soll.' Jüdische Autorin Inge Deutschkron wird zunehmend bedroht," *Der Tagesspiegel*, 4 November 1992.
15. "Wer kennt Ignatz Bubis?" *Die Woche*, 18 February 1993.
16. The contents of the telegram were distributed through DPA, the German press agency.
17. Hundreds of women had protested for one week against the arrest of their Jewish husbands and sons. Between 1500 and 2000 men were released as a consequence of this action. See Marianne Heuwagen, "'Gebt uns unsere Männer wieder.' Vor 50 Jahren in Berlin: Protestaktion gegen die Deportation von Angehörigen," *Süddeutsche Zeitung*, 27–28 February 1993; Zafrir Cohen, "Ehrung des Mutes," *Berlin Umschau*, 2.3 (1993; Nachrichten aus der Jüdischen Gemeinde). A report on this protest was broadcast also on the television channel "West 3," on 24 February 1993, at 10:30 p.m. About the topic "Jewish Resistance," see Alice Zadek, "Frauen des Widerstandes," *Jüdische Korrespondenz*, 3.3 (March 1993).
18. The Jewish Community in Frankfurt decided to hinder the staging of the play. See Edith Kohn, "Ignatz Bubis verteidigt die Demokratie gegen die Antisemiten," *Tempo*, December 1992, 39.
19. See Alexandra Schwerin von Krosigk: "Zwischen Überlebenskampf und politischer Aktion. Eine Ausstellung in Berlin Mitte erinnert an Juden im Widerstand 1939–1945," broadcasted by the state radio station

Sender Freies Berlin, 5 April 1993, 7:05 p.m.; see also Klaus Trappmann, "Das Warschauer Ghetto—Überleben im Endlösungswahn," broadcast by Sender Freies Berlin, 19 April 1993, 7:05 p.m.; Ferdinand Kroh, "Chasak – sei stark! Eine jüdische Widerstandsgruppe im Kampf gegen die Nazis," broadcast by the Sender Freies Berlin, 28 April 1993, 10:00 p.m.

20. Horst Schlitter, "Jüdische Italiener rächen sich. Prügelei mit Neofaschisten nach antisemitischen Schmierereien," *Frankfurter Rundschau*, 11 July 1992.

21. See, for example, the case of Mario Offenberg. The representative of the Orthodox Adass Isroel Community in Berlin, he has tried in dubious ways to convince the Senate of Berlin to recognize his Community as legal successor of the prewar Adass Isroel, Community. When confronted with "sensitive" issues, the media tend to avoid it—or employ a Jewish journalist (preferably Henryk M. Broder) to write about it. See Henryk M. Broder, "Tote Seelen in Berlin oder: Die wundersame Auferstehung der jüdischen Gemeinde Adass Isroel als Familienbetrieb—eine deutsch-jüdische Posse aus der Wendezeit," *Die Zeit*, 26 September 1991.

22. Peter H. Wyden, *Stella* (Göttingen: Steidl, 1993). See *Der Spiegel* 43, 44, 45 (1992).

23. See Ferdinand Kroh, *David kämpft. Vom jüdischen Widerstand gegen Hitler* (Reinbek: rororo, 1988), 163–74.

24. Hans-Ulrich Jörges, "Für Deutschland streiten! Die Bonner Parteien sind ratlos, ihre Kandidaten verbraucht. Die Republik braucht Ignatz Bubis als Bundespräsidenten," *Die Woche*, 18 February 1993, 5. In the subsequent edition a number of letters to the editor of *Die Woche* commented on Jörges's proposal. They confirmed Bubis' assessment that anti-Semitism has again become acceptable in polite society. See *Die Woche*, 25 February 1993.

25. See also the articles on "Jews and Reunification." See Gisela Dachs, "Der nationale Traum als Trauma. Die deutschen Juden tun sich schwer mit der Einheit," *Die Zeit*, 5 May 1990. This liberal weekly paper quotes exclusively Jews who were critical of unification. Dachs does not even mention the approval that Heinz Galinsiki gave to reunification—to the disappointment of younger and leftist Jews. In need of Jewish approval for reunification, the conservative press published an article by Michael Wolffsohn, "Vertrauen in das neue Deutschland. Die Juden und die Wiedervereinigung," *Frankfurter Allgemeine Zeitung*, 8 November 1990.

26. The program is presented once a month on one of the private channels. Julius H. Schoeps, the director of the Moses Mendelsohn Institute for Jewish European Studies in Potsdam, is planning another program in cooperation with the public broadcasting company Ostdeutsche Rundfunk Brandenburg.

27. Asked what it meant for her to write for a non-Jewish audience, Esther Dischereit declared in an interview: "prostitution." Interview with Esther Dischereit, Ithaca, New York, 27 March 1993.
28. The Jüdische Kulturtage, which took place in March 1993 in Chemnitz presented the Moshe-Effrati-Dance-Compagnie from Tel Aviv, George Tabori's play *Goldberg Variationen*, staged by Schauspiel Dresden, and Oleg Jurijew's play *Kleiner Pogrom am Bahnhofsbuffet*, staged by the Hans Otto Theater, Potsdam.
29. Mariam Niroumand, "Deutsch-jüdisches Coming Out," *Die Tageszeitung*, 23 November 1992.
30. Tilmann Krause, "Schtetl in der Großstadt der Neunziger," *Der Tagesspiegel*, 30 November 1992.
31. Krause, "Schtetl in der Großstadt."
32. Interview with R. Seligmann, 27 March 1993.
33. Henryk M. Broder, "Leiden an Deutschland. Deutsche Juden und Deutsche," "Juden und Deutsche," *Spiegel Spezial* 2 (1992), 27.
34. The exhibition drew 350,000 visitors during a three-month period.
35. Ulrich Motte, "Ostjuden sollen uns willkommen sein," *Süddeutsche Zeitung* 252 (31 October–1 November 1992), viii.
36. Krause, "Schtetl in der Großstadt."
37. Avraham Ehrlich, "Judentum und Kultur. Zur Klärung der Möglichkeit 'jüdischer Kultur' als Anregung und Einladung zur Kulturarbeit," *tachles-Bühne* 2 (May 1992).
38. Richard Chaim Schneider, "In der Haut der Eltern. Deutsche Vereinigung—Verlust der jüdischen Identität?" *Die Zeit*, 7 December 1990.
39. Y. Michal Bodemann, "Die Endzeit der Märtyrer-Gründer. An einer Epochenwende jüdischer Existenz in Deutschland," *Babylon: Beiträge zur jüdischen Geschichte der Gegenwart* 8 (1991), 7–14.
40. Quoted by Anita Kugler, "Was macht die Sachertorte jüdisch?" *Die Tageszeitung*, 13 June 1991.
41. Michael Brenner, "Der falsche Glanz entliehener Pracht," *Jüdische Allgemeine Wochenzeitung*, 18 February 1993.
42. V. Michael Wolffsohn, "Ein Ritual für gute Menschen," *Der Tagesspiegel*, 10 February 1992; Rafael Seligmann, "Die Juden leben," *Der Spiegel* 47 (1992), 75–76; Hanna Rheinz, "Flucht vor dem Anderssein. Juden in Deutschland: Auch eine Wiedervereinigung?" *Süddeutsche Zeitung*, 16 June 1990.
43. See Judith Hart, "'Es ist an uns herauszutreten und endlich Zeichen zu setzen.' Der Jugendkongreß in München legt Identitätsdilemma bloß," *Jüdische Allgemeine Wochenzeitung*, 26 November 1992.
44. "The passing of time," writes Schneider, does not allow "the second and third generation to play the favorite game: help, I am being persecuted.'" Richard Chaim Schneider, "In der Haut der Eltern."
45. Moishe Waks said in an interview: "These things [anti-Semitism] which the younger generation did not really ever experience but were trans-

mitted to them by their parents now have a correspondence with reality in the current political situation. "'Dann bin ich weg über Nacht.' Die Jüdischen Gemeinden und der wachsende Antisemtismus in Deutschland," *Der Spiegel* 51 (1992).

46. The Jewish Community "is being courted and wooed by all officials," and are, as Broder puts it, elevated to "moral watchdogs of the Germans." "How can Jews live in Germany?" Henryk M. Broder, who came to live in Germany when he was still a child, answered this question: "There is probably no second country in the free world where one as a Jew could lead a better life than in the Federal Republic." Henryk M. Broder, "Wie können Juden in Deutschland leben?"

6. The "Ins" and "Outs" of the New Germany: Jews, Foreigners, Asylum Seekers[1]

Jeffrey M. Peck

On December 16, 1992, I heard Ignatz Bubis, the recently elected leader of the Jewish Community in Germany, give a speech in Berlin. I posed the first question. "Mr. Bubis," I asked, "Are anti-Semitism and xenophobia [*Fremdenfeindlichkeit*] the same thing?" He responded unequivocally, "There is no great difference [*grosser Unterschied*] between the two."[2]

Since Hoyerswerda, Hünxe, Rostock, and especially Mölln and Solingen, the lives of foreigners, Jews, and asylum seekers in Germany have changed dramatically. Since the events that have put these towns on the map of the new Germany, I have asked myself the question I addressed to Bubis. While Jews have not been violently attacked or murdered, Jewish cemeteries have been desecrated, the Jewish barracks at Sachsenhausen was burned down, and, as Bubis states, anti-Semitism has become "salonfähig."[3] If for Bubis, "Fremdenfeindlichkeit" and "Antisemitismus" are the same, are attacks on a Tamil asylum seeker, a Turkish "Gastarbeiter," or a German Jew equally heinous? One must ask today if Jews and foreigners are mutually exclusive categories, as "Deutsche und Juden," the nomenclature that is still, even with its Nazi heritage, in everyday use. While comparisons as to the degree a particular group is hated can indeed lead to grotesque results, I think a number of new questions are surfacing. What is the relationship between Jews living in Germany and foreigners, including refugees, asylum seekers, the former "guest workers," and even Americans? Has the growth of right-wing radicalism and neo-Nazism realigned the relationship between Jews and foreigners, and what does that mean for the self-understanding and self-image of these peoples and more importantly for the Germans? Should one even differentiate among the groups that are the object of hostility because they are viewed as *fremd*, and, if so, what do these differences mean? These questions are not merely semantic but address the differing roles, status, and histories that these groups have in Germany.

In fact, the move I have made from anti-Semitism and *Fremdenfeindlichkeit* to discussing Jews, foreigners, and asylum seekers emphasizes that what appear to be all non-German minorities are linked precisely because of the prejudices against them. To talk about these groups in Germany is most often to speak of desecrations, attacks, and charges of criminality and exploitation. In other words, at least since Hoyerswerda, minorities that are perceived to be different than the majority of the German population are consistently acknowledged by the negative impact they have on society. Apparently Jews insist on remembering the Holocaust, foreigners (Turks) insist on speaking their language and maintaining uncivilized customs (wearing headscarves),[4] and asylum seekers insist on taking advantage of Germany's generous asylum laws and social welfare system.

Even if the brunt of hostility in Germany has been toward foreigners and asylum seekers, any discussion of the reemergence of Jewish culture in Germany has to take into account attitudes toward the foreign population to which the Jews are again being counted. Although attacks on Jewish cemeteries have not increased to a great extent, the burning of the Sachsenhausen barracks, a memorial to the Holocaust in "anti-fascist" East Germany, broke a taboo and qualitatively changed attitudes toward the status of Jews in Germany. While no Jews were physically attacked, a symbol of Germany's extermination of the Jews was destroyed, which in the East German context could be interpreted as a clear rejection of the anti-fascist ideology.

Anti-Semitism was in the news again and so was Ignatz Bubis, who is aggressively drawing the public's attention to the relationship between xenophobia and anti-Semitism. Newspapers and magazines such as *Die Zeit, Der Spiegel,* and *Stern* among others all within days of each other asked the question again—which had appeared to recede—whether Jews can continue to live in Germany today. Bubis was interviewed in newspapers throughout Germany, East and West. Although Jews were not the main targets of right-wing attacks, the appearance of skinheads and neo-Nazis yelling "Sieg Heil" and marching with a Nazi salute has given rise to serious concern by Jews around the world. Bubis was called to speak in New York before two dozen Jewish groups to brief them on the situation in Germany. The World Jewish Congress wanted to call a boycott on tourism and trade against Germany. American newspapers such as *The New York Times* and the *Washington Post* reported daily about Germany with a frequency unknown since reunification. Attacks have now quieted down, Germans are marching in the street, and the world is relieved. Candlelight and clasped hands are indeed better than Molotov cocktails and Nazi salutes. The demonstration of civil courage by Germans is new and praiseworthy for what it shows about their rejection of violence toward foreigners. And in America it shows those still fascinated by fascism, to invoke Susan Sontag's title, that every German is not a potential Nazi. In short, neither side is free of stereotypes and clichés about the other.

And just as all Germans cannot be uniformly categorized either under the simplistic rubrics of hero or villain, neither can all those who are not "German" be categorized as victims of the same kind. Just as Jews were nearly erased as victims under the term "anti-fascism," *Fremdenfeindlichkeit* elides important differences among those who are considered different. Ralph Giordano even rejected the stigmatization of Jews as victims when he called on them to arm against attackers if the German government were unable or unwilling to provide protection. I want to explore what I see as a new and significant relationship between Jews and foreigners, where Jews, according to *Zeit* reporter Gisela Dachs reporting on Alphons Silbermann's new study on anti-Semitism, "jetzt wieder zu den Fremden im Land zählen."[5]

The pages of the *Allgemeine Jüdische Wochenzeitung* notably use the term *fremd* or a generalizing equivalent when talking about attacks on foreigners. An editorial in the paper in the week following Hoyerswerda declares, "Wenn sich in Deutschland Zukunftsangst wieder in Gewaltaktionen gegen die entlädt, die man für 'anders' hält, dann ist das keine Erklärung, die beruhigen könnte."[6] In the same paper the following week, the subtitle of an article reads, "Hoyerswerda und der Terror der Rechtsradikalen: die Mehrheit der Bürger schaut dem Fremdenhaß gelassen zu." This statement appears with anti-GDR sentiment thrown in: "Aber Hoyerswerda war nicht der erste Ausbruch von Gewalt und Terror gegen Ausländer in Ostdeutschland, vielmehr war es der bislang traurige Höhepunkt einer langen Kette von Feindseligkeit und Haß gegen Fremde und Andersdenkende in der Ex-DDR."[7] In the following week, headlines appear such as "Die Welle von Fremdenhaß," "Ablehnung des Fremden. Was früher die Juden waren, das sind nun die Ausländer."[8] Like the category "North American" that generously includes Canadians when American is meant, the word *fremd* performs the same function, namely to include Jews in a discussion that primarily has to do with *Ausländer*. Those who are *fremd* are different than the Germans, who are essentially those whose identity is based on being white and Christian.

Although for many years Germany has had inhabitants who were racially, ethnically, or religiously different, the dramatic changes in attitudes toward foreigners took place when the rush of asylum seekers entered the West after the breakdown of Eastern European regimes and the reunification of Germany. The fact that Germany was officially not a "land of immigration," although four million foreigners lived there, did not disturb its citizens until reunification, when economic and social upheaval in both western and eastern Germany created competition for space and economic resources. Repressed racism and anti-Semitism resurfaced. Attacks began against those who could be easily identified as *fremd*, and in Hoyerswerda these were black and Asian guest workers from Mozambique and Vietnam. But the night air in Hoyerswerda was filled with cries reminiscent of the Nazi period, and the young men involved styled themselves as Nazis. The citizens applauded, and the comparisons were there with Pogrom-nacht 1938. Although many people for years had thought of the Turks as the "new Jews," suddenly with Hoyerswerda xenophobia and anti-Semitism coincided in a decidedly different way. All foreigners who were recognizably different appeared to be the new Jews, marked by color (rather than merely race—even a fallacious notion of race drummed up by real Nazis).

Why are Jews in Germany today thrust into the limelight again? In part this attention is linked to being different, that is, Jews are not only non-Christian, but the distinction between their ethnicity and religion is ambiguous and casts doubt on their Germanness. Attacks on cemeteries, distribution of anti-Semitic writings, and the public circulation of words and symbols also elicit obvious comparisons with the Third Reich. The position of Bubis (and some American responses to him) represents the complexity of German-Jewish relations today and the impact for the Jews of the attacks on foreigners. In one interview Bubis states, "Juden sind in Deutschland eine Art bessere Ausländer, so wie Italiener."[9] Elsewhere he declares, "Ich bin lieber ein Fremder."[10] Bubis clearly acknowledges the Jews' solidarity with all of those who are considered to be different than the Germans on the basis of *Menschenrechte*, and proudly recounts how Jews have marched and spoken out against the attacks on foreigners. But as important as it is, does the human rights issue really address what makes Germans in particular susceptible to right-wing violence? Bubis himself admits that anti-Semitism has not grown in Germany, only the willingness of Germans to act it out violently or to identify themselves by name when they call or write Bubis with anti-Semitic messages. On the other hand, those who would like to mollify criticism constantly draw attention to the virulent anti-Semitism and xenophobia in neighboring France or England. Even the United States, that cradle of ethnic pluralism, suffered the Los Angeles riots where Koreans shot blacks, blacks beat up whites, and Hispanics looted black stores. And let us not forget the serious tensions between blacks and Jews, tragically exemplified in Crown Heights, New York. Are Germans any better or worse than Americans when it comes to human rights? What does being German and living in Germany have to do with the way all groups of foreigners are being treated? Does ethnic or racial specificity supersede universal criteria for the treatment of all human beings? Are we in the midst of the debate between internationalism and multiculturalism?

I am offering more questions here than answers, and I am only sketching here the contours of the newly complicated relationships provoked by recent events. Relations among Jews, foreigners, and asylum seekers on the one hand, and "the Germans" on the other is, of course, fraught with discursive and semantic confusion. Jews apparently are again considered as foreigners, some analysts say, as if they indeed had managed to become German. I disagree. While the issue of living in Germany had ceased to be worthy of journalistic interest, Jews living in East and West Germany continued to have an uneasy relationship to the nation and national identity as the Germans did to the Jews in their midst. While very few Jews are of German origin, most "Jews in Germany" have a national identification, such as the Soviet Jews who themselves were distinguished in the Soviet Union as an ethnic group. The term "asylum seeker" already stigmatizes by reducing this person to a function of his or her political status. Like "die drei Türkinnen" in Mölln who were not individuals but merely the convenient ethnic category accorded all so-called *Gastarbeiter* (the two children were, however, born in Germany), the discourse of asylum politics and foreigner politics functions similarly to erase difference by establishing objectifiable and generalized criteria. Broadest of all terms, the word *Ausländer* encompasses all those who are not German regardless of their religious, ethnic, or religious status, although the term *Ausländer* does not differentiate adequately between the American tourist and the African seeking asylum.

Germans gather in cities all over the country to protest the attacks on *foreigners*, yet "fears rise," as a *Washington Post* journalist declares. Reporting on German responses to a fearful American schoolteacher who worries about bringing his students to Germany, the journalist writes: "Many letters tried to explain that Germans are not angry at foreign visitors, but at the hundreds of thousands of asylum seekers who have entered the country since the fall of the Berlin Wall."[11] Hostility is not based only on money, length of stay, and status, but also on racial and ethnic criteria that have to do with the willingness of Germans to accept the distinctions readily apparent in difference itself. In short, some foreigners are better than others. It is even possible to establish a hierarchy according to color from (1) the Germans, including the former *Übersiedler* from the GDR; (2) what I call the "almost Germans," or "ethnic" Germans from Eastern Europe, officially called *Aussiedler*; (3) Eastern European *Ausländer*, Poles in particular; (4) the "real" *Ausländer*, including Turks, other Mediterraneans, Pakistanis, Tamils, blacks (African, American, or otherwise); (5) Asian *Ausländer*, Vietnamese in the former GDR; (6) Sinti and Roma (so-called Gypsies), who are lowest in this hierarchy.[12] This last group requires even further differentiation, since the former have established some stability in Germany and regard the latter from Romania and Yugoslavia with disdain, since their bad reputation threatens to jeopardize the Sinti's achievements. *Ausländer*, who are (white) Americans, French, Dutch, Scandinavians, are at the top of the list and are even termed "noble foreigners" by the sociologist Dietrich Thränhardt.[13]

And what of the Jews in Germany? Complicated by the fact that their identity is crossed between being sometimes *deutsche Juden* and other times *Deutsche jüdischen Glaubens*, "*Juden in Deutschland*" today are always more or less Jewish, German, foreign, or political refugee, based on the historical contingency of the Holocaust and the imperatives of nationalist, ethnic, and religious demands. Jews in Germany are only about 15 percent of German Jewish heritage, the rest are of other nationalities, including immigrants from Eastern Europe and the former Soviet Union, Israel, and the United States (many of whom are artists, musicians, journalists, writers, and academics specializing on Germany). Ignatz Bubis and Jews throughout Germany were shocked by the *Vorsitzender des Innenausschusses der Rostocker Bürgerschaft*, Karl Heinz Schmidt, when he asked the leader of the German Jewish community, "Sie sind doch Deutscher jüdischen Glaubens, doch Ihre Heimat ist Israel?" Bubis offers many such examples from even well-meaning Germans. In general, Bubis and others have indicated that anti-Semitism and racism have statistically not increased within the population; one member of the Jewish community reminded me that since the war, not one year has gone by that Jewish cemeteries have not been desecrated, and foreign children were burned in Hünxe as well. What has happened that has made these recent events more powerful, more compelling? Why are Jews more frightened, even though they have not been the focus of attacks? And are in fact the "symbolic" attacks on Jewish cemeteries and especially the barracks at Sachsenhausen to be feared like the murders in Mölln?

Clearly, violence or the potential for violence has dramatically increased against all those people who are different, that is, those recognizable as thinking, acting, or looking different, not falling under the normative categories of what it means to be German. To be German, according to Article 16 of the Basic Law, means to be born of German parents (*ius sanguinis*), not merely to be born on German soil (*ius solis*). The ramifications are not only about race and ethnicity, but also about citizenship and the access to certain jobs (to become a civil servant [*Beamter*] or to vote) Such status confirms participation in and protection under the law, for example, the possibility for a Turkish youth born in Germany to become a policeman and to work in his own community. Unrepresented and unprotected, non-Germans are weaker and more vulnerable to attacks. This includes handicapped people and gays and lesbians, as well as asylum seekers, Jews, and foreigners. Attacks have increased against the former groups as well.

But just as the norms and prescriptions for becoming German are imprinted on the body politic, so too does the color of the body itself distinguish foreigners from each others, and make Jews (at least German Jews) indistinguishable from the rest of the German population. Unlike Hitler who needed to develop a racial ideology and program to set the Jews (even the assimilated ones) off from the "Aryan" Germans, today's Jews have the "benefit" of being white and being able to be assimilated into the general population. While their last names may "give them away," unless they speak out publicly they are invisible to attackers. A high official in the Verband told me that his wife asked him not to appear on television for fear of reprisals from the right wing. Of course, this status is only an advantage as long as one chooses to hide or remain silent, and Jews in Germany have indeed stood up against the attacks on foreigners. The pages of the *Allgemeine Jüdische Wochenzeitung* are filled with reports on these events and reflect the solidarity of the Jewish community.

One wonders, however, if simply being non-German or foreign is enough to bring Jews together with Turks, Tamils, or black Africans. In a sense the class distinction that traditionally divided German Jews from their Eastern European counterparts and from many of their Christian fellow Germans now separates them from Turkish laborers. In the early days after Hoyerswerda, a leader in the Jewish community told me that many Jews did not feel moved to speak out or demonstrate since they felt that these attacks had nothing to do with them. As the hostility has intensified, the community at least has taken a demonstrative stand of solidarity against any kind of violence toward foreigners. Some Jews indicated off the record that the Jewish community could do more, for example, inviting Turkish leaders to the synagogues or encouraging dialogue with other foreigner groups. He also mentioned that after the burning of the barracks at Sachsenhausen only one official Jewish leader (Marion Offenburg from Adass Isroel) went to the camp. Neither Jewish leaders nor progressives and leftists spoke out against the deportation of Roma back to Romania. These attitudes reflect, I think, the ambivalence of Jewish leaders and Jews in Germany toward this altered situation.

The future of Jewish life in Germany is one of the most striking examples of this bind. Previous warnings of the World Jewish Congress resonate again when Jews considered whether they could continue to live in Germany. Were they to sit on the proverbial packed suitcases? The possibility of developing a German and Jewish identity which had seemed more normalized was now provoking an identity crisis. *Heimat*, overdetermined with *völkisch* ideology, had become a problematic notion for Jews in Germany who, before such an intrinsically German idea of homeland was destroyed by the Nazis, could believe it might signify a place that provided trust, security, and a sense of belonging. Now Germany might be a home, but not a *Heimat*. It appeared that the Jew would be a *Weltbürger* again, forced to seek community outside of Germany with other Jews rather than with other Germans. The hyphenated identity of "German-Jews" marked the ambivalence of identifying themselves with their so-called fellow citizens (*Mitbürger*). If democratic principles and the safety of citizenship could not be counted on to protect them, then Germany did not deserve their allegiance.

The issue of citizenship of course distinguishes the majority of Jews in Germany from the other "foreigners" living in their midst. Turkish *Gastarbeiter*, African asylum seekers, and even an American tourist do not have the rights that most Jews have in Germany. If the Jews are vulnerable to attack, even if they are citizens, then one asks how important is the citizenship issue for insuring the safety of foreigners. There is some contradiction here, since becoming a citizen should in theory preclude being "foreign." As of now citizenship does not protect foreigners who look different. Bluntly stated, to a neo-Nazi skinhead a black man is a potential victim whether he has a German, American, or Nigerian passport. However, it must be said that second- and third-generation foreigners, especially Turks, who recognize that citizenship will not protect them from discrimination or attacks, still feel that this legal status offers them security and shows their German fellow citizens that they are going to stay.

However, citizenship has a much greater effect if the laws concerning the granting of citizenship—*ius sanguinis* to *ius solis*—are changed in order to effect a massive shift in the population of "Germans." With the change in law, millions of foreigners born in Germany would "become German," and with time the normative notions of what defines Germanness could be revised. This transformation could very well change the images of what it means to be German. Foreign faces would be visible in more and varied areas of German life: television, advertising, and public offices. Unfortunately, the only time foreigners are seen in advertising is in specifically multicultural spots such as the infamous Bennetton and the Peter Stuyvesant cigarette ads in which the fact that they "look different" is overly self-referential.[14]

The ability to deal with difference in an unselfconscious fashion has not yet been achieved in Germany. While foreigners are the victims of right-wing attacks, they are also the victims of patronizing and patriarchal attitudes from the left. During many demonstrations against the attacks, some Germans proudly announced, "Ich bin Ausländer" or "Laßt mich nicht allein mit den Deutschen." For Germans to identify with the oppressed by denying their own national identity contributes to a further polarization between *Deutscher/Ausländer* and the fossilization of positions: being either *ausländerfeindlich* or *ausländerfreundlich.* This tendency toward reifying positions is even more problematic regarding attitudes toward Jews, since it could be said that the very same kind of thinking prevents Germans from criticizing Jews or even voicing their reservations about positions that the Jewish community might take. Do Jews have a special immunity from criticism because of the Holocaust that we would expect all other "foreigners" to bear? Ironically, the Roma and Sinti, who were also major victims of the Holocaust are not being accorded the sympathy or recognition that they deserve either from the German authorities or the Jewish community.

After forty-five years it is still difficult for many Germans to let the word *Jude* cross their lips and the *Zigeuner* remain the most despised of foreigners. One wonders if the word *Ausländer* is also accumulating this kind of negative signification. By continuing to reify the binary opposition *Deutscher/Ausländer,* it will not be possible to generate more differentiated terms for describing an increasingly heterogeneous population. Richard von Weizsäcker in his Christmas speech finally drew attention to the continued generic reference to the "drei Türkinnen" who died, and for the first time in my knowledge a political figure of that stature publicly addressed the German tendency to objectify and instrumentalize human beings simply because they were non-Germans.

I do not want to overemphasize the discursive aspects of this problem at the expense of the materiality of the violence committed against human beings. It is clear, however, that the circulation of language and images associated with National Socialism has contributed to encouraging an atmosphere where a well-timed "*Sieg Heil!*" can engender responses that have more to do with protest than with ideology. A swastika, until recently forbidden in Germany, appears on the cover of the German news magazine *Der Spiegel.* While the mere presence of such symbols may not inspire violence, it does lend a vocabulary and ritual to the right-wing movement. Such symbols represent a meaning-full (in the literal sense) community that attracts young men who have lost meaning or any hope for a secure future to neo-Nazi groups. The lines of signification that go back to the 1930s establish them as part and even a continuation of a *völkish* tradition that connects them to the "real Nazis" of the 1930s. I make this point in order to draw attention to the frequent comparisons between the two periods.[15] To question such comparisons does not in any way underplay the seriousness of the present situation in Germany. On the contrary, confronting both the differences and the similarities draws our attention to this new historical situation in Germany for the Jews, where the potential for violence against those who are different permeates the population. This is not to say that "the Germans" are essentially more racist, more xenophobic, or more anti-Semitic than other national groups. But the burden of history demands a special vigilance against such tendencies. Because of this inheritance, I do not think that the Jews are as much in danger as those who are poor, without civil protection, and without a home. The Jews are protected by the world Jewish community, especially in America, that watches events in Germany carefully. Israel's presence also reminds the world of the Germans' special responsibility to the Jews. But what protection do the asylum seekers have who have no extended support system beyond themselves?

The leaders of the Turkish community are clear about how the events in Mölln have mobilized their people. They are no longer *Gastarbeiter* but a minority among others in the Federal Republic, like the Jews, who, however, were better organized. Turkish people want to live in Germany among other groups no matter what their religion, ethnic, or national identity. Two-thirds of all non-Germans have lived over fifteen years in the Federal Republic and have no citizenship. Community leaders want their people to have double citizenship, local voting rights, and the right to keep their culture and language intact while they live among the Germans. One of these leaders reminded me that there are no Turkish school directors in all of Berlin and no Turks ranking high in the administration at the Office of Foreigners in Berlin. Most important, however, is the fact that the foreigners, especially the former guest workers, are no longer guests and plan to stay in their former host country. As far as the Turkish community is concerned, a mode for living together must be found.

The candlelight marches of late may be a sign that Germans and non-Germans can manage to create what is often called, for lack of a better term, a multicultural society. Members from all the minority communities show their solidarity by such demonstrations. Yet while these show that the infamous lack of German civil courage can be mobilized when necessary, it covers up the issues around citizenship that I think go to the root of *Fremdenfeindlichkeit* of all sorts. Multiculturalism stimulated by migration implies a constantly changing body politic and reinforces the insecurities of those who are already uncertain about where they belong. The call for "Deutschland nur den Deutschen" reminds us of desires for a unified and homogeneous body politic where brown, yellow, and black foreigners or Germans cannot find a place. I am not convinced that the marches are anything more than demonstrations against violence (important as this is) and do not reflect how committed those people are to erase anti-Semitism, xenophobia, or racism from their midst. In other words, while the marches will show the world that the Germans are not as bad as they might think, or that they can have solidarity with the oppressed, it does little to ameliorate relations between ethnic groups or races. In short, the *völkisch* tradition of German identity based on blood is obviously not questioned, no matter how many people march in the street. The gap is still wide between what it means to be German and what it means to be against violence: the former is an ethnic category, the latter is a question of human rights. These two issues need to be confronted in Germany as part of the same problem, one that is (not surprisingly) controlled by the dominant culture that holds the legal, economic, and cultural power.

Minorities could perhaps work together to change the terms of the debate. While it is a mistake to designate all non-Germans with the all-purpose term *Ausländer* and to ignore the significant differences among the various groups by race, class, ethnicity, religion, and color, I wonder if more solidarity among the foreigners might affect a change in policy. Like black Americans who decided that the term "African-American" was more appropriate to describe their identity, could not similar groups in Germany try the same? The use of the term "Afro-Deutsch" in some German circles at least indicates that the possibility is there. This suggestion still may be in fact too naively American, since it is precisely the fact that African Americans are citizens and have voting rights that make them and other minority groups a force to reckon with in American society. But as Germany takes on the face of an immigration country and multicultural society—whether it wants to or not—American solutions might be helpful, especially if parallel changes allowing political participation ensue.

Whatever program Germany pursues, it has finally been forced to acknowledge that the "foreigners" of all kinds who live in Germany are not going to disappear. While the change in the asylum law may limit access for those who are not "really" politically persecuted (as if economic disadvantages prompting people to immigrate from the Third World were not the result of the political and economic policies of advanced capitalist countries), Germany will have to acknowledge its responsibility to the millions of foreigners and Jews already living on its soil. While an immigration law would regulate the movement of foreigners wanting to come to Germany, it too would not necessarily change German attitudes toward foreigners. The change in laws to deny privilege of citizenship to "ethnic Germans," to the detriment of those peoples living and working in Germany no matter what their ethno-national identity, would break the *völkisch* tradition that is still intimately linked to Nazism and its racial laws. To be able to prove ethnicity for German citizenship today by using membership documents from the SS exemplifies the way that Germany's history grotesquely resonates for contemporary politics around citizenship and identity.

The changes I am suggesting go deep; they are an attack on a literal "Blut und Boden" mentality linked to a specific German cultural-political tradition. Germany does indeed have a particular task, one that looks more toward the future than to the past, even as the Holocaust continues to cast its shadow on present-day notions of German identity. The reemergence of German Jewish culture after Hoyerswerda, Hünxe, Mölln and Solingen is already couched in different terms than before these events, no matter to what extent they affect Jews directly. Differentiations must be made among the various minority groups and the kinds of hostility directed at them, but at the same time prejudice, discrimination, and violence of any kind against minorities should touch the Jews and especially the Germans. The responsibilities lie with the German population and with their politicians. Our role as Jews and as (Jewish) Americans who study Germany is to educate and to provide expertise not only for our fellow citizens here but also for the Germans. This is a more difficult task. It is important for scholars, such as those in this volume, to consider ways that our thinking, clearly different from colleagues in Germany and benefiting from our unique double perspective, could have some influence beyond academic circles. The reemergence of German Jewish culture is nourished at least in small part by its representation abroad, especially in North America. We who are scholars on Germany write, speak, and teach about this culture. It is also our responsibility, in addition to journalists, policy makers, and politicians, to effect change through the discourses we produce, as in this case, the discourses on Jews and foreigners.

In countries like the United States and Canada where the notion of heterogeneous identity is much less problematic than in Germany, we draw attention to identity without second thought. If we want to influence thinking in Germany, we must support the continued presence of the Jewish community by educating non-Jewish Germans to what it means to be Jewish today and to live in a diaspora. To live as a Jew is to acknowledge one's difference at all times from those with whom one lives. It is the openness and tolerance of the society that determines the degree to which one feels at home or as a stranger (*Fremder*) with this multiple identity. Life in the United States and Canada has proven that at least for Jews to be different is not necessarily to be marginalized and not to be the object of physical hostility. For blacks and other people of color this security has not yet been reached. North Americans react to these attacks on those considered different in Germany, because it is precisely the freedom we have to move back and forth across the boundaries of our different identities that the Jews in Germany and certainly foreigners and asylum seekers lack. For many Germans, North American Jews are their introduction to a population that lives among them. As part of our unique professional status as "foreigners" of a privileged sort, we often draw more attention to what it means to "be Jewish," since we have the benefit of a heterogeneous and hyphenated identity that is considered "normal" for North America.

Ignatz Bubis is contributing to constructing a different identity for Jews in Germany. In one article, he declares "ich 'bin' ein deutscher Jude, nicht 'ich verstehe mich als deutschen Juden.'"[16] While he can acknowledge that anti-Semitism and *Fremdenfeindlichkeit* are the same, he differentiates as well, "Ein Antisemit ist nicht immer fremdenfeindlich. Aber wer Ausländer haßt, ist immer auch ein Antisemit."[17] Anti-Semitism then is in fact a specific form of prejudice that is usually but not necessarily linked to specific traits, beliefs, or behaviors of Jews. In the case of contemporary Germany where the majority of Jews (aside from Soviet immigrants) are financially secure and "integrated," financial status may be a determining factor. In the East, it may well be the privileges that Jews received from the Honecker government or the old linkage of Jews with communism that inspire anti-Semitism. Anti-Semitism will not disappear with the change in asylum laws, or even with the transformations in German society that I have imagined occurring through some of my suggestions. Some of the hate against Jews and foreigners can be mollified by the reinstatement of economic and social security that many now lack after reunification. However, while the apparent threat may diminish that encourages many of these people to join neo-Nazi organizations or to simply stand by while foreigners are attacked, it will not wipe out anti-Semitism and xenophobia.

Hostility to those who are different will remain, but hopefully in less virulent forms. Jews and foreigners in Germany today and in the future may only be able to attain peaceful integration (rather than assimilation). Bubis is willing to recognize the realities of German Jewish life as part of this new Germany. He realizes Jewish identity must be reconfigured as part of all those who are considered different. To call himself a "deutscher Jude" is a step toward breaking the common distinctions made by Germans and Jews alike between "Deutsche(n)" and "Juden." To call himself a German Jew, especially in the context of hostilities toward foreigners of all kinds, is to take a strong stand for tolerance and openness toward all who are considered non-Germans. While to be a German Jew may still be easier for the Germans to understand as long as they only think of being Jewish as a religious determination, his presence represents not only the 40,000 Jews in Germany, but also those minority groups whose spokespersons are not as forceful and who cannot command the attention of German politicians and the world. Today German Jewish culture could lead the way in the debate over foreigners and asylum in Germany; now those representing this culture must speak up.

Notes

1. This article is based on interviews with members from different sectors of the Jewish community and the Turkish community in December 1992 in Berlin. I am grateful for the support from the Center for German and European Studies at Georgetown University, which allowed me to make this trip.
2. Lecture given at the Paul-Lobe-Haus.
3. *Der Spiegel* 51 (14 December 1992), 57.
4. For a very interesting and important analysis of the Turkish headscarf as a "sartorial symbol" for both Turks and Germans, see Ruth Mandel, "Turkish Headscarves and the "Foreigner Problem": Constructing Difference Through Emblems of Identity," *New German Critique* 46 (Special Issue on Minorities in German Culture, Winter 1989), 27–46.
5. Gisela Dachs, "Die Juden sollen sich nicht verstecken," *Die Zeit* 47 (20 November 1992), 2.
6. Karla Müller-Tupath, "Wendepunkt Hoyerswerda?" *Allgemeine Jüdische Wochenzeitung* 46/39 (26 September 1991), 2.
7. *Allgemeine Jüdische Wochenzeitung,* 46/40 (3 October 1991), 3, 11.
8. See the newspaper from 17 October 1991 and following.
9. Giovanni di Lorenzo, "Ein Drahtseilakt in Deutschland," *Süddeutsche Zeitung,* 19/20 December 1992.
10. *Neue Zeit,* 12 November 1992. For other interviews with Bubis see *Die Zeit,* 2 November 1992; *Der Spiegel,* 5 November 1992; *FAZ Beilage* 669 (23 December 1992); *Die Wochenpost,* 1 November 1992 and 29 November 1992; *Der Tagesspiegel,* 18 December 1992; *Die Tageszeitung,* 18

December 1992 and 21 December 1992; *Neues Deutschland,* 16 October 1992; *Junge Welt,* 12 November 1992; *Neue Zeit,* 3 November 1992.

11. In an article by Marc Fisher entitled "Germans Debate Image: 'How Ugly Are We?'" 25 January 1993, A12.
12. This discussion is elaborated in my article, "Rac(e)ing the Nation: Is There a German Home"? *New Formations* 17 (Summer 1992): 75–84.
13. See Dietrich Thränhardt, "Patterns of Organization among Different Ethnic Minorities," *New German Critique* 46 (Winter 1989): 10–26.
14. I analyze this ad in greater detail for its "multicultural" significance in the German context. See "Refugees as Foreigners: The Problem of Becoming German and Finding Home," Forthcoming.
15. I discussed the comparison between the 1930s and recent events in a paper presented at the 1991 German Studies Association Convention. It was entitled, "The Ethics of Comparison and the Recourse to Race in the Foreigner Debate."
16. *Neue Zeit,* 12 November 1992.
17. *Süddeutsche Zeitung,* 19/20 December 1992.

7. The Persian Gulf War and the Germans' "Jewish Questions": Transformations on the Left

Kizer Walker

This volume is concerned with the reemergence of Jewish life in contemporary Germany—the emergence, that is, of new German Jewish identities in the postunification Federal Republic. In this chapter, I reexamine an early crisis for Jewish life in the short history of Germany since 1990: the debates surrounding the Persian Gulf War and the opposition to it in Germany, as well as the bitter disputes that arose around Israel, the German Left, and anti-Semitism. My treatment of the so-called *Antisemitismusstreit* pushes somewhat against the current of the other contributions in this collection in that—while I consider Jewish voices in the German Gulf War debate—I devote considerable attention to discussions of anti-Semitism and "the Jews" on various parts of the mainly white, non-Jewish German Left and the implications of these discussions for the viability of a political Left in Germany. I hope thereby to contribute to the mapping out of the political terrain on which Jews are articulating new identities. I comment on rather far-ranging aspects of the Gulf War discussions and make no claim to cover the most prominent or influential interventions; two excellent pieces that have appeared in English can provide such an overview.[1]

I

Abraham Melzer, editor of the Left-liberal, German-Jewish magazine *Semit*, begins the April 1991 issue with the following:

> The Gulf War has ended and on the battlefield, next to the many Iraqi and Allied victims, lies the probably stillborn new German-Jewish and German-Israeli relationship. We stand before a pile of shards, as if a SCUD missile had struck right in the heart of these relationships. How could this happen when just a few short months ago these relationships stood at the high point of their "normalcy"?
>
> The Gulf War opened all our eyes and showed that it was all along only a matter of a normalcy of lies and hypocrisy. . . . Under the cover of this apparent normalcy gaped an abyss over which only a very few Germans and Jews were able to jump.[2]

A sense of a hopelessly shattered German Left likewise emerged in the aftermath of the Gulf War. At a discussion in the spring of 1991, Jan Phillip Reemtsma of the Institut für Sozialforschung in Hamburg registered his dismay: "It's a fact that all at once those people who before [the war] thought they belonged in common with others to something called "the Left" are now slinging vehement denials back and forth at each other. Something has happened here; a tone is being set that is new. . . . [There is] nothing detectable left of a consensus that one used to assume somehow united a certain sort of Left. And I wish I understood this phenomenon somewhat better than I understand it at present."[3]

In the months preceding the bombardment of Iraq by the United States and its allies, details surfaced about the extent of German contributions to Baghdad's chemical arms program. Not only was German industry reckoned to have been responsible, through technical assistance and the delivery of materials, for some 90 percent of Iraq's capability to produce chemical weapons; German firms were also involved in reoutfitting Soviet SCUDs to bring Israel into range of these weapons. The firms involved in this project were guaranteed protection against financial loss by the Kohl administration. The prospect that survivors of Auschwitz could in 1991 be gassed by a collusion of German capital and the

German state pushed Israel to the center of the Gulf conflict in the German discourse and tore up lines of political allegiances in Germany.

Moribund for several years after its flourish in the early 1980s, the peace movement was reborn during the period of mobilization for the Gulf War; but by the time the first Iraqi SCUDs were launched toward Haifa and Tel Aviv, a number of prominent Left intellectuals had already announced their support of the war against Iraq. Two weeks before the commencement of Operation Desert Storm, Henryk Broder had accused the German antiwar movement of indifference to what he called "a second Final Solution"; for Broder, the failure to address the Iraqi threat to Israel was in perfect accord with the German Left's philo-Semitic "enthusiasm for dead Jews" that always had as its flipside "difficulties . . . with living ones."[4] An avalanche of critique from the Left directed at the antiwar movement was to follow, and by no means were the critics mostly Jewish. Unresolved issues around a complex of problems—(German) Leftism / Israel / anti-imperialism / anti-Zionism / anti-Semitism—that had accompanied the New Left in Germany since its infancy, as more or less private "family" antagonisms now erupted on the pages of the mainstream and "movement" press. During the course of the war, several surprising figures appeared among the *Bellizisten*—as Gulf War supporters from the Left were dubbed, in contradistinction to *Pazifisten*. Hermann L. Gremliza, editor of the magazine *Konkret*, concluded that "this time, for the wrong reasons and with the wrong justifications, it appears the right thing is being done. . . . Iraq must be robbed of its ability to—as Saddam has announced—attack and liquidate Israel."[5] Between *Bellizisten* and *Pazifisten*, the German discourse did not appear to admit a position that would without compromise both oppose the war against Iraq and thematize anti-Semitism as a problem of the Left. Declaring his support of allied actions at the outset of the Gulf War, Klaus Hartung of the Left Berlin daily *taz* would seem to have articulated the parameters of the German debate: "Frieden oder rettet Israel"—"make peace or rescue Israel."[6]

The dispute over this pair of alternatives—"peace" *or* "Israel"—concerned not only the question of military force against Iraq, but also the role to be played by the German government and military in the war. With the realities of the costly project of unification just beginning to set in, the Bonn government was at first disinclined to fully back an intervention in the Gulf; this early reticence allowed critics of the burgeoning popular protests against the war to point to an apparent "alliance of government passivity and movement activity."[7] But this "alliance" was not to last. Two weeks into the Gulf War, Helmut Kohl declared that "for Germany there must be no flight from responsibility"; not only were subsidies forthcoming, but some 3,200 German soldiers were soon stationed in Turkey and the Mediterranean, the largest such mobilization since 1945.[8] In view of the threat to Israel, one Bundeswehr general argued for the deployment of German troops against Iraq as a form of "praktische Trauerarbeit"—practical work of mourning for Hitler's victims.[9] One of the decisive divisions on the Left occurred over the question of whether German anti-SCUD missiles should be stationed in Israel. Before the Gulf War had ended, plans for a revision of the Basic Law's proscription of "out-of-area" deployment were on the table in Bonn.

Despite the relatively marginal role played by the Bundeswehr, the war seemed to be experienced with a particular immediacy precisely in Germany. Micha Brumlik writes: "In no European country . . . did the war and the events that led to it arouse feelings in the way they did in newly reunified Germany. Hardly anywhere else did so many friendships go to pieces, did people who had survived the same political and intellectual battles over more than twenty years stop talking to one another."[10] White bedsheets—flags of surrender—hanging from windows; candlelight vigils; silent marches and prayerful entreaties for peace at demonstrations: the pathos of the symbolism employed by large parts of the antiwar movement caused opponents and supporters of the war to question what besides the immediate political emergency was at stake for German demonstrators.

Above all, many critics of the peace movement were struck by a ritualistic preoccupation with one's own *Betroffenheit*—an insistence in slogans, actions, symbols, on one's own pain and grief. A nationwide demonstration in Bonn, for instance, was held under the motto "Against the Destruction of Our Future." Brumlik sees in reactions to the Gulf War a return of the repressed:

In Germany, the Second Gulf War was experienced by most of those who took part in the debate publicly and in an engaged manner, as a collective remembrance of the Second World War, particularly of the last months of it. This became clear by no means solely from surface phenomena . . . but more from the way people privately, in their therapy sessions, in arguments with friends, children, and parents, again and again articulated fears, experiences, and perils that even in the most pessimistic prognoses had no reality content whatsoever.[11]

Brumlik refers to fears expressed by many in Germany, also publicly and in the context of demonstrations, that the theater of war could spread to Northern Europe or, more commonly, that the ecological catastrophe unleashed by the war would be such that Germany would not be spared. For Brumlik, the reaction is an indication that "in the rage about the [Gulf War] Allies," the Germans had broken through their notorious "inability to mourn" the German losses of World War II.[12]

Wolfgang Schneider, a writer for *Konkret,* similarly sees in the German protests a return of the collective past. Assembling traces of actual slogans, headlines, and declarations from the German public sphere in the first hours of the Gulf War, Schneider sketches a panorama of *Germany* 1991 under attack by Allied bombers, the population erupting in panic and outrage. On the night of the "attack," demonstrators call from city streets: "Neighbors, wake up! The Amis have brought war," "Defend yourselves! Resist!" The next day food shortages are reported in Munich. The magazine *Stern* reports that "in the first hours of the war, the nation is standing together like seldom before." Churches, unions, and parties take to the streets; school children carry banners that read "We are too young to die." For Schneider, it is a scene from a madhouse:

The Germans . . . are imagining that the attack launched on January 17 by the Americans, the British and the French against Iraq was really meant for them. But this is not an empty delusion. It feeds on a murky mixture of guilty conscience, self pity, . . . angst, and a need for revenge that is reflected in the refusal to take on the consequences of the Nazi mass murders. But it results, at the same time, from knowledge of the fact that Iraq has largely

German industry to thank for its ability to continue with the eradication of the Jews where the parents and grandparents of today's antiwar demonstrators were interrupted by the military intervention of the Allies.[13]

Intended as a critique of the German Gulf War opposition, Schneider's comments are themselves part of a discourse that overlaid the Second World War as a template for responses to the Gulf War from every quarter. Recurrent invocations, by opponents of the war, of the effects of Allied bombing in Germany in World War II indicate the extent to which this moment of relocation of the Gulf conflict to German soil involves a renegotiation of the relationship to the German past. Gregor Gysi's Party of Democratic Socialism, the successor to the East German Socialist Unity Party, made wide use of the slogan "Denkt an Dresden!" ("Think of Dresden") in its campaign against the war. A headline in the party's newspaper *Neues Deutschland* read at the start of the Gulf War: "For the first time in 45 years, Anglo-American bomber squadrons drop their deadly load." Likewise, the Left Berlin daily *taz* wrote: "Today old people are remembering with tears in their eyes the bombardments they themselves experienced."[14] In his piece in *Die Zeit* (his "coming out" for the war as it was dubbed, in English, by critics), Wolf Biermann counters such references with his own gruesome childhood memories of the bombardment of Hamburg—an action he could only welcome as the destruction of the regime that killed his Jewish father at Auschwitz. But Biermann draws his support of the war from a similar schema: the bombardment of Iraq is a reenactment of the bombardment of Germany; the alternative is "appeasement" and a new holocaust.

Analogies to the Second World War could allow segments of the antiwar movement to employ the Persian Gulf War as a tool to reorder their relationship to a national past, as a vehicle for anti-Semitism or revanchism vis-à-vis the "victorious powers," or as an opportunity to try on the vestments of the victim. But such analogies were also employed in support of the war and functioned just as surely to relativize German history. Hans Magnus Enzensberger's piece in the *Spiegel* in support of the war is subtitled "On Saddam Hussein in the Mirror of German History."[15] He begins by proclaiming that the notion of the singularity of the history of

National Socialism and the Holocaust, which had been insisted upon "with good reason" in the post-World War II period, has proven illusory. The Saddam-Hitler analogy, one of George Bush's earliest and most often repeated popular justifications for troop deployment in Saudi Arabia, is for Enzensberger "no journalistic metaphor or propagandistic exaggeration, but rather the essence of the matter." And it is primarily in terms of "essence" that Enzensberger argues. Hitler and Hussein appear as the first incarnations of a twentieth-century creature called "The Enemy of Humanity" from which Enzensberger erases concrete political and historical particularities. "It is a fatal mistake," he writes, "to attribute convictions to Hitler or Saddam." The Enemy's real motive is "the death wish," and "entire peoples," also acting on suicidal yearnings, "summon [his] coming with their wishes." "[Saddam] is not fighting this or that particular domestic or foreign political opponent; his enemy is the world." Neither was Hitler interested, Enzensberger insists, "in defeating one or another internal or external opponent. He was the deadly enemy not only of the Jews, the Czechs, the Poles, the English, the French, the Dutch, Belgians, Scandinavians, the Baltic peoples, the Russians, and the Americans, but ultimately of the Germans as well." After placing the Germans at the end of a long list of Hitler's enemies and victims, Enzensberger goes on to write that what is essential in Hitler cannot be localized in Germany: "The time has come to take leave of such illusions once and for all. The new enemy of humanity behaves no differently than his predecessor. . . . This continuity proves that we are dealing not with a German fact, not with an Arab fact, but with an anthropological fact." Ingrid Strobl, writing in *Konkret*, recognized in the deployment of the Saddam-Hitler analogy by Left intellectuals like Enzensberger a moment of repression of the past coupled with an abandonment of any serious critique of the exploitation of the "Third World" by the "First":

> The German intelligentsia . . . projects the crimes of its own fathers onto the Arabs of today and thereby kills two birds with one stone: If Saddam Hussein is Hitler, then one can finally forget about one's own Hitler and at the same time one's guilty conscience about the fact that he or she is shamelessly profiting from the imperialist appropriation of resources and the op-

pression of the Arab people in the so-called Near East. Thus begins a process that will redetermine for the future one's position vis-à-vis the South—and why not vis-à-vis the fathers at the same time?[16]

The war front is transferred to Germany; Hitler is exported to Iraq. Experienced in Germany, as in the United States, through abstract, highly controlled and mediated video images, the war in the Gulf was open to occupation with various fantasies of war. The Left's concerns with the problems of historical analogy involving the Third Reich in the *Historikerstreit* of the mid-1980s give way in the Gulf War *Antisemitismusstreit* to a proliferation of analogies. The conflict between *Bellizisten* and *Pazifisten* becomes a struggle between two: "Baghdad = Dresden" versus "Saddam = Hitler."[17]

II

Advertised as the event that would inaugurate the post-Cold War era and waged in the name of a "New World Order," the Persian Gulf War of 1991 followed German unification by only two months. German unification—this other emblem of the *end of the Cold War*—had recast overnight Germany's position in the order of the world and marked in Germany the *end of the post-World War II era*. The first response of many Left intellectuals in West Germany to the prospect of unification had been a profound crisis of identity at the dissolution of actually existing socialism in the German Democratic Republic. As has been much discussed elsewhere, there was a widespread reaction, regardless of one's ideological distance from the East German state, to the loss of the GDR as the loss of a potential utopia. This response was quickly rejoined by a flurry of self-criticism for past naiveté vis-à-vis conditions in the GDR, and, eventually, by a surprisingly broad endorsement of unification on the part of the Left. Especially among veterans of the 1968 student movement, the collapse of Eastern European socialism destroyed for many Left intellectuals in Germany a set of coordinates by which their generation had perceived the world: this much, of course, mirrors the continuing international crisis of the Left. But if internationally, this political crisis has been conceived in geographical terms as a dissipation of the global East-West opposition, in Germany unification has meant that the discussions have been carried out in large part with reference to the national map. Cut loose ideologically, Left intellectuals were left to renegotiate their positions vis-à-vis the German state and its official politics, just as the expanded Federal Republic was initiating a massive project of refashioning the German nation.

"Out of utopian reflection, and into what is already happening anyway. . . . This is the profitable lesson the intellectuals learned from the reunification crisis and put to use in the Gulf War."[18] Indeed, among intellectuals on the Left, support for the war against Iraq did correlate, generally speaking, with support for German union. Forsaking the outsider position it had occupied since its inception, much of the intellectual New Left came in from the cold in 1990 and 1991, betraying in numbers unprecedented before 1989 a willingness to engage in Great Power *Realpolitik.* The Gulf War debates, and especially the logic of the German *Antisemitismusstreit,* facilitated an integration of large parts of the Left into the official political culture of the Federal Republic. Extending his support for the deployment of German missiles in Israel against Iraqi SCUDs, Detlev Claussen called for the Left to return "to the logic of politics," to enter, that is, into the discourse of statecraft. This "normalization" of Left intellectuals[19] ran parallel to the integration of the "normalized," united Germany into the community of nations. *Bellizisten* countered the "ethic of conviction" (*Gesinnungsethik*) that supposedly informed an antiwar position with an "ethic of responsibility" (*Verantwortungsethik*) that demanded global activism at the level of the state. Thomas Voss of the Greens called for an end to German "neutralism," an acceptance by the government, but also by the Left, of Germany's new role as a Great Power and the responsibilities, "financial, but if necessary also military," that this status entails. Social Democrat Brigitte Seebacher-Brandt echoed Karl-Heinz Bohrer's critique of German "provincialism" in her assessment of the Gulf War debate: "The German contemplation of navels in the Leftist camp was provincial in both instances. The pro- and antiwar variants have a common denominator—the flight from reality that amounts to a flight from responsibility."

Responsible action would have demanded the "political imagination" and "self-consciousness" necessary to accept a military role in the Gulf for Germany in line with "its weight, determined by history and the present." In tandem with the normalization of the Left, then, could proceed its *nationalization.*

The disputes around the Gulf War were at the center of a process by which parts of the Left sought to reform, transform, or, in some cases, dismantle themselves. Both Dan Diner and Micha Brumlik, editors of the Jewish journal *Babylon* and central figures in Frankfurt's Left intellectual circle, the Jüdische Gruppe, took the Gulf War and the German protests as points of departure for book-length essays—each is a postsocialist stock-taking and leave-taking of a range of Left positions and traditions. For Diner and Brumlik, the lifting of the bipolar division of the Cold War world has disrupted the "binary code" (Brumlik) of "Left" and "Right." Brumlik is aware of the ideological uses—from French fascism of the '20s and '30s to Cold War theories of totalitarianism—of the notion of Left-Right convergence. These earlier attempts necessarily missed "the essential": "[A]t their core, the Left radicalisms that were influenced by Marxism were bound to the concept of a *different economy* which de facto cannot be said of the historical Right. . . . The Right stood and stands for a capitalist economy, just as the radical Left, even in its most distorted forms, would not acquiesce to it."[20] But Brumlik goes on to claim that "in any politically meaningful sense, the much invoked obsolescence of the classical Left/Right schema only becomes true and reasonable when there is no longer an alternative to capitalism."[21] This condition, as Brumlik would have it, was met with the collapse of Soviet socialism.

The events of the Gulf War sealed the fate of the bipolar order, but the Left's response, in both Brumlik and Diner's view, was to stubbornly force the new situation into old categories—to "verticalize" the horizontal East-West division into a conflict between "North" and "South" and insist on the character of the war against Iraq as an imperialist war waged over the control of resources. According to Diner, the Gulf War was, in fact, fought to secure the principle of the inviolability of borders. The new multilateralism to which global bipolarity has given way depends for its stability on the reemergent principles of state sovereignty and territoriality; the sovereign state replaces ideology as the guarantor of order. The point of the offensive against Baghdad, in fact, was less to defend Kuwait or disarm Iraq per se than, in a period of transition, to uphold the state in principle.[22]

In Diner's analysis, the insistence on supposedly obsolete categories of analysis sprang from a need to shore up a Left identity in crisis. But with the sudden dissipation of political moorings, familiar Left discourses of the Cold War era begin to resonate, in the movement against the U.S.-led Gulf War, with older, national discourses:

> [A]gainst the background of the united German nation state, the spreading rage touched those latent but certainly still operative lines of continuity that ultimately mix up that reassuring difference of conviction historically stipulated as Left and Right and reduce it to nothing more than a street sign pointing the direction in traffic. For that which bubbles up in the form of allegedly social analysis no longer has anything in common with social critique. The latter is hardly able to keep hidden its character as mere camouflage for national *ressentiments* that had endured these long years in a collective half-sleep.[23]

At issue, for Diner, is the question of Germany's traditionally ambivalent relationship to "the West." With the breakup of global bipolarity, the "political concepts of 'East' and 'West,' metaphorically conceived in terms of the points of the compass, regain their old cultural-geographical significance":[24] a reinstatement of Orient and Occident. Precisely in the German movement against the Gulf War, Diner sees a reemergence of "a deep-seated anti-Western sentiment" that is now cut loose from the ideological framework of the Cold War Left.[25] In view of the changed global situation, solidarity with "Third World" struggles mobilized against the Gulf War can show up little more, for Diner, than a "German affinity for peoples in colonial situations" rooted in a discourse of resentment against the successful colonial powers and Germany's traditional enemies.[26] Similarly, protest against the Gulf War as an intervention to secure U.S. control of the world oil market resonates with a traditional European anti-American critique with its "images and metaphors that lament uprootedness, alienation, and the globalized power of the pecuniary." "Metaphors of circulation" link images of America and the Jew, and Diner postulates that "European and above all German anti-Americanism," also as it was supposedly expressed in the movement against the Gulf War, represents "something like a displaced anti-Semitism."[27]

In the aftermath of the Cold War, Diner can affirm "the West" as "a field of force and center of innovation [from which] guiding, civilizing impulses emanate."[28] The role of the Unites States is central to this conception and its "civilizing impulses" are apparently inseparable from a capitalist economy: "It happens to be the United States that, even more than other Western commonwealths, represents a universalism of values and doctrines that correspond to the abstraction of the world market."[29] "[A]fter the collapse of the utopia of socialist internationalism," it is for Diner precisely "the values of a democratic and republican universalism," encoded in a fortified conception of international law and enforced by institutions like the United Nations, now freed from Cold War constraints, that "should become the respectable foundation of a future Left."[30] Brumlik, too, sees the "question of a politically serviceable universalist ethic of action on a global scale . . . pushed to the foreground."[31] Diner and Brumlik's Gulf War interventions no doubt offer astute and necessary critiques of Left discourses; their solutions leave little maneuvering space for a radical anticapitalist politics or for a Left that would problematize neocolonial relations of power.

III

Micha Brumlik ends his reflections on the Gulf War with two predictions—one for the Jews and one for the Left. In view of what came to light with the German movement against the war, "Jews and historically conscious people may live in Germany for a long time to come and in certain cases live very well; they will never be at home here. Overtaken by its own history, the German Left stands before a pile of rubble. It no longer has anything to impart to the new historical epoch."[32] Did the Gulf War render the Left obsolete, then, dividing what remained of it along the lines of the *Antisemitismusstreit* between a politically integrated post-Left and an entity that can only recycle reactionary national discourses? Rummaging among the rubble—is truly nothing "Left"?

Here it is necessary to turn briefly to the 1990 unification debate. In another Gulf War retrospective, Oliver Tolmein and Detlef zum Winkel reiterate that it was the intellectuals on the Left who had supported unification in 1990 who also tended to support the Allies' objectives in Iraq, while that segment of the activist Left that had opposed German union opposed the war in the Gulf as well. But between the two events—German unification and Persian Gulf War—Tolmein and zum Winkel note a migration of the problematic of Germany's National Socialist past from one camp to the other. If the forces mobilized against unification had taken the problem of the legacy of National Socialism as a point of departure for an antinationalist politics, this frame of reference was more or less neglected in the movement against the Gulf War. Those Left intellectual "opinion makers, on the other hand, for whom the restoration of Germany had presented no problem, who, with no consideration for the opinion and interests of the victims of the Nazis, had placed themselves on the side of their government... now suddenly remembered their history books . . . [and] proclaimed a special German responsibility for Israel."[33]

Organized protest against German unification took place largely in the context of the so-called Radikale Linke, a loose confederation of disparate Left groups and activists that came together in 1990 to this end. Dissident Greens played a leading role in its formation, but the Radikale Linke became a collecting vessel for various remnants of a disintegrating West German Left. It is possible to point to at least a current in the Radikale Linke that was engaged in 1990 in a nuanced discussion of anti-Semitism as a contemporary problem for, as well as in the German Left. A number of articles and speeches appeared in the context of the "Nie Wieder Deutschland" ("Germany—never again!") campaign against unification that addressed anti-Semitism as a force in the everyday lives of Jews in Germany today and stressed the need for white, non-Jewish Leftists and feminists to acknowledge their own positions of power in any approach to anti-Semitism.[34] Like emergent discussions of racism that are compelled by second-generation immigrants' and black Germans' public articulation of their experiences in Germany, this kind of discussion of anti-Semitism depended on the self-assertion of a new generation of German Jews. The highly charged polarization of the Left between *Pazifisten* and *Bellizisten* served to alienate some participants in the discussion from the Gulf War opposition and, within the antiwar movement, to largely stifle a discussion of anti-Semitism. But amid the damningly hasty dismissals of critiques of the Left in this regard, it is possible to make out, also in the radical spectrum of the German Left, cells of a continuing engagement with the problem of anti-Semitism, through the months of the Gulf War and after.

Arbeiterkampf, the newspaper of the former Kommunistischer Bund, ran numerous articles during the Gulf War that sought to introduce elements of the critiques leveled at the antiwar movement into the discourse of the radical Left. Writing under the *nom de guerre* "Jürgen," an activist with the Radikale Linke admonished the movement against the Gulf War for its failure to maintain the "anti-German" focus of the "Nie Wieder Deutschland" campaign. Jürgen diagnoses the German Left as split between a "crude anticapitalism" that "ignores the German past" and a "vulgar antifascism" that neglects the "German present." Either tendency in isolation, he charges, leaves an "open flank for nationalism."

Jürgen in no way suggests relinquishing the category of imperialism in an analysis of the Gulf War; he does contend that to make the United States the center and "popular vehicle of . . . anti-imperialism" in Germany is a grave error in a post-Cold War "multipolar world" in which Germany is reemerging as an imperialist power in its own right. Not only does such a move fail to apprehend the changed global terrain, but, Jürgen suggests, it is also eminently compatible with right-wing discourses. In the context of opposition to the Gulf War, an insistence on what Jürgen calls "German guilt in the past and present" would have centralized scrutiny of the mechanisms of German imperialism at work both in the arming of Iraq and the mobilization of the Bundeswehr against Iraq. Instead, the Left was drawn into a debate over

"German *responsibility*" that could legitimize an expansion of the role of the German military—Jürgen points to the way in which the Left was caught up in the controversy over Foreign Minister Genscher's offer of German Patriot missiles to Israel. Following the mainstream discussion, the Left paid little heed to the fact that the initiative came largely from the German side; the Israeli government's ultimate refusal of the German weapons went nearly unnoticed. Provocatively calling for "support [for] anti-German protests in Israel," Jürgen asks why the German Left was unable to make use of critiques coming out of the Left in Israel which put together the issues of chemical arms-mongering and renewed German militarization: "Instead of taking up the Israeli critique offensively in this way, for our struggle against German militarism, we allowed ourselves to be pressured and duped onto the defensive by the German politicians and their media. A Frankfurt leaflet aptly describes this deceptive maneuver: "It is the height of cynicism that the Federal Government and its media are suggestively portraying it as though they were asked by Israel to enter the war."[35] In attempting to recover the radical antinationalist orientation submerged in the movement against the Gulf War, Jürgen suggests the contours of an alternative Left politics that would have uncompromisingly opposed the war against Iraq while yielding radically different answers to questions raised in the *Antisemitismusstreit.*

The last survivor of the communist K-Gruppen formed in the early 1970s, and always the most independent and dynamic, the Kommunistischer Bund split during the process of German unification into a majority faction that allied itself with Gysi's Party of Democratic Socialism and a minority that tended to overlap with the Radikale Linke. With this minority faction originated a number of articles attacking anti-Zionism on the Left from the standpoint of a critique of the reified anti-imperialist politics that have been a mainstay of the post-1968 German radical Left. Problematizing the focus on *national* liberation in an anti-imperialist position that opposes "the enemy defined as 'imperialism'" with "the friend defined as a 'people' and the 'popular masses' ['*Volk*' and '*Volksmassen*']," [36] these critiques point to a tendency to displace home-grown nationalist energies onto "third world" struggles. Less than a month after the end of the Gulf War, the Kommunistischer Bund was dissolved, not least owing to divisions around issues of nationalism and anti-Semitism.[37] However, *Arbeiterkampf*, whose readership for years had vastly outstripped membership in its parent organization, continues to be published, and its editorial board still reflects the formal division of the Kommunistischer Bund from 1990. The minority communists, now called "Gruppe K," have maintained an emphasis on questions involving anti-Semitism and the German Left; the focus, significantly, is on *contemporary* problems *inside* the Federal Republic. During the protests in the spring of 1992, mostly by Orthodox Jews, against plans to build a shopping center on the site of Hamburg Jewish cemetery, it was in *Arbeiterkampf* that one could read critiques of the Left's (mostly absent) response.[38]

In the Black Forest town of Freiburg, the *Antisemitismusstreit* came to a head in a dispute over a series of broadcasts by an alternative Left radio station, almost a month after the Gulf War had officially ended.[39] Of the several attempts in the 1970s and 1980s to establish alternative radio in Germany, Radio Dreyeckland in Freiburg is the only station in the country that has maintained an entirely noncommercial broadcast. The project, which originated in the movement against nuclear energy and the Left regionalism of the late 1970s, has been transmitting legally from Freiburg since 1988, after more than a decade of underground operation from a mobile studio.[40] The station is a central component in Freiburg's thriving counter-public sphere.

In March 1991, in the context of its "Background to the Gulf War" coverage, a group of Radio Dreyeckland programmers broadcast a three-part round-table discussion on "Israel-Palestine and the Federal Republic." Participating in two of the three discussions was Dr. Helmut Spehl, a professor at the University of Freiburg's Institute of Physics who in his spare time has made a small name for himself in some anti-imperialist circles for his work on the history of Zionism that centers on allegations of ideological affinities, as well as pragmatic political cooperation, between Zionism and National Socialism. According to his own description, Spehl is "not Left,"[41] nor is his alleged defense of the Palestinian people part of a context of international solidarity

("What did Vietnam or what does Chile mean to me? What is Angola supposed to mean to me?"). Rather, his research proceeds from a notion of a powerful "Zionist" conspiracy that makes German politicians and media dance to a tune of guilt played on the Israeli "pipe organ." Spehl has conducted a twenty-year, one-man crusade to banish German inhibitions with regard to this "Zionist plague," to expose Israel as the successor state to the Third Reich that is perpetrating a holocaust on the Palestinians. In numerous self-published tracts and two books, Spehl follows on the trail of "the Jewish sponge machine" that soaks up dollars and channels them to Israel, that "barren desert of Mendelsohns."[42]

Radio Dreyeckland programmers apparently invited Spehl to speak on the air without having read any of his material first hand—his name was known from a series of nested cross references in various Leftist publications.[43] The overt anti-Semitic vocabulary was kept to a minimum in Spehl's radio appearances; his analogies between Zionism and National Socialism were received without much comment by the other discussants.

A few days after the third program with Spehl, a local activist broadcast an explication of Spehl's *Fortzeugung des Behemoths* over Radio Dreyeckland, calling the book a product of "'classic' anti-Semitic thinking." Then, in early May, a group of "friends, listeners, and coworkers of Radio Dreyeckland" occupied the studio, calling for an "end [to] the dissemination of anti-Semitic stereotypes at 102.3 megahertz." Carried out by a number of local political projects and organizations—including pillars of alternative Left culture in Freiburg with close ties to the radio station—the studio occupation and the campaign that followed were spearheaded by the Initiative Sozialistisches Forum, "a circle of independent Left communists in Freiburg." The political biography of Joachim Bruhn, the central figure in the ISF, stretches from the 1968 student movement, through the K-Gruppen in the 1970s, to a move in the 1980s in the direction of critical theory. In his work with the initiative, Bruhn has sought to reintroduce a revolutionary politics at the philosophical niveau of the Frankfurt School. A Marxist analysis of anti-Semitism has been central to the project of the ISF and its polemic critique of the Left; the group has been in conflict with certain segments of the anti-imperialist Left in

Freiburg since at least 1988, when the ISF targeted local groups in a series of events on the topic of anti-Semitism and anti-Zionism.

The Radio Dreyeckland dispute, carried out through the summer months of 1991 on the air and in crowded membership assemblies, tended to run aground amid a pedantic search for an acceptable definition of "anti-Semitism." The often inflationary accusations of anti-Semitism from the ISF and other critics of the station met with intransigence and a "bunker mentality" on the part of the programmers responsible for the Spehl fiasco and their supporters. Radio Dreyeckland's bureaucratic solution was to adopt a set of guidelines for acceptable handling of issues involving Israel, Zionism, and anti-Semitism; when their access to the airwaves was temporarily restricted on this basis, the "Background to the Gulf War" programmers eventually issued a halting self-critique.

In its journal *Kritik und Krise*, in the publications of Bruhn's ça ira Verlag, and also in discussion groups where it exercises significant influence in local circles, the ISF continues to address questions involving anti-Semitism. At Radio Dreyeckland, the immediate dispute was followed by a long silence regarding the issues raised in the conflict. A year after the Gulf War ended, a group formed at the station to pick up the discussion again and pursue it in an ongoing way; the direct impetus came not from the ISF, but from an open letter composed by a group of jailed militants in Frankfurt in response to the 1991 events at Radio Dreyeckland.[44] The letter sharply criticizes Spehl's invitation and the subsequent defensive posturing of the responsible programmers. The authors distance themselves from many of the positions taken by the ISF and other critics in the broader German *Antisemitismusstreit*, but they urge a thoroughgoing engagement with anti-Semitism on the part of the radical, anti-imperialist Left. The Freiburg group, referring in an early discussion paper to the resistance met by women challenging sexism on the Left after 1968 and black German women confronting racism in the feminist movement in the 1980s and 1990s, articulated a central problem for any approach to anti-Semitism on the German Left: "Who will put on the pressure needed to force an engagement with anti-Semitism? Will it be up to the Jewish refugees from the former

Soviet Union, or will we as Leftists finally manage to carry out the necessary discussions ourselves, without having our feet stepped on?"[45] The Leftist "we" implied in the question is rather clearly white and non-Jewish, but the fact that such a question is posed at all in regard to anti-Semitism would seem at least to indicate that not only "dead Jews" or Jews in the abstract are at issue, but living Jews in Germany.

In Berlin, Nozizwe, a multicultural feminist project, promotes discussion and political work among women immigrants and refugees, black German women and Jewish women. The fragile relationships among these groups of women survived the Gulf War and the divisions it revealed in Germany, but it did not survive undamaged. More than a year after the Gulf War, the differences and in some cases mutual distrust that arose in that context remained a topic of ongoing discussions. In regard to the public Gulf War debates, however, there was a sense of estrangement at Nozizwe. Gotlinde Lwanga, one of the coordinators, notes in retrospect that "the fact that the Left is anti-Semitic and racist was already clear" before the Gulf War and the "pseudo-front" that developed between *Bellizisten* and *Pazifisten* did not address the concerns of the women at the project.[46] Another Nozizwe coordinator, Jessica Jacoby, a Jewish woman, recalls the discussions in the German public sphere:

> [O]f course all the blame was pushed onto the peace movement; but the peace movement only reflects what goes on in the society as a whole and, of course, also at the level of government—and that is a fundamental disinterest in Jews. . . . [T]he peace movement presented itself, so to speak, as a scapegoat for one's own anti-Semitism. And that leads, of course, to the need for legitimation on the part of the Left; they have to prove they are not anti-Semitic. It is a game among Germans. And if I am in the game at all, it is only as the object; I am a nonparticipant.[47]

Jacoby's comments underscore the distance of the Gulf War *Antisemitismusstreit*, which centered on an abstracted "Jewish victim" in Israel, from the lives of contemporary German Jews. As they were carried out, the Left's discussions facilitated a self-dissolution that for segments of the Left clearly also presented a welcome opportunity for *rapprochement* with the new Germany. Both sides of the Left's public debate, with the frantic, last-minute thematization of anti-Semitism, bypassed difficult, ongoing engagements with the problem already underway in less visible spheres; at the small Nozizwe project, questions of anti-Semitism, racism, and sexism are being addressed together, by the people affected, in the specific German context. If an oppositional Left is to reinvent itself in Germany, these voices will have to be heard.

Notes

1. Anson Rabinbach, "German Intellectuals and the Gulf War," *Dissent*, Fall 1991, 459–63 and Russell A. Berman, "The Gulf War and Intellectuals, in Germany and the United States," *Telos* 88 (Summer 1991), 167–79.
2. Abraham Melzer, "Unter Bomben begraben . . ." *Semit*, March–April 1991, 4–5.
3. Jan Phillip Reemtsma, "Bankrott der Linken?" *Konkret*, May 1991, 15.
4. Henryk M. Broder, "Beredtes 'friedliches' Schweigen," *taz*, 2 January 1991.
5. Hermann L. Gremliza, "Richtig falsch," *Konkret*, March 1991, 8.
6. Klaus Hartung, "Frieden oder rettet Israel," *taz* , 19 January 1991.
7. max., "Von der 'zitternden Provinz' zur Kriegsmacht," *Arbeiterkampf* 327 (11 February 1991), 10.
8. Ibid.
9. Quoted in Jürgen, "Die anti–deutsche Orientierung in der (Golf–) Krise," *Arbeiterkampf* 328 (11 March 1991), 19.
10. Micha Brumlik, *Weltrisiko Naher Osten: Moralische und politische Perspektiven in einem Konflikt ohne Ende* (Hamburg: Junius, 1991), 27.
11. Ibid., 31–32. The designation "*Second* Gulf War" was frequently used in the German context to historicize the 1991 event in relation to the Iran–Iraq war. The term's resonance with "Second World War" serves to underscore Brumlik's point.
12. Ibid., 39–40.
13. Wolfgang Schneider, "'Lazarett Deutschland,'" *Konkret* Februar 1991, 10–13.
14. Quoted in ibid., 11.
15. Hans Magnus Enzensberger, "Hitlers Wiedergänger," *Spiegel*, 6 (4 Februar 1991), 26–28.
16. Ingrid Strobl, "Neue Untermenschen,'" *Konkret*, April 1991, 22–23.
17. Cf. Ilse Bindseil, "Die Intellektuellen und der Golfkrieg," *Kritik und Krise* 4/5 (Summer 1991), 75.

18. Ibid., 77.
19. For a critique of Left "normalization," see Gunter Hofmann, "Wenn die Linke normal sein will," *Die Zeit* 15 (Februar 1991). Also Helmut Kellershohn, *"Frieden oder 'Rettet Israel'?" Die linken Kritiker der Friedensbewegung und ihr Beitrag zur neuen deutschen Normalität* (Duisburg: Duisburger Institut für Sprach- und Sozialforschung, 1992).
20. Brumlik, *Weltrisiko*, 17.
21. Ibid., 17.
22. Dan Diner, *Krieg der Erinnerungen und die Ordnung der Welt* (Berlin: Rotbuch, 1991), 9–17.
23. Diner, "Den Westen verstehen. Der Golfkrieg als deutsches Lehrstück," *Kursbuch* 104 (June 1991), 145.
24. Diner, *Krieg*, 57.
25. Diner, "Westen verstehen," 145.
26. Diner, *Krieg*, 44.
27. Ibid., 62.
28. Ibid., 59.
29. Diner, "Westen verstehen," 147.
30. Diner, *Krieg*, 80.
31. Brumlik, *Weltrisiko*, 22.
32. Ibid., 158.
33. Oliver Tolmein and Detlev zum Winkel, *Herr P. und die Bombe: Vom Krieg der Polemiker* (Hamburg: Konkret, 1991), 14.
34. Maria Baader und Gotlinde Magribi Lwanga, "Redebeitrag auf dem Kongreß der Radikalen Linken"; Jessica Jacoby and Gotlinde Magribi Lwanga, "Was 'sie' schon immer über den Antisemitismus wissen wollte, aber nie zu denken wagte," *Kongreß der Radikalen Linken Pfingsten 1990* (Frankfurt/Main: internationale sozialistische publikationen, 1990), 19–65, *passim*.
35. Jürgen, "Die anti-deutsche Orientierung," 19.
36. Ulli K., "Antiimperialismus als Feind des Internationalismus," *Arbeiterkampf* 327 (11 February 1991), 17.
37. Ulli K., ". . . vom Ende," *Konkret*, June 1991, 32–33. On the *Kommunistischer Bund* and its demise, see also Georg Fülberth, "Der Tod des linken Trüffelschweins," *Konkret*, January 1991, 52–54.
38. O., ZF, Be, Gruppe K Hamburg, "Jüdischer Friedhof in Hamburg-Ottensen"; Tjark Kunstreich, "Wounded Knee in Ottensen," *Arbeiterkampf* 342 (6 May 1992), 5, 7.
39. The Radio Dreyeckland affair generated reams of printed commentary. I wish to thank the staff of the Archiv für soziale Bewegungen in Freiburg for their help in locating and making sense of the various interventions. I would also like to thank the members of the Projekt interredaktionelle Zusammenarbeit at Radio Dreyeckland for alerting me to materials I would otherwise have overlooked.

Both sides of the controversy assembled documentation packets: the station's critics published *Radio Dreyeckland: Antikapitalistisch, antiimperialistisch, antirassistisch, antisexistisch—jetzt auch antisemitisch?* (Freiburg/Br.: ça ira, 1991). Radio Dreyeckland made available its *Dokumentation* (Freiburg/Br.: Radio Dreyeckland, 1991). A good overview in Bonnie and Claude, "Freiburg hat was—alle suchen: Der Antisemtismus-Streit im Radio Dreyeckland," *Arbeiterkampf* 333 (26 August 1991), 29–30.

40. Radio Dreyeckland, "*Wie sieht so ein freies Radio eigentlich von innen aus?*" *Das Freie, antikommerzielle, linke Regionalradio: Geschichte—Aufbau—Programm* (Freiburg/Br.: Radio Dreyeckland, 1991), 4–8.
41. Helmut Spehl, *Israel–Palästina und die BRD*, debate, part 2, Radio Dreyeckland, Freiburg, 27 March 1991, quoted in Joachim Bruhn, "Der antisemitische Professor und der 'antizionistische' Agitator," in *Jetzt auch antisemitisch?*, 18.
42. All from Spehl, *Fortzeugung des Behemoth* (Freiburg/Br., 1978), quoted in Thomas Haury, "Professor Dr. Helmut Spehls 'Fortzeugung des Behemoth,'" in *Jetzt auch antisemitisch?*, 8.
43. See the programmers' account of the matter: "Stellungnahme der Goldfredaktion," *Dokumentation*, 12.
44. Bernhard Rosenkötter, Ali Jansen, and Michael Dietiker, "Der Erlkönig lebt! Zur Hebung der antizionistischen Verkehrsicherheit bei Nacht und Wind," unpublished open letter, July 1991.
45. Projekt interredaktionelle Zusammenarbeit bei Radio Dreyeckland, unpublished discussion paper, 1992.
46. Lwanga, personal interview, 11 June 1992.
47. Jacoby, personal interview, 2 June 1992.

PART THREE

Literature and Sexuality

8. What Keeps the Jews in Germany Quiet?

Rafael Seligmann

By the time Adolf Hitler committed suicide on April 30, 1945, he had long since plunged Germany into the most appalling political, military, and moral defeat in its history. Only on one single front did the Führer and his henchman triumph. They had succeeded in murdering most of Continental Europe's Jews. In Poland, Europe's largest and most vigorous Jewish community was obliterated. In other countries, with the exception of France, the situation was not much better.

Most Jews whose mother tongue was German survived the Holocaust, at least physically. But more than 90 percent of them refused to return to Germany or to start a new life there. Only about a quarter of postwar Germany's 40,000 Jews were born there. But a number of prominent German Jewish writers did stay in or return to Germany or Austria after the war: Arnold Zweig, Friedrich Torberg, Hans Weigel, Hilde Spiel, and many others. German Jews have published assiduously since the Holocaust; more than a thousand books have been written by Jewish authors in postwar Germany. On closer inspection we find that these writings fit into some remarkably consistent categories: more than four hundred of these books are autobiographical records or narratives; most of the books deal exclusively with the Holocaust; virtually all of them are what I call "hate-sterile," which means that nowhere is there any hate expressed against Germans—not even against the murderers in the SS, much less against German citizens in general. As an almost inevitable consequence, until the late 1980s no German Jewish fiction was written about contemporary life in Germany.

All German Jews were affected by the Holocaust. They were either in exile, in hiding, or in concentration camps. The traumatic experience of the Holocaust dominates their literature. This has not changed in almost half a century. If we compare this literature with the works of Jewish authors from around the world, we notice a striking difference. The writings of Jewish authors outside Germany contain, implicitly or explicitly, a considerable measure of aggressiveness against the actual German perpetrators, their accomplices, and sometimes even *all* Germans. This is true even in countries that were not directly affected by the Shoah, for example the United States. But in the writings of Jewish authors in Germany itself, this aggressiveness is completely absent. Why?

All Jews in Germany witnessed their neighbors voting for the Nazis, humiliating Jews, robbing them, beating them up. Many Jews feared for their lives and fled, while their brothers, sisters, parents, children, and other relatives were murdered. Is it really possible that no Jewish writer in Germany has ever hated? Not a single one? There is the theory that only those Jews who never felt anger or even hatred toward their tormentors came back to Germany, but this idea has been proven false. Equally fallacious is the assertion by postwar Germany's most renowned literary critic, the redoubtable Marcel Reich-Ranicki. This "pontiff of German letters," who happens to be Jewish, says that Jewish literature in postwar Germany is impossible because all the German Jewish writers are dead. As we have seen, a number of them returned after 1945. What keeps the Jewish writers, and for that matter German Jews in general, from expressing their anger and even their hate? The answer is banal: fear and shame.

Whoever had to flee from the Nazis, whoever was tortured by them (often enough for years on end), whoever lost loved ones will never, as long as he or she lives, completely overcome his or her fear—either of the so-called direct culprits or of the German nation as a whole. And what Diaspora Jews, except for the Israelis, would ever dare to provoke renewed "anti-Semitism"? After all, almost all Gola Jews live under the illusion that simple appeasement will mollify their antagonists. They think that expressing hatred will stir the anti-Semites to new actions or even make new anti-Semites out of those who don't care one way or the other. All Diaspora Jews, including the writers, are afraid of this. But Jewish writers in America, Holland, or Russia are most probably in agreement with the majority of the population when they rail against the Nazis or even the German people. In Germany, however, anti-German aggressions set the Jewish writer apart from the majority. It is not only fear of "the Germans" that keeps German Jews from expressing their feelings about individual or all Germans. *Shame* is an equally effective muzzle.

Hate is a feeling which a society usually does not sanction, unless of course this hate is directed against an "enemy." The majority of the population, or at least the political leaders and other molders of public opinion, target and define these enemies: witches, criminals, Christ killers, or enemies due to race, nation, heritage, or even athletics. Against such persons and groups, hate and violence are sanctioned, even demanded. But when a member of a minority expresses hatred of a majority, this is considered highly despicable indeed—at least by the majority.

What Jew wants to give the impression of a venom-spewing Shylock?—especially in the Federal Republic of Germany, the democratic successor to the Nazi regime?

Utterances of hatred by Jews in Germany are stifled not only by external constraints. The ego is just as effective—especially the egos of the intellectuals. Unlike an ordinary citizen, the intellectual has to justify his or her thoughts and actions constantly. At least this is what he or she believes. But how are Jewish journalists, writers, and philosophers to justify their return or their immigration to Germany? Intellectuals are different from businessmen; they cannot say it was money that brought them here—even if it really was money. The German language also does not provide a sufficient motive: he or she could have gone to Switzerland. The intellectuals need a more solid, ethical reason. They generally formulate it, to themselves and to others, as follows: "I've come here to call for and contribute to German-Jewish reconciliation. This cannot be achieved through hate, but only through love of one's fellow human beings." The situation in postwar German literature proves that this is not just empty talk. Until 1986, in spite of thousands of books about and by Jews in Germany, there were no novels by Jews about contemporary German life. Amidst all the nonfiction and autobiography, why are there no novels about the contemporary German scene? The answer is obvious. Novels deal with the feelings of people and thus, indirectly, with the sore points of society. Using such tools as exaggeration and parody, it seeks to capture that which objective analysis often misses—the emotions of human beings.

After 1945, but especially after the founding of the Federal Republic in 1949, West German society embraced its Jewish members with typical German thoroughness. In particular the political, ecclesiastical, and publicistic circles, plagued as they were by guilt feelings, embraced the Jewish survivors so tightly that the bones of the latter almost broke. Many Germans who considered themselves intellectuals had despised and discriminated against the Jews. They had voted for Hitler, either because they hated the Jews or because the fate of the Jews was not important to them. They had accepted the murder of the Jews without protest, and some of these people were even accomplices. The despised Christ killers were classified as *Untermenschen,* whose annihilation was the duty of the master race. But after the Nazi regime had been smashed, the opinion makers in the new and democratic Germany—frequently the same people who had supported Hitler—elevated the Jews from *Untermenschen* to the status of near *Übermenschen,* or supermen. The same Jews who during the Third Reich were regarded as interested only in "exploiting and eroding host nations" were now exclusively good and decent men and women who thought only of helping their neighbors. Every Jew was a personification of Lessing's Nathan the Wise. And the German Jew even received a new label: Jewish *Mitbürger.* This word can be roughly conveyed in English by "fellow citizen."

The "good" West German nation was ponderously generous in its material reparations. The word for reparation or compensation is highly significant: *Wiedergutmachung,* or "making-good-again." Individual Jews as well as the Jewish state of Israel were the beneficiaries of this *Wiedergutmachung.* In every German city, a Society for Christian-Jewish Cooperation arose. Twice a year the Republic looks into its own heart, celebrating in spring the Christian-Jewish Brotherhood Week and being overcome with remorse in autumn as it commemorates the 1938 *Reichskristallnacht,* or Night of Broken Glass. These official commemorations were only the start. The intelligentsia began, again with German thoroughness, to "get involved" with Judaism. Countless books about Jews were published and read. As early as 1945, a Munich publishing house brought out a volume of poetry called *Three Years in Theresienstadt.* The author, Gerti Spies, had been a prisoner in Theresienstadt. But Spies and her book were soon forgotten. At that time it was experts for the Christian-Jewish dialogue who were in demand.

The unbroken interest in the Christian-Jewish dialogue (with almost no Jews taking part) contrasted saliently with the obvious lack of interest shown by German intellectuals for the Jews who were living in their midst—40,000 Jews in a population of 80 million. But this tiny minority contained a number of Jewish writers. Why didn't anybody notice that none of these Jewish writers, somewhere in their never-ending reams of lectures, essays, and books, ever dared to make an aggressive remark against individual murderers or the German people in general? Did these "good" German intellectuals really believe that "their" Jews did not or could not hate? They knew the writings of Jews in Israel, the United States, France, Italy, and Sweden. Germans read Primo Levi, Samuel Pisar, Cordelia Edvardson, or Yoram Kaniuk.[1] These and many other Jewish authors have sometimes vented their rage against the Germans. None of them preach eternal hate. They merely do not shrink back from crying out in their rage. Until recently, however, there was nothing comparable in books by Jewish authors in Germany. Not a single Jewish writer in the Federal Republic dared to express rage or hate in public.

This complete abstinence from hate unmasks both Germans and Jews. Could the German critics really accept the idea that "their" Jews were better than those beyond their borders? That the German master race had come to be replaced by a Jewish master race that was morally pure, forgiving of everyone, loving everyone—even the murderers of their own families? Nobody, not even a German intellectual, could be so immeasurably naive. Many so-called friends of the Jews are voyeurs of the Holocaust and the life of its survivors. They remind one of butterfly collectors: they know a lot about the object of their love—age, history, behavior, structure—but they are most comfortable when the specimens are dead. There are countless experts on German Jewish literature in Germany, including the Marcel Reich-Ranicki. All of them should have noticed that Jewish writers in Germany were afraid to write about their feelings toward Germans, to the extent, of course, that they were interested in living Jews at all. It is remarkable that this body of experts, along with legions of ordinary readers, overlooked the fact that no Jewish writer in Germany could muster the courage to say what he or she thought and felt about the mass murderers and their children. *That there was not a single line of German Jewish literature about the feelings of Jews in contemporary Germany.*

It was more than four decades after Auschwitz that a Jew in Germany was able to muster this courage. In 1986 the Suhrkamp publishing house in Frankfurt brought out Jurek Becker's novel *Bronstein's Children.* This book was special in a number of ways. It was a story published in West Germany and written by an immigrant from East Germany about the life of a Jewish family in the German Democratic Republic. Becker forthrightly presents the hate of the father, a former concentration-camp inmate, for his tormentors in the SS. It is remarkable that this first book about Jewish sensibilities in postwar Germany received rather little attention from the critics and the reading public. This is all the more remarkable because Becker was already an established author. His *Jacob the Liar,* the story of a ghetto Jew in Poland during the Holocaust, was far more interesting to readers and critics alike.

When *Bronstein* appeared in the bookstores, I had already been trying for two years to find a publisher for my novel *Rubinstein's Auction,* the story of a twenty-year-old student in Munich at the end of the 1960s. In it I describe the life and feelings of a young Jew living in Germany. Although I was an established journalist and the author of a well-received book on Israel's national security policy, no one was willing to publish my novel. The reasons given were quite remarkable. The publisher of the SS memoirs of Franz Schönhuber, head of the ultra-right Republican party, found my book, not Schönhuber's, "anti-Semitic." Other publishers didn't like all the space devoted to sex. They thought this would make the Jews appear despicable. One editor at the prestigious Hoffmann & Campe house said that she found the book "fascinating" but the way the "hero" spoke to his mother was so execrable that the publisher could not in good conscience subject the readers to it. Would they become anti-Semites if they found out about a Jew who was *not* a Nathan the Wise?

After four years, I gave up trying to find a publisher for *Rubinstein* and had it printed at my own expense. The reaction to the book was mixed. Some important critics ignored it, while the official Jewish press was hypercritical. The weekly *Allgemeine Jüdische Wochenzeitung* labeled me a "defiler of the nest." The Munich monthly *Jüdische Zeitung* which I had founded some years before, called my book "wretched." But there was a handful of Jewish intellectuals who were rather taken by the book. One of them even wanted to make a film version, "so that the hair of the Germans would stand on end." But he didn't want to accept the watered-down high-school love story version desired by official and private funding groups, so they refused to finance the project. A number of non-Jewish critics also liked *Rubinstein*. They praised the novel's "authenticity and nonconformity." They thought that finally the *goyim* could learn the feelings and thoughts of Jews who lived among them. But not too many German readers were interested in this opportunity.

Irene Dische, a German-American Catholic author, has met with similar reception. Her father was Jewish. In 1989 her book *Pious Secrets*, a collection of seven short stories, appeared in a German translation. Dische's biographical background plays a prominent role in these stories, which present a kind of game of hide-and-seek between Germans, Jews, Nazis, and Americans. All the figures are unable to free themselves from the fears of the past. The critics were overwhelming in their praise. Here, too, was Jewish authenticity, rendered more palatable by the double prism of irony and a chastened style. But despite almost unanimous critical enthusiasm, the commercial success of *Pious Secrets* was far from spectacular. Average German readers, regardless of critical reviews, are after all not very interested in the actual lives and feelings of their Jewish *Mitbürger*.

My second novel, *A Yiddishe Mama*, came out in 1990. The story deals with a Jewish man's neurotic interactions with women—predetermined by phobias and his relationship to his mother. Non-Jewish critics were mostly positive and occasionally enthusiastic. The interest of the reading public was again rather modest. But, as before, Jewish critics were far from modest in their comments. A typical example was Eva Elisabeth Fischer, a Jewish editor with Munich's *Süddeutsche Zeitung*, who called me a pornography-monger and a "callboy." Maxim Biller had to go through a similar critical gauntlet with his volume of short stories *If I Become a Rich and Dead Man*, also published in 1990. Drawing on his own life, Biller focuses on Jews and non-Jews growing up in the Federal Republic. Biller, Dische, and I share some remarkable biographical similarities. All of us were born outside Germany. None of our parents were concentration-camp inmates. Biller grew up in the former Czechoslovakia, Dische in the United States, and I in Israel. Biller and I both came to Germany when we were ten years old; Dische arrived as an adult. So our childhoods were free of the horrors and fears of the Nazis or, as the case may be, the German anti-Semites. Living as I was in Israel, I had no experience with anti-Semitism at all. This may be one reason why I write directly against the avowed enemies of the Jews, and why I have the fewest qualms about describing Jewish fears and phobias.

The four books I have mentioned remain the only German Jewish literature available *at present* about contemporary life in Germany. Why? The development was interrupted by an event that aroused fear in Jews around the world: the reunification of Germany. Many Germans didn't like the articulation of these fears, for example by Eli Wiesel or Israel's Prime Minister Shamir. Rudolf Augstein, editor of the weekly news magazine *Der Spiegel*, disdained what he called this meddling in Germany's internal affairs and proffered the opinion that Germany should not be made the eternal hostage of its history. I happen to share this opinion. I think that it would be of no use to anyone if 17 million people, the vast majority of whom were born after the war or were children during the Third Reich, continued to be held in dictatorship and oppression. But I did not like the crusader mentality which Augstein shared with his supporters and also with his opponents. Aggressiveness and know-it-all arrogance set the tone of the discussions for and against reunification. Common sense had gone off on leave, as had respect for individuals and for divergent opinions. I described the situation in my nonfiction book *Limited Hope: Germans, Jews, Israelis,* published by Hoffmann & Campe in 1991.

At the time, I could not foresee the amount of indifference, intolerance, and hate which unleashed itself against foreigners and minorities in the wake of reunification. Instead of rejoicing over the newly won freedom and national unity, many Germans began to wallow in a new feeling of what they perceived as strength but what really arises from weakness and inhumanity, and to harry those unfortunate people who were the targets of their frustration. Other Germans, who have not participated actively in this new trend, have watched and applauded from the sidelines. Most Germans, however, have simply closed their eyes to this injustice—as their parents had once done. A great many, especially among the intelligentsia, are afraid. These people retreat to the safe and tranquil precincts of classicism and aestheticism. Criticism of contemporary society—now more necessary than ever—is seldom voiced. Timidity and cowardice reign triumphant. In such a situation it is highly unrealistic to expect contributions to a renaissance of German Jewish culture from a small band of frightened survivors and their children—contributions which under different circumstances might indeed report on fears and desires, aggression and love.

The Hoffmann & Campe publishing house approached me after the partial success of my novels. But they asked me to postpone my planned novel about a German Jewish family under the Kaiser, Hitler, and the Bonn democracy and to produce a nonfiction book instead. This is how I came to write *Limited Hope.* In it I took a critical approach not only to Israel and Jewish functionaries but also to the German government, German politicians, German journalists, and so-called friends of the Jews. A Hoffmann & Campe editor tried to get me to tone down the critique. I refused. The publishing house responded by refusing to advertise the book. Finally I started to write the novel about the German Jewish family, and the new editor attempted to convince me to "bracket out" the Jewish theme because most readers would not be interested in it. Because I followed his advice only in part, Hoffmann & Campe reacted by refusing to publish the book. Their rationale: the book was "not a novel."

A year ago I wrote a play called *Talkshow: Good Night, Germany*. In the course of a talk show featuring prominent Jews and Gentiles, the mendacity of German-Jewish postwar relations is drastically brought to light. The renowned S. Fischer publishing house immediately bought the rights to the play. But up to now only small theaters have performed it. The head of one of Germany's greatest theaters at first expressed strong interest. However, when the play *Singer* by Ariel Dorfman found very little favor with the public, he distanced himself from my play, saying that "there is no interest in Jewish matters."

These are of course only subjective experiences. But they are indicative of certain tendencies. As in other countries, the majority of intellectuals in Germany are surely not anti-Semitic—at least no more than they were years ago. But the German intellectuals are afraid. They sense a renewed increase in nationalist tendencies. They sense that most people are interested primarily in themselves, that many Germans don't want foreigners (at least not poor ones), that although the Germans don't hate Jews, only a third of the population wants to acknowledge any historical responsibility. In the current intellectual climate, a full-scale renaissance of Jewish culture in Germany is impossible. There are just not enough Jews. And those few Jews who do attempt something in this direction awaken too little interest among non-Jews. Judaeocentric considerations aside, the behavior of a society toward its Jews is a measure of that society's stability and humanity. The increasing German indifference to the life and feelings of German Jews is therefore a general cause for concern—not only for the mere 40,000 Jews in Germany but also for the Germans as a nation, and for neighboring countries as well. The muteness of postwar Germany's Jews—after the first cautious utterances in the late 1980s on the post-Holocaust—remains a lasting triumph of the Third Reich. This is a distress signal for Germans and Jews alike.

Note

1. See esp. Primo Levi, *Die Untergegangenen und die Geretteten* (Munich, 1990); Samuel Pisar, *Das Blut der Hoffnung* (Reinbeck bei Hamburg, 1979); Cordelia Edvardson, *Gebranntes Kind sucht das Feuer* (Munich, 1989); and Yoram Kaniuk, *Der letzte Jude* (1990).

9. En-gendering Bodies of Memory: Tracing the Genealogy of Identity in the Work of Esther Dischereit, Barbara Honigmann, and Irene Dische

Karen Remmler[1]

Ich habe es satt, das inkarnierte Leiden im Gesicht zu tragen.

—Esther Dischereit[2]

Es fällt mir so schwer in so vielen Welten zugleich zu leben, es fügt sich alles nicht zusammen.

—Barbara Honigmann[3]

The unsettling rise of xenophobia in unified Germany and the concomitant call for recognizing the multicultural makeup of German society coincides with the portrayal of a genealogy of different Jewish identities within German culture in literary works by Jewish women writers publishing in Germany. Their work expresses the desire to break down monolithic images of the "Jew" and examine the relationship between tropes of femaleness and Jewishness in contemporary Germany, while at the same time reassessing the parameters of German identity. One could argue that Jewish identity in post-Wall Germany is as controversial and constructed as the unification process itself. Similarly, female identity in unified Germany is as ambiguous and contested as the rights of German women to control their bodies, as the German High Court decision to restrict abortion has demonstrated.

In a forthcoming collection of essays, stories and images about Jewish female identity in present-day Berlin, the contributors, a diverse group of Jewish women of both German and non-German descent, express a growing uneasiness with living in a society that continues to stigmatize them doubly.[4] Contemporary Jewish women writers living in Germany often find themselves situated at a busy intersection where associations of Jewishness clash and merge with tropes of female otherness. The double stigma of Jewishness and femaleness perpetuated by the historically changing, yet recurring normative stultification of difference is implicitly addressed in texts by Honigmann, Dischereit, and journalists such as Lea Fleischmann, and Austrian filmmaker Ruth Beckermann.[5] The place of gender in their work suggests that the position of women in an imagined German Jewish culture is one of redefinition not only within Jewish culture but also within contemporary German culture.[6] As Hazel Rosenstrauch implies in her essay "Verwurzelt im Nirgendwo" ("Rooted in Nowhere") on her confrontation with being Jewish, Jewish women are not searching for roots so much as establishing a place in the present from which to benefit from not having roots: "It is obvious that the Federal Republic is not the ideal home for a communist Jewish Viennese child of emigrants, who also happens to be female."[7] By recognizing gender as an important mark of difference that constitutes Jewish identity in today's Germany, I develop a feminist reading of texts published in Germany by contemporary Jewish women writers, and raise questions about how to approach their recent publications in Germany.[8] Not surprisingly, the three writers considered here, Esther Dischereit, Barbara Honigmann, and Irene Dische, have ambiguous relations to Germany and to the German language.[9] By labeling them Jewish writers, one, in fact, consolidates conflicting and often ambiguous identities. Any generalizations about the representative nature of their work are, at best, tentative.

Esther Dischereit was born in the former Federal Republic in 1952 and lives in Berlin. Her mother, a Jew, survived Nazi Germany in hiding. Her father was a non-Jewish German. Barbara Honigmann, born in 1949 to German Jews who had returned to East Berlin after the war, grew up in the former German Democratic Republic, but left in 1984 to live in Strasbourg. The third author, Irene Dische, writes in English but publishes in German. The child of German Jewish emigrants, Dische was born in New York in 1952. She was raised as a Catholic. Honigmann published her first collection of prose, *Roman von einem Kinde*, in 1986, following her emigration to Strasbourg. Dischereit has published two novels. The first, *Joëmis Tisch: Eine jüdische Geschichte*, appeared in 1988, and was followed by *Merryn* in 1992. Dische's collection of short stories, *Fromme Lügen*, translated from English, received generally positive reviews in 1989, as did her first novel, *Ein fremdes Gefühl*.[10] Given the different geographical, political, and cultural contexts in which these three authors write and live, their work cannot be read as representative examples of Jewish female identity as such. Rather, by contrasting the contradictions in their writing, we can develop a methodology of reading that does not replicate stereotypical or binary attributes imposed upon them as members of groups both stigmatized and abstracted in German society. Accordingly, the historical context of their lives, and the locations in which they write, play a major role in fashioning the reception of their work and possible readings of them. Moreover, their varying degrees of participation in religion and self-identification as Jews further complicates an all too easy subsumption of Jewish identities under one rubric.

Each author chose to take on a repressed (or previously inconsequential) Jewish identity in adulthood, if under different circumstances.[11] To what extent are Jewish women writing in Germany engaged in writing a minority discourse? To what extent does the (cultural) representation of their identities and their bodies in German (cultural) spaces affect the way they write? Not all Jewish women writing in Germany speak the voices of minority literature, although they do move across territories, cross borders, and traverse the spaces in between. For German Jewish women writing in German, the attachment, however ambiguous and painful, to German culture through memory, family, or language positions them in spaces not shared with non-German women of Turkish, African, or Eastern European origin. It is not the degree of victim status but rather the positioning of identities that are not static nor stable that often determines the relations between Jewish women and other minority cultures in Germany. Writers like Honigmann or Dischereit, who are native speakers of German, engage in the discourse of the dominant culture. Granted they engage in this language not without horror, disgust, or pain, since it reverberates with the language of the Nazis that has alienated them as Jews from their mother tongue.[12] Unlike other female minorities in Germany, however, as Jewish women, they experience a marginalization as others not solely based on gender and ethnic difference. Similarly, historical contingency (the Shoah) has symbolically abstracted them into an absence that makes their presence invisible, but at the same time places pressure on them to come out publicly in order to fill the absence with the material reality of their bodies.

In tracing the process by which bodies continue to be transformed into missing objects, however, Dischereit and Honigmann also map out the sites where an ambiguous en-gendering takes place—one that locates the discontinuities and the disunified remnants of female Jewish identity within a historical context in which the female body figures as the implicit reminder of difference. In their texts, they recall, remember and rename the disrupted and obscured genealogies of Jewish identity by recovering missing bodies of memory and locating them in the present-day experience of being Jewish and female in contemporary Germany. In addition, the representation of re-membered bodies in their texts counters the sanctioned memorializing of Jews in German public spaces such as monuments, museums, and sociocultural events. Furthermore, by en-gendering the bodies of memory and by positioning female Jewish bodies as images that both convey and embody sites of remembering, these works are testimonials not only to the victims of the Shoah but also to the living presence of Jews in Germany today. By writing from a decidedly gendered position, these writers also indicate the differences within the Jewish community in unified Germany and raise controversial questions about the marking of Jewish identity through the male Jewish body.

In contrast to the emphasis many male Jewish writers place on the social, sexual, and cultural consequences of circumcision for Jewish males as both a signifier of difference and of absence,

Jewish women writers seem to focus on the female Jewish body as a site of mourning and dubious agency.[13] Through representations of the re-membering process and attempts to reconnect with the past, the texts demonstrate both the realities of being marked Jewish and the limitations of a consolidating gesture that measures the perception of Jewish identity from a male perspective. The female body becomes a site of remembrance, a topography that exhibits the contours of a constantly shifting identity that takes not just sexuality into account but also the location of this body vis-à-vis other bodies in German culture.

In addition to examining the bodies of remembrance, Honigmann and Dischereit, in particular, problematize the act of remembering. Their writing is less a reconstruction than a delicate probing of the body of remembrance. By en-gendering bodies of memory, they implicitly construct a theoretical framework through a writing process that conjures up metaphors associated with acts of critical remembering. The representation of remembering, Jewish identity, and the female body takes place through a genealogical practice that questions fixed notions of identity and expresses the desire to recover lost or thwarted moments of subjective agency. The possible correspondence between genealogy as a critical counter-remembering, and en-gendering as the construction of a nonunified but viable female Jewish identity are played out in the texts by Dischereit and Honigmann upon the metaphorical body of the female protagonists.[14] By en-gendering memory through the female body and through sites of mourning and obscured remembering, these texts demonstrate the actual diversity of Jewish identity in Germany by incorporating metaphorical operations: (1) the genealogical formation of identity; (2) the pathological operations and dissection of corpses; and (3) the excavation of ancient artifacts. All these methodologies have a particular connotation for a memory work that does not retrieve or obscure the past, but rather makes its presence felt in the present. Therefore, Dischereit and Honigmann manifest female Jewish identity and memory not only by exposing the absence of space for such remembering but also by representing en-gendered memory through metaphorical operations that uncover repressed associations with the past without obscuring the transformations of Jewish identity in the present.

As a re-membering process, genealogy locates the many-layered bodies of identity that reject a nostalgic return to an origin or to unity. Although the remembering of the dead through the stories or the silences of their parents or friends who experienced the concentration camps firsthand is a major trope in many works by second- and third-generation Jewish women writers, the bearing of witness is everything but a return to *tikkun*, to the repaired vessel. Instead, many writers trace the broken family lines and the inheritance of the pain. Accordingly, genealogical practice becomes a method for breaking down overly centralized categories of gender and identity. Texts by Dischereit and Hongimann are not genealogical in a biblical sense, but rather in a Foucaultian sense. Foucault explains the concept of genealogy as follows: "What is found at the historical beginning of things is not the inviolable identity of their origin: it is the dissension of other things. It is disparity."[15] A genealogist "sets out to study the beginning—numberless beginnings whose faint traces and hints of color are readily seen by an historical eye" (145). Thus the work of a genealogist identifies the errors, and the incongruities of a history fragmented, yet not derivative from an intact origin. In works such as *Joëmis Tisch: Eine jüdische Geschichte* and *Merryn* by Dischereit or *Eine Liebe aus nichts* by Honigmann, the act of remembering is also an act of en-gendering a female Jewish identity that is neither fixed nor homogeneous, but rather fragmented and heterogeneous, yet not without agency.[16]

In their practice of remembrance and of resistance, Honigmann and Dischereit often explore not only the pathology of German society but also of the body of practices that constitutes the remembrance of the Shoah. By maneuvering between the present and the repressed past, they expose the legacy they have both inherited and dis-inherited. Their literary figures are neither completely Jewish nor completely female, and the dilemma of incompleteness, the necessity of remaining fragmented in order to perceive the danger of political or socially constructed wholeness, plays itself out upon the body of their writing as it is inscribed upon real bodies by a society that sees their bodies as representative of a single body.

While their en-gendering conjures up images of birth and creation, these writers also take on the task of forensic pathologists who analyze the diseased organs of corpses in order to ascertain the cause of death. Accordingly, their texts become the location in which to dissect the body of misremembrance in German culture. The textual constructions of remembrance function as archeological digs that uncover the fragmentation of a Jewish identity as a tragic consequence of the Shoah and as a necessary condition for writing a genealogy of Jewish identity, one that both mourns the loss and celebrates the possibility of establishing a multifaceted identity. Although the genealogy conveyed in the texts acknowledges the victimization of the Jews during the Shoah, it also objects to a second victimization of a Jewish presence in German society that perceives Jews only in terms of their absence in post-Shoah Germany. In other words, Dischereit and Honigmann practice a genealogy that follows family lines as webs, woven across the branches of dead family trees that no longer bear fruit but whose roots remain alive in the stories told by distant relatives. By tracing the family lines not backwards but in diverging shapes marred and drawn by the experiences of the Shoah and its aftermath, these Jewish women writers do not return to the family fold nor to a home. Instead, they dissect the body or corpse of memory and search for signs of violently imposed disease in organs which they refuse to transplant into their own bodies. They strive to remove the stigma of dis-ease without succumbing to the dubious health of normalcy. The female Jewish body figures in this process as both a conveyor of genealogical networks and as the excavation site of pathological amnesia—and thus of archeological remembering altogether. Like the rememberer in Walter Benjamin's much quoted passage on excavation and remembering in his *Denkbilder*, the women writers stand at the edge of the excavated site (of German indifference) that constitutes the past in the present.[17]

How does a genealogical, pathological, and archeological en-gendering of memory function in the works by Dischereit and Honigmann? The representation of the female body as a different rememberer—in fact, one abstracted to a greater extent than that of the circumcised male Jewish body—distinguishes female Jewish identities in the works I will explore: *Joëmis Tisch: Eine jüdische Geschichte* and *Merryn* by Dischereit, *Eine Liebe aus nichts* by Honigmann, and Irene Dische's "Eine Jüdin für Charles Allen."[18] Each work exemplifies an en-gendered remembering that incorporates methodologies of genealogy, pathology, and archeology within the task of writing. These three methodologies provide a framework for explaining the resurgence of a multi-faceted Jewish culture within German society that often skirts the issue of gender. The force of re-memory in these texts contextualizes Jewish identity vis-à-vis other identities and, equally importantly, questions the reduction of Jewish identity to the male sex organs. Granted, the circumcised penis remains a crucial signifier, as Sander Gilman has shown in his work on male Jewish writers writing in Germany.[19] Nevertheless, the texts by Jewish women writers suggest another body of signification at work—that of the fragmented, gendered body of remembrance. The re-membering of family genealogy recovers the missing parts of family stories and feminine identity, while simultaneously dissecting German bodies of misremembrance, thereby complicating the elision of Jewishness with femaleness and thus with otherness.

The experience of being other often coincides with a literal border crossing—one reaction to a sense of isolation and absence in a society without a viable Jewish community. For Honigmann, leaving East Berlin in 1984 became a necessary catalyst for writing about her Jewish identity in the former East Germany. Her work retrospectively dissects the ambiguities of Jewish identity from the vantage point of Strasbourg, a city that provides her with a thriving Jewish community not available to her as a daughter of parents whose allegiance to the GDR socialist ideology all but eclipsed their Jewish identity. Consequently, Honigmann left the GDR in search of a community that reflected her own desire to regain her Jewish heritage. Her work must therefore be read within the context of her chosen exile—an exile all the more permanent in the wake of the fall of the Berlin Wall and German unification.

Honigmann's collection of short stories, *Roman von einem Kinde*

(1986), reveals her struggle to recall remnants of a Jewish identity from the ruins of the past. In her short story "Doppeltes Grab," she describes Gershom Scholem's visit to the site of his family's tomb in the Jewish cemetery in Berlin-Weißensee: "We freed the grave from the old leaves and twigs, branches and half trees, and from the boundless ivy that crept over all the graves, from one to the other, from tombstone to tree and from tree back to tombstone, taking and swallowing everything, until the entire stony order grew back to a forest and not only the body of the dead, but also this entire work of remembering the body, became earth again" (89). Standing in front of the tomb, Scholem remarks that "in order to visit an ancestor's grave, one needs an ax to cut a path through the overgrowth of time" (89). Indeed, time's choking of the graves of Jewish relatives and obscuring the memorial inscription of their names has an ambiguous connotation in Honigmann's story. It is not a "natural" passing of time that has obstructed the inscriptions of names, but the rapid consolidation of Jewish memory within German culture that leaves little room for different formations of Jewish identity. Consequently, Honigmann's recollection of Scholem's remark at the grave of his deceased family situates her work and that of other Jewish women writers within the context of genealogy and remembrance.

Instead of dwelling on her position as other within German culture, the female Jewish protagonist in Dischereit's *Joëmis Tisch* similarly questions the "normalcy" of that dominant culture. The novel intersperses images of the narrator's dead Jewish mother, Hannah, with her encounters with Germans, whose apparent naiveté and defensiveness reveal a pathological state of denial. Thus, the narrator undertakes a genealogical task complicated by pathological studies of German misremembrance. The narrative of more than fifty scenes moves back and forth between the past and present, between individual experience and imagined history, and between third- and first-person narration. Ostensibly, the semi-autobiographical fragments remember the relationship between Hannah, a survivor of the Shoah, and her daughter. The daughter imagines her mother's history against the backdrop of her own sense of alienation in postwar Germany and her decision to reclaim her Jewish identity.

Dischereit's act of remembrance in *Joëmis Tisch* begins with the narrator's *decision* to be Jewish: "After twenty years of being an un-Jew [*un-Jude*], I want to become a Jew again. I've thought it over for ten years" (9). In reconstructing her mother's life, the female protagonist gathers the images of her childhood in a constellation that suggests the impossibility of remembering in isolation; for the ritual of conjuring the past is not simply a practice in the company of the Jewish community, but also in the company of Germans. By engaging with the "resident other," as Karl Plank calls the "German" Germans, the narrators in Dischereit's trek through the landscape of Jewish identity in Germany confront the prejudices, the anti-Semitism, and the ignorance that relegates the Jew to the status of an image.[20] The female Jewish narrator performs in constant contradiction to the "resident others." In an almost voyeuristic manner, the narrator listens to and comments on the patronizing words of German counterparts whose insensitivity implies the impossibility of a symbiosis between Jews and Germans. In refusing to take on the status of victim, the narrator offers ironic commentary to illuminate the grotesque normalcy in the social and cultural formations in which Germans function. The voices of Germans are often placed in quotation marks—a seemingly mechanical move that nevertheless signals a degree of absurdity in their statements. The body of German misremembrance is thus mapped out by empty words leading nowhere, the self-pity of the Germans who see themselves as victims or passive onlookers, and the insertion of the narrator's sarcastic responses to the Germans' blindness to their own insensitivity. By silently completing the recollections by German interviewees that trail off as "und so weiter" ("and so forth"), and by demonstrating their undifferentiated use of National Socialist jargon, the narrator exposes the speakers' unwillingness to take responsibility for the past or to articulate their repressed guilt. One central passage in *Joëmis Tisch*, for example, tells the story of a German, one of the "Vertriebenen,"[21] who describes his treatment after the war:

"We were there in the collection camp and then we ended up in Hohenfurt, Kaplitz, Bahnstation and were then loaded into cattle cars."

My ears repeat: Hannah loaded into cattle cars.

"I was twelve years old at the time. . . . At that age it was even a bit of an adventure."

. . .

She was six years old.

"Until cold reality set in and we had to stand in line for food in the camp . . .

"The only thing I haven't forgotten. It was a beautiful May day. We had a large dog at home, and he ran after us."

The sister ran after her . . . and stumbled. (60)

The antiphony between the perspectives of the German (in quotation marks) and the inner monologue by Hannah's daughter undermines the parallelism that ahistoricizes the experience and relation between Germans and Jews. Although deportation takes place in both cases, the crass difference between the process and end result of the dislocation becomes amplified by the narrator's silent interjections:

"We had to leave everything behind. In Butzbach we were distributed among families. There were people there who took in refugees."

Where were the people who took in refugees? In England? Germany? Where?

"We were treated exceptionally well . . . 1956-57, the church congregation gave us a piece of land. Then everything became part of a co-operative project [*Gemeinschaftsarbeit*].—Yes—there was also financial compensation [*Lastenausgleich*]."

Restitution [*Wiedergutmachung*], you know. (60–61)

Similarly, in another passage, Ruth, a Jewish character, notes ironically the tactlessness of her German friend, Martha Elisabeth, who asks her to find her husband's grave in France, where he died a hero's death (*Heldentod*) as a soldier in the Wehrmacht. Ruth notes with bitterness that it would be unthinkable to ask Martha Elisabeth to find the mass grave of her father and brother:

Ruth travels in this direction for Martha Elisabeth. South of Valence. Ruth takes the scrap of paper out of her pocket. It must have been here—25 to 30 km to the left of the street—that's what she did—south of the industrial site. Ruth tries to remember. "While driving along this road, your husband was struck by a bullet from the right so that he fell against the steering wheel . . ."

Ruth drives along the entire route, gets out, do you see a respectable military grave? There isn't one here anymore, she will tell that to Mrs. Steder. She did her best.

Imagine, if she would ask Mrs. Steder to go with her to her father's, brother's mass grave, to search. . . . Maybe, that the earth a fragment of a tooth or jaw—one should still be able to recognize most by that . . . (108–9)

Ruth is asked to share in the grief of the German woman over the loss of her husband, yet it would be taboo for Ruth to ask the same of the German woman. The ritualized re-creation of a soldier's burial contrasts sharply with the understated brutality with which Ruth's brother and father are denied not only a proper burial but a place in memory: "Ruth's father was not killed in battle. He was burned and reduced to ashes. The brother also doesn't have a respectable military grave—always on top of one another—he climbed on top of corpses, naked, because clothes can be removed more easily from the living. When the bullet finally hit him, his body landed on top of the other bodies with a smack. His hands grasped into flesh already cold" (108). In contrast to the re-creation of the imaginary body of the German soldier through the burial ceremony, the absence of Jewish bodies remains final. The finality of the absence reflects the injustice of a continued mis-remembrance in the present. Even in Ruth's memory, it is the burned and maimed bodies of her father and brother that remain, not the living images of them.

Yet it is through the bodily gestures of the female survivor that bodies forever lost are remembered. The recurring image of hands in Dischereit's text functions as a metonymic link to the past that reminds one of the power of the body to re-member the location of death and its affective presence in the bodies of the survivors. Hannah's mother's story is personified in the affective remnants of the past embodied in her hands and those of possible perpetrators:

The landlord is *Sudetendeutsch. Sudetendeutsch*—may one still say that? Of course, one can still say that. The landlord from the Sudetes now has two apartment buildings, all the work of his own hands—and financial compensation [*Lastenausgleich*]— which I find out later.

At our place no one worked with their hands, because my mother's

> hands trembled. For no reason at all, they trembled. They could really stop trembling now. But they tremble. For this trembling she receives restitution. In contrast, she can say that she doesn't have a career, a high school diploma, parents, siblings—her life and this trembling. (57)

The trembling hands are an image of the denial of proper burial, of a missing farewell to a loved one, a gesture of distancing and dismissal, all common tropes throughout Dischereit's novel. The hands embody silenced memories; gestures of the hand not only represent the act of remembering through body parts but also through the act of coaxing the images of the past from behind the wall of the present. Childhood memories of her mother's hands frequently allude to the painful detachment Hannah's daughter records in her retelling of these memories. Hannah's hands represent the connection to the past and a reminder of the correspondence between the body of memory shared intermittently between mother and daughter.

The en-gendering of memory through the female body reveals the genealogical and pathological structures of Dischereit's text. How does the text constitute archeological remembering? Just as the gestures of mourning are often denied the survivors and their children, so too the recovery of ancestors' property and, thus, memories. In Dischereit's second novel, *Merryn*, the broken chain of inheritance and disrupted legacy is exemplified in the irretrievable loss of access to the things of the past that embody the memories of the protagonist's grandparents in Berlin. In no uncertain terms, the loss is a result of the persecution masquerading as "law" during the Nazi regime: "Prenzlauer Allee. The fall of the Wall, the collapse, the victorious breakdown opens the gates. Property to be reclaimed. Should she reclaim her grandparent's judaized [*verjudete*] flat? Already lapsed. The sewing nook in the backroom, clothes iron, chairs, table, chest and the usual table ware, estimated at 800 Reichsmark, according to the files. Vermin checked off. 10.3.43, on the file cover, underneath, the number of the trend. Auschwitz-trend [*Auschwitzwelle*]" (77). The missing artifacts inscribed into the well-kept files of the Nazi bureaucracy can only be imagined in the narrator's archeological re-membering of the remnants of her grandparent's dislocated and destroyed lives. By interspersing the reprehensible vocabulary of the Nazi rhetoric with slightly bitter sarcasm, Dischereit demonstrates the inextricable confrontation with the layers of grief in the midst of repressed responsibility on the part of many Germans.

Like Dischereit, Honigmann seeks to write the life of her past by reconnecting with a dead Jewish parent—in her case, her father. Not until the end of her novel *Eine Liebe aus nichts* does the vivid image of her filling the blank pages of her father's diary represent the genealogical task undertaken by her in her own search for home: "Because I didn't want to take the calendar back to Paris simply as a memento and because so many pages were left blank, I wrote in it myself and dated the weekdays according to the present year. I entered the date of my father's death and the date of his funeral and the date in which we saw one another for the last time, and then I began to fill the empty pages, so that our entries ran together in the English calendar that was long out of date anyhow" (99–100). The female protagonist retrieves the mostly blank diary from her father's room in the Belvedere Schloß in Weimar after his death—a death she foresees weeks earlier in a dream. This novel, too, is filled with scenes of leave-taking that expose the intrusion of real time into the mythical time of ritual remembering. The scenes of railroad stations in Honigmann's work imply that the fragile vase of perpetual anticipation has cracked open completely to reveal the broken pieces of dreams that remain forever unfulfilled.[22]

Honigmann's novel does not focus on Germany *per se*, but on the transience of Jewish existence within Germany's borders. Germany is no *Heimat* for the Jews. On her journey from East Berlin to Paris, the narrator stops in Frankfurt am Main. Despite the fact that her father was to be in Frankfurt to greet her at the train station, she looks for him in vain. Disappointed, she searches unsuccessfully for traces of his ancestors. Later, after she has been living in Paris, she receives news of her father's death. She travels to his funeral, returning via the same route of her departure from the former GDR.

Just as the places remain silent that could conceivably speak to her from the past, the artifacts of her father's existence also appear empty of memory. They are no longer of memorial value:

I wanted to see my father's room one last time, to take along a keepsake, but it was difficult and depressing to choose something, his clothes lay in the room looking as lost as his body now, and all the other objects that had belonged to his life and that bore memory, seemed like deserted remnants that had lost their grip and were now meaningless. . . .

But I understood that memory had departed from the objects—now they would be thrown out or given away and other people would fill them anew with their story, but my father's story was no longer a part of them, it no longer remained in the things. (9–10)

The end of her father's history signals the beginning of her own, one that continues that of her father yet accentuates the discontinuity of Jewish identity in Germany. Honigmann's genealogical work is not meant to reclaim the past but to come to terms with the fragmented identity and the differences between her identity and that of her father. Her father's corpse is present at his funeral: he has a proper burial, although the cantor conducting the services is a stranger to him. The estrangement of the Jews from the German environment continues even after death. And one proper burial does not reconstitute normalcy in a place where so many were sent to their death and left unmourned.

The ambiguity of relying on artifacts for transmitting identity and memory is apparent in Dischereit's *Joëmis Tisch* as well. Hannah's three-armed candelabra conveys Jewish tradition as much as individual peculiarity:

Friday toward evening, Hannah gets the candelabra from the cupboard. She takes the middle candle holder out of the opening and places a small vessel with flowers in its place. As such it stands with two arms in the middle of a white table cloth. After the Rabbi arrives she lights the candles. No one opens the front door. Schabbes begins.

What's the matter with the woman who buys a three-armed candelabra when she only needs a two-armed one? (17)

On the other hand, the presence of decidedly German artifacts, such as the oak bedroom set in Hannah's apartment, illuminates the contradiction between an alienated existence as a Jew in German society and the desire to be at home in that society. Hannah's daughter both balks at and desires to do justice to her mother's memories: "Her unlived life shall live on in me. A famous, intellectual woman, who would converse with important men in politics and industry" (42). By relating her lineage (an imaginary one) to Rahel Varnhagen and Henrietta Herz, the mother is given a genealogy that aligns her with the "pariah" existence of Jewish women in German culture.[23]

The Jewish female body in the texts by Dischereit and Honigmann is inscribed with Jewish icons that are portrayed as means of self-empowerment *and* of humiliation.[24] Hannah's daughter repeats the survival techniques forced upon her mother in Nazi Germany. With her body she crosses borders, learns to perform a non-Jewish body, or, at the very least, pretend to be invisible. Nevertheless, her body is metaphorically marked by her Jewish identity: "But if they demand that I should disrobe—why should they demand that—if they demand that I should disrobe and I would undress. And one would see the star through the clothes—one does not see it—through the clothes, burned into my skin—it is not burned, I wasn't ever there—burned into my skin, and the dogs would come to me" (35). The crossing of the physical border, in this case between Germany and France, marks the location of Jewish identity, as much as it reminds one of the apparent impossibility of recovering an identity free of territorial exclusion and embodied otherness as a Jew in Germany.

In positioning the identities of her protagonist in spaces shared with other "others" in German society, Dischereit exposes a lasting legacy of racism in German society. The Jewish body of the protagonist is aligned with the body of the present-day other in German society, the *Ausländer*, a euphemism for Turk and more recently for political refugees. By an admittedly problematic association, the Turk is the present-day Jew in Germany.[25] Upon hearing a conversation between a father and a son, the narrator considers her status as other:

His son caught a bit of our conversation. "Papa, what's that, Jew?" The papa can now say, be quiet, my dear, after all, we are all human beings. A Jew is a human being too, just like you and I. "No," says the child, "not me. I am German! I won't be burned like the others." The papa says nothing—I, human-being-too [*Auch-Mensch*] wonder, whether or not there are other human-beings-too, like me. Turkish human-beings-too [*Auch-Menschen*] live across the street. Should one establish a community of human-beings-too

[*Auch-Menschen*]. . . .
Can one simply be a Jew again?
I'll become a Turk—at the very least. Then, at least, we could populate our side of the street quite thickly. (23)

To dismantle the designation of Jews as "Auch-Menschen," the narrator reverses the roles and takes her German counterparts to task. She investigates their psyches, their reminiscences, their sorrows, their diseases and differences, in order to disrupt the hierarchical dichotomy that makes Jews others. Why not make Germans the "other"? Dischereit's text is punctuated with sudden stabs of irony that jolt the reader. What seems normal becomes grotesque when placed within the context of apparent continuities between Nazi Germany and present-day Germany.

Honigmann and Dischereit engage in archeological forays into genealogical pathology. Their texts gather the remnants of Jewish female identity in order to record the places in which they were found in relation to the finder, not as a petrified object of a lost culture to be put on display. The object of their writing is not to create a replica of Jewish identity and artifacts but to expose the meaning of such artifacts and their fragmentation in the present. The major artifact is the body—as a representation of cultural identity. Writing like archaeologists who gather artifacts of the past, Dischereit and Honigmann weave the varied bodies of both Jews and non-Jews, men and women into a series of entangled webs, while at the same time retrieving them from being turned into corpses (for the distorters) of history.

Irene Dische's texts, in contrast, accomplish a related yet ambiguous task. Unlike Dischereit and Honigmann, Dische's relation to her possible Jewish identity must be seen as one in part externally fabricated in conjunction with the publication of her first collection of short stories, *Fromme Lügen*. Although Dische did not identify herself as Jewish, the frequent portrayal of Jewish figures in her works and her Jewish ancestry became catalysts for German reviewers to identify her as a Jewish writer.[26] Thus her texts could be read by a German reading public as representative of a "Jewish" perspective, aligned artificially with the works of Honigmann and Dischereit. Given her ethnic background as a

New Yorker of German Jewish descent raised as a Roman Catholic, her approach to Jewish female identity greatly differs from that of Dischereit and Honigmann. Unlike the two German Jewish writers, Dische has neither the experience of growing up in West or East Germany as the child of Jewish parents, nor does she share the dilemma of writing in German. She writes her stories in English and has them translated into German for publication. One could argue that the rediscovery of her Jewish heritage resembles the delayed confrontation that Honigmann and Dischereit experienced with their Jewish identity.[27] Yet the construction of Dische's Jewishness by the German press more likely reflects the current fascination among Germans for things Jewish than the memory work evoked in her texts.[28] Dische's apparent subversion of typical Jewish bodies in her texts through a reinstatement of anti-Semitic representations of them is actually overlooked by a reading public that is as much invested in constructing her work as Jewish and non-German as it is in maintaining negative images of Jewish men and women. Rather than disrupt Jewish stereotypes, Dische's work appears to incorporate them.

Nevertheless, Dische practices a strategy of genealogical, archeological and pathological remembering in her work as well. Dische knows the insides of morgues. As a child in Manhattan, she often visited her mother, a forensic pathologist, at her workplace. Dische was born in 1952 in New York. She moved to Berlin in the early eighties, after jaunts as a teenager in Africa, studies of anthropology under Leakey until his death, and studies in comparative literature at Harvard. Of her own identity she said in a *taz* interview: "My family might be Jewish, but I was raised Catholic. And I come from a neighborhood, that might have been Jewish. But I went to school with 'white Anglo-Saxon Protestants.' I don't really understand much about Judaism. But I am a New Yorker. And when you grow up in New York you are automatically somehow a Jew. All New Yorkers are Jews—that's right—that's just 'traveling culture' here."[29] In her collection *Fromme Lügen*, written in English but first published in German, one story similarly attempts to disrupt any semblance of clear-cut Jewish identity only to reconfirm it. The main protagonist, Charles Allen, a bookkeeper for the Immaculate Conception convent in

Oregon, whose residents took him in when he became an orphan at age sixteen, is the child of German Jewish parents who emigrated in 1939 from Berlin. He was raised Catholic. After receiving notice that he had inherited property due to his father's death, he travels to Berlin. Charles barely knew his father, who left him and his mother after the war to reclaim property where his store had been destroyed by the Novemberpogrom in 1938. While in Berlin, Charles waits almost a month before seeking out his father's "Trödelladen," called ironically the "Schöne Heimat," where he encounters Esther. Esther was his father's employee and apparent lover, and as the story unfolds, Charles discovers that she made a great deal of money by engaging in black market-type import/export exchanges, including selling white Bethlehem candles produced in Hungary to the Jewish Community, which thinks the candles came directly from Jerusalem. Charles finds himself caught in the mixed emotions of being a male Jewish virgin in a Berlin rampant with corruptness and deceit, embodied in the text by Esther, a sharp-tongued "Jewish" woman with black hair. He begins a love-hate relationship with Esther until, on November 8—a date of obvious significance—the eve of his departure as well as the deadline given him by German bureaucracy to claim his inheritance, he discovers that Esther is in fact an impostor. Her hair is dyed black to conceal the blonde strands and her story about being born in 1944 to a Jewish woman in hiding in Alsace is exposed as outright fiction by her mother, a resident at a home for the elderly. Esther's motives for play-acting the role of an obnoxious, corrupt Jew is not revealed. The interplay between Charles, a Jew turned Catholic, and her, a German turned Jew, has a violent end.

In "Eine Jüdin für Charles Allen" Dische seemingly confuses identities in order to "unfix" any attempts to normalize relations between Germans and Jews. At the close of her story, we are left with bodies that do not fit. Instead, the body of the text mimics the construction of one-dimensional images of Jewishness and Germanness in grotesque manners, thus drawing attention to the dominant discourses about Jews and gender in German society. Dische does an autopsy on the body of the Shoah by transplanting the diseased organs out of one body and into another one. The post-Shoah body survives because of the transplant, but suffers as the ruptured organs make themselves felt in the pain of remembrance and the wake of repression. The anamnesis of the absent body situates the body that has inherited the memories of the violent abuse next to the preceding bodies who are in the precarious position of having to vouch for a memory they have only second-hand.

By switching identities and confusing them, Dische at first glance realigns the markers and creates dissonance for the reader. As Jack Zipes has shown in his essay on double identities in Hilsenrath's novel, the transfer of physical traits from a Jewish body to a German body and vice-versa disrupts the expectations of the reader.[30] By having her German female protagonist take on a Jewish body and the Jewish male take on a Catholic one, the roles are not simply reversed but exposed as constructions that erase identity as much as they bear it. The female protagonist, Esther, passes as a Jewish woman by dyeing her hair black and incorporating idioms of Jewish self-irony and prejudice into her everyday banter. She herself comments on the negative stereotypes of the Jews by herself voicing them. Once it is revealed that she is a daughter of an SS man and is only posing as a Jew, the disgust at her corrupt character emerges full force. The male protagonist, fittingly a virgin, not having to expose his Jewishness (the sign of which is the circumcised male organ), rapes the woman whose betrayal of identity only accentuates his own denial of his heritage as a Jew. By acting out the culturally inscribed text of the Jewish body, the figure of Esther reveals both the external and internal markers that culturally relegate bodies to single identities, when in fact identities are shifting poses, staged in different contexts.[31] Yet in her attempt to disrupt stereotypes and fixed identities, Dische undoes the memory work accomplished by Dischereit and Honigmann. As a constructed Jewish writer in Germany, she herself seems to reconstruct negative relations between Jews and Germans that mirror anti-Semitic stereotypes, instead of addressing and protesting against them. Unfortunately, the shifting of identities from one body to another in actuality reinstates the negative image of a Jewish male violating a German female body.[32]

Consequently, the framework suggested at the beginning of

this essay for reading the work published in German by Jewish women writers exposes the precariousness of relying solely on one category of identity without questioning the agent of its designation and the radical differences between the construction of female Jewish identity in texts by Jewish women writers. By entwining memory and female Jewish identity, texts by Dischereit and Honigmann give voice to the silenced victims of the Shoah without speaking for the dead or displacing them into metaphorical tropes. It is not the language *per se* which is of the female gender but the arrangement of places, bodies, and images in disarray. The stories are uneven, unstable, fragmented, and disjointed because that is the way female Jewish identity is embodied in a constant process of reassemblage. In their writing, Dischereit and Honigmann resist the labels and restrictions placed upon them as Jews and women in everyday life in Germany today. Although, at first glance, dealing with the disruption and reconstructing of families appears central to their work, Dischereit, Honigmann, and, and to a lesser extent, Dische do not reconnect and regather the remnants left behind in the wake of the Shoah but write texts that practice a genealogical, pathological, and archeological engendering of memory. By playing the role of the rememberer, they expose the ambiguity inherent in an identity founded on victimization. The discontinuous and anti-nostalgic tone of their work exposes the precarious position of Jewish women living in Germany today who refuse to succumb to the role of the victim as the only feasible stance in light of German history. Instead of dwelling on the return to "ruined places," they seek to establish their living presence. They oppose the sole reliance on the inscription of presenced absence on monuments and memorial plaques for reminding others of the past atrocities that culminated in the erasure of remembrance through annihilation. Whereas the monuments serve the important function of marking the ground of both Jewish life and death, they consolidate many experiences into one. Though the inscriptions give names and thus limited subjecthood to the remembered, the petrification of the name in stone breaks down in texts, themselves fluid inscriptions of the past and markers of the present. By recognizing gender difference as a sign of the unequal equation, texts by contemporary

German Jewish women writers call for dis-closure rather than closure and dis-harmony rather than harmonious co-existence. Thus their writing is a reminder of the difference and complexity of relations in a paradoxically unified but postmodern Germany. Their genealogical work is not the fashioning of a subject with capital I but of an ever-changing "we" in search of a place from which to speak as a community with bodies of their own in a place that can only rarely, if ever, be their own.

Notes

1. I would like to acknowledge the helpful comments of Alberto Sandoval, Leslie Adelson, Jack Zipes, and Sander Gilman on earlier versions of this essay.
2. Esther Dischereit, *Joëmis Tisch: Eine jüdische Geschichte* (Frankfurt/Main: Suhrkamp, 1988), 68.
3. Barbara Honigmann, *Roman von einem Kinde* (Frankfurt/Main: Luchterhand Literaturverlag, 1986), 30.
4. I am grateful to Jessica Jacoby and Wendy Howard, co-editors of the volume, for discussing their project with me during the summer of 1991 in Berlin.
5. See Lea Fleischmann, *Dies ist nicht mein Land: Eine Jüdin verläßt die Bundesrepublik* (Hamburg: Hoffmann und Campe, 1980), and Ruth Beckermann, *Unzugehörig: Österreicher und Juden nach 1945* (Vienna: Locker, 1989).
6. As Jewish feminists such as Susannah Hechsel and Shulamit Magnus have pointed out, the issue of gender has only recently been an object of study in Jewish Studies and in Jewish historiography. Due in part to the influence of women's studies and feminist criticism, scholars have begun to study the differences between female and male experiences of Jewish experience and interaction. See Susannah Heschel, "Women's Studies," *Modern Judaism* 10.3 (1990): 243-58; Shulamit Magnus, "'Out of the Ghetto': Integrating the Study of Jewish Women into the Study of 'The Jews,'" *Judaism* 153.39 (1990): 28–36.
7. In *Fremd im eigenen Land: Juden in der Bundesrepublik,* eds. Henryk Broder and Michel R. Lang (Frankfurt/Main: Fischer, 1979), 341. Unless otherwise indicated, English translations of German text are my own.
8. In addition to contemporary writers such as Esther Dischereit, Barbara Honigmann and Irene Dische, who belong to the same generation, writers such as Jeanette Lander and Ronnith Neumann have also received attention in recent years. See Leslie Adelson, "There's No Place

Like Home: Jeanette Lander and Ronnith Neumann's Utopian Quests for Jewish Identity in the Contemporary West German Context," *New German Critique* 50 (1990): 113–34. In her analysis of Jeanette Lander's semi-autobiographical novel *Auf dem Boden der Fremde,* or Ronnith Neumann's *Heimkehr in die Fremde,* Leslie Adelson develops the notion of "polylogue" in order to address the multiple identities a Jewish woman faces in Germany. Her reading of Lander and Neumann suggests that Jewish identity as portrayed by female writers exhibits a "polylogue" of voices and changing "subject positionality." Whereas being Jewish in Germany makes the protagonist in Lander's novel a "stranger in foreign territory," it also gives her a "grounding in precisely that foreignness" (117). The "constant traversing of boundaries" that comprises the search for Jewish identity in the novels breaks down a clear-cut division not only between Jewish and German but also between Jewish male and female. Such a heterogeneous approach includes gender as an integral definer in the reevaluation of what exactly constitutes German Jewish or non-German Jewish writing in the newly unified Germany.

Similar to the notion of difference implied in the term "polylogue," another approach to the writing of Jewish writers and, in particular foreigners in Germany, places their texts within the auspices of a minority discourse that shares characteristics with what Gilles Deleuze and Félix Guattari term "minor literature" in their analysis of Kakfa's writing. Heidrun Suhr, among others, has found evidence of a similar phenomenon at work in writing by Turkish writers living in Germany. See Heidrun Suhr, "Minority Literature in the Federal Republic of Germany," *New German Critique* 46 (1989): 71–103. When reading any minority voice in German culture, especially one that echoes back to times before Germany could be used to designate a cohesive territory, studies on minority discourse or "minor literature" help to shape the approach by pointing out the contradictions. See Gilles Deleuze and Félix Guattari, "What Is Minor Literature?" *Mississippi Review* 11.3 (1983). Compare the *Special Issue on Minorities in German Culture,* ed. Russell A. Berman, Azade Seyhan, and Arlene Akiko Teraoka, *New German Critique* 46 (1989). See also Jack Zipes's discussion of minor literature in this volume.

9. Dische's German Jewish identity is an anomaly, despite the description of her on the book jacket of her collection of short stories, *Fromme Lügen,* as a "German American Jew raised as a Catholic." See Irene Dische, *Fromme Lügen: Sieben Erzählungen,* trans. Otto Bayer and Monika Elwenspoek (Frankfurt/Main: Eichborn, 1989).
10. *Ein fremdes Gefühl* (Berlin Rowohlt, 1993).
11. Honigmann describes her determination to become Orthodox in her short story, "Bonsoir, Madame Benhamou," in *Roman von einem Kinde,* 111–17. Dischereit's relations to her Jewishness frame her novel *Joëmis*

Tisch: Eine jüdische Geschichte, while Dische's Jewish identity is extremely ambiguous, a topic I deal with toward the end of this article. Dischereit attributes her ambivalence toward her Jewish identity to her parents' divorce and her mother's subsequent renewed attachment to Jewish tradition.

12. For further discussion of the relations between Jews and other minorities living in Germany, see Jeffrey Peck's article in this volume. For a more in-depth consideration of minor literature, see Jack Zipes's article in this volume.
13. Compare Sander Gilman's essay in this volume on the significance of circumcision as both a physical and metaphoric sign for Jewish identity in Germany and in writing by German Jewish authors.
14. Although Judith Butler criticizes Foucault's somewhat deterministic description of the body as the site of the inscription of power relations, she acknowledges the valuable insights his redefinition of genealogy provides for recognizing the instability of identity. Thus, Foucault's genealogical inquiry "investigates the political stakes in designating as an *origin* and *cause* those identity categories that are in fact the *effects* of institutions, practices, discourses that multiply and diffuse points of origin" (viii–ix). Accordingly, genealogical practice becomes a method for breaking down overly centralized categories of gender. See Judith Butler, *Gender Trouble: Feminism and the Subversion of Identity* (New York: Routledge, 1990), and Michel Foucault, "Nietzsche, Genealogy, History," in Donald F. Bouchard, ed., *Language, Counter-Memory, Practice: Selected Essays and Interviews* (Ithaca, N.Y.: Cornell University Press, 1977).
15. Foucault, "Nietzsche, Genealogy, History," 145.
16. Honigmann, *Eine Liebe aus Nichts* (Berlin: Rowohlt, 1991), and Dischereit, *Merryn* (Frankfurt/Main: Suhrkamp, 1992).
17. According to Benjamin's comparison of the archaeologist to the rememberer, the scene of remembrance says more about the relationship between the past and the present than the cataloguing of the found objects—themselves fragmented and only reconstructed in imagination: "And he cheats himself out of the best, he who only takes an inventory of his findings and cannot designate the exact spot in the present ground where the old is stored up. Therefore, authentic memories must proceed less as a report than as a precise marker of the location in which the investigator took possession of them." See Walter Benjamin, *Gesammelte Schriften: Werkausgabe* 10, ed. Tillman Rexroth (Frankfurt/Main: Suhrkamp, 1980), 400–401.
18. In Dische, *Fromme Lügen*, 5–74.
19. See Gilman's article in this volume.
20. See Karl A. Plank, "The Survivor's Return: Reflections on Memory and Place," *Judaism* 38.3 (Summer 1989): 274.
21. In this context, *Vertriebene* (refugees) refers to refugees of German nationality who came west at the end of World War II from territories in

the east formerly occupied by Germany.

22. See Walter Benjamin's image of departure in his rendition of the Orphean myth: "Gewiß: heute im Zeitalter des Autos und Flugzeugs sind es nur sachte, atavistische Schrecken, die unter den schwarzen Hallen noch ruhen und jene abgespielte Kommödie von Abschied und Wiedersehen, die man vor dem Hintergrunde der Pullmanncars aufführt, macht aus dem Bahnsteig eine Provinzbühne. Noch einmal spielt man uns das abgelebte griechische Melodram: Orpheus, Eurydike und Hermes auf dem Bahnhof. Im Kofferberge unter dem sie steht, wölbt sich der Felsgang, die Krypta in die sie versinkt, wenn der hermetische Schaffner mit der Signalscheibe, die feuchten Blicke des Orpheus suchend, das Zeichen zur Abfahrt gibt. Narben des Abschieds, die wie der Sprung einer griechischen Vase über die dargehaltenen Leiber der Götter zuckt." Walter Benjamin, *Das Passagen-Werk: Erster Band*, ed. Rolf Tiedemann (Frankfurt/Main: Suhrkamp, 1982), 512.
23. See Hannah Arendt, *Rahel Varnhagen: Lebensgeschichte einer deutschen Jüdin aus der Romantik* (München: Piper, 1981).
24. As Sander Gilman shows in his work on contemporary Jewish writers, female bodies are also marked, if invisibly, by the stigma of Jewishness. Being born Jewish leaves the "mark of Cain" inscribed into the Jewish body, and the Jewish star functions as a declaration of Jewish identity, while, at the same time, being hidden and exposed as a point of provocation. See "Male Sexuality and Contemporary Jewish Literature in German" in this volume. If we stay within the realm of representation and follow Gilman's logic, the primacy of the male Jewish body as representative of all Jews implies that female Jewish bodies are even more absent than their male counterparts. As Gilman acknowledges, more work needs to be done on understanding the ways in which the female Jewish body itself has been represented and misrepresented.
25. See Jeffrey Peck's argument for a more differentiated recognition of different forms of otherness and degrees of discrimination experienced by people of color and white Jews in Germany in this volume.
26. In an interview in the *taz*, 30 March 1990, 15–16, Dische repeatedly criticizes reviewers who designate her as a Jew. She blames the media for creating the image of her as a Jew.
27. The fact that these three writers are not the only ones of their generation who began exploring the significance of their Jewish heritage shortly before or around the time of unification strongly suggests that the attempt by many Germans to establish a national German identity free of the burden of the past conversely brings about an increased urgency among Jews living in Germany to reconnect with their Jewish past.
28. Compare Katharina Ochse's essay in this volume.
29. See "Frei von Pathos," *taz*, 30 March 1990, 16.

30. See Zipes, "Die kulturellen Operationen von Deutschen und Juden im Spiegel der neueren deutschen Literatur," *Babylon* 8 (1991): 34–44.
31. Dische's story raises an issue that I believe is becoming more prevalent in studies of German Jewish relations—that of the reduction of victim/victimizer status to nonbinary linguistic markers. I welcome the exposure of the illusion of absolute opposites and the rights of historical victims to a retrospective agency in language. But what of their misuse by those who would have the status reversed or become interchangeable? It is one thing to textualize the psychological and physical crossovers or de-familiarize differences as Hillsenrath does in his novel, *Der Nazi und der Friseur,* or as portrayed in the film *Europa, Europa,* but it is quite another to suggest that one can erase the differences altogether. The junctures where German and Jewish meet, retract, and retreat from one another are multiple, yet in concrete situations they may remain dependent on the discourses that claim to replicate them and on the material reality that tears any relation asunder.
32. Compare Gilman's more critical reading of Dische's story in "Male Sexuality and Contemporary Jewish Literature" in this volume.

10. Male Sexuality and Contemporary Jewish Literature in German: The Damaged Body as the Image of the Damaged Soul

Sander L. Gilman

Jewish Literature in German Deals with an Old Question

In the past decade a new literature written by Jews has begun to appear in the German language, representing the "negative symbiosis" of culturally embedded Jews in the new Germany.[1] The writers of these works feel themselves to be both part of this new Germany yet alienated from it. For these Jewish writers this new Germany always existed in their fantasy. Their literature is marked not only along the expected line of demarcation between the "German" and the "Jew" (while calling that boundary into question), but it is also clearly marked by the gender of the author. There is a special status to the discourse of the Jewish male writer in contemporary German letters. In reading this literature one can speak of a marking of the literary text through a writer's internalization of a fantasy of his own body. Jews—especially Jewish males—continue to be perceived in post-Shoah German society as indelibly different, and these Jewish male writers represent this difference when they inscribe their fantasies into their texts. Within the Western tradition, it has been the Jewish ritual practice of infant male circumcision that traditionally placed the male

Jewish body into a separate conceptual category. Jewish males were anatomically different, and this difference was represented by a clearly defined sign, the artificially altered shape of the penis. This sign came to signify the inherent difference of the Jew in all matters, from the form of the Jewish body to the creativity of the Jewish spirit.[2]

In the early twentieth century the internalization of the debates about circumcision, especially among the Jews of Central Europe, provided a heightened sense of their vulnerability because of their visibility. In the 1920s, Jacob Wassermann chronicled the ambivalence of German Jews toward their own bodies, their own difference. Wassermann articulates this difference within the terms of the biology of race. He writes: "I have known many Jews who have languished with longing for the fair-haired and blue-eyed individual. They knelt before him, burned incense before him, believed his every word; every blink of his eye was heroic; and when he spoke of his native soil, when he beat his Aryan breast, they broke into a hysterical shriek of triumph."[3] Their response, Wassermann argues, is to feel disgust for their own body, which even when it is identical in *all* respects to the body of the Aryan remains different: "I was once greatly diverted by a young Viennese Jew, elegant, full of suppressed ambition, rather melancholy, something of an artist, and something of a charlatan. Providence itself had given him fair hair and blue eyes; but lo, he had no confidence in his fair hair and blue eyes: in his heart of hearts he felt that they were spurious."[4] The Jew's experience of his or her own body was so deeply impacted by anti-Semitic rhetoric that even when that body met the expectations for perfection in the community in which the Jew lived, the Jew experienced his or her body as flawed.[5]

Such moment is reflected in the debates about the need for circumcision among acculturated Jews in Vienna in the first half of the twentieth century. Albert Drach, in perhaps the greatest satirical representation of the meaning of the Jewish body in Austrian culture written during the late 1930s, has his Eastern European Jewish protagonist, Zwetschkenbaum, respond to the question of "what is the difference between a man and a woman?"[6] His answer, which is to be used by the court in judging Zwetschkenbaum's competency, is that "men are circumcised and women are not." For the Jew of the 1930s and 1940s, circumcision was the primary mark of male, Jewish identity. And that image is negatively charged. The extraordinary, anonymous tale of "Herr Moriz Deutschösterreicher," written in the mid-1940s, begins with the argument between the father and the mother of this "Mr. Average Austrian Jew":

> Moriz Deutschösterreicher was born on June 2, 1891, in Vienna. His mother did not want him to be circumcised: "It's crazy, Sandor, to purposely violate my child, think about when he goes into the army and they all have to bathe naked together, or what if he marries a Christian, how embarrassing. . . . If you are dumb enough and don't have him baptized, don't do this to him. Does one have to send such a poor worm with such a handicap into the world?" She cried day and night. But it didn't help a bit. Sandor agreed with his old mother—by himself he would have perhaps hesitatingly agreed, because he did not place much store in such things.[7]

Circumcision has no positive meaning in this context, except as a means of pleasing someone of an older generation. The context of the writing by male Jews about their body is thus a central one in determining their sense of identity with the literary culture in which they live. The framing of the meaning of circumcision for male Jews in Germany during the nineteenth century provides the background to this discourse of dissatisfaction with one's own body—for it is not only the infant "Mr. Average Austrian Jew" who is to be circumcised and will grow up ill at ease with his body, but also his father whose sense of the oddity of his own sexual body is stressed by the one person who would know it best—his wife.

After the Shoah, the meaning attributed to circumcision for Jews in Europe was as the ultimate sign of betrayal and recognition. The Parisian psychotherapist Susann Heenen-Wolff, in her recent book of interviews of Jews who remained in Germany after 1945, uncovered the continuing power of this anxiety about the male body. Hans Radziewski, a Berlin Jew, tells her of his capture at the beginning of 1943 on the streets of Berlin.[8] He is asked how he was recognized: "Well, you had to tell your name. They asked about the [Yellow] Jewish Star, and if everything else failed, one had to drop one's pants." When he is asked how the Germans could tell a Jew from a Moslem, he remarked that because of their Arab specialists, the SS could tell whether the cut was made on the eighth or the twenty-eighth day. This powerful fantasy about the immediate visibility of the Jewish body was shaped by the sense that his body was indeed inherently different. And yet the marker of circumcision remains a powerful sign of identity for Jews in Germany. In her interview with Rolf K., born in 1932, whose criminal activities in postwar West Germany led him to extended periods in prison, she asks about whether his son feels himself to be Jewish. The answer is no. The child's mother is not Jewish. And yet, he notes, he is circumcised—and not for medical reasons. His mother explains: "No, no, he is circumcised because I wanted it. And at his age he couldn't refuse. He was seven days old" (112). Jewish anxiety in contemporary central Europe about the meaning of the Jewish body after the Shoah becomes part of the definition of the gender role ascribed to the male Jew as circumciser and circumcised.

The Meaning of Circumcision

The very core of the definition of the Jew for medical science during the latter half of the nineteenth century is also the most salient popular fact in defining the body of the Jew. It is the practice of infant male circumcision. "In the folk-mind scarcely anything was more important than circumcision. Circumcision *made* the Jew," as the American historian Jacob R. Marcus has cogently observed.[9] In terms of the late nineteenth century, the anthropologist Richard Andree noted that in "Yiddish the very term 'to make into a Jew' (*jüdischen*) means to circumcise."[10] Thus the male Jewish body is the baseline for the definition of the Jew. Circumcision marked the Jewish body as unequal to that of the Aryan and the male Jew as the exemplary Jew. What would circumcision have meant to a Jewish scientist who had internalized the negative associations with this practice? As the anti-Semite Ezra Pound once remarked to his friend Charles Olsen: "There was a Jew, in London, Obermeyer, a doctor . . . of the endocrines, and I used to ask him what is the effect of circumcision. That's the question that gets them sore . . . that sends them right up the pole. Try it, don't take my word, try it. . . . It must do something, after all these years and years, where the most sensitive nerves in the body are, rubbing them off, over and over again."[11] The rub was a social as well as a scientific rub, as we shall see.

The centrality of the act of circumcision in defining what a Jew is makes the very term "Jew" come to mean the male Jew in the nineteenth century. Thus we have an immediate dichotomy—all Jews, male and female, are different from the "neutral" scientific observer (who is male and Aryan in his ideology), but male Jews are uncanny, in that they superficially appear to be males but are not because of the altered form of the genitalia. (Jewish women are different too. They are different—different in a manner other than women are different from men, but different from the Aryan male observer.) The anti-Semitic British explorer and author, Richard Burton, commented that "Christendom practically holds circumcision in horror."[12] The perspective of this supposedly neutral observer becomes one with the space of scientific observation. The male, Aryan scientific gaze becomes the means of defining the healthy perspective. Jewish scientists, their bodies marked through the act of circumcision, cannot share in this sense of community.

It is not that the circumcised penis was in itself the most unusual biological feature of the anthropological image of the male Jew in nineteenth-century science—indeed the debates about the specificity of all of the physiological and psychological markers of difference invented by eighteenth- and nineteenth-century ethnology, from skull capacity, size, and shape (cephalic index) to skin and hair color were employed to document the difference of the Jews from all other races.[13] But it was in the arena of this specific ritual practice that the pathological nature of the Jews was seen to manifest itself most clearly. The *brit milah*, the practice of infant male circumcision, became for the thinkers of the late nineteenth century the major sign of Jewish difference.[14] And all of the controversies over circumcision within the medical literature were colored by its centrality as the means of distinguishing between the healthy and the diseased, between the Aryan and the

Jew. As an anonymous author stated in the leading German pediatric journal in 1872: "The circumcision of Jewish children has been widely discussed in the medical press as is warranted with topics of such importance. But it is usually discussed without the necessary attention to details and the neutrality that it deserves. Indeed, it has not been free of fanatic anti-Semitism."[15] This association continues strongly even as the practice of circumcision becomes widely practiced (in countries such as the United States and Great Britain). Indeed, as late as 1920 one can read in the *British Medical Journal* the following comment on circumcision: "This injurious procedure, like that of keeping women in bed after childbirth, we owe to the Jews, and we have nothing to thank them for as regards these two of their religious rituals."[16] One might add that in most of the anti-circumcision literature to the present, there is a constant strain of blaming the Jews for the dangers perceived as inherent in this procedure.[17] Circumcision marks the Jew as damaged and as potentially damaging. In German popular culture of the 1980s the sign of circumcision marked the group fantasy about the hidden nature of the male Jew's body even when the body in question was uncircumcised.[18] And for German Jews, the internalization of the sense of their body's difference cannot be underestimated.[19]

The social significance of reliance on circumcision as the marker of Jewish difference in European medicine of the late nineteenth century can be located in the overt fact that Western European Jews by that time had become indistinguishable from other Western Europeans in matters of language, dress, occupation, location of their dwellings and the cut of their hair. Indeed, if Rudolf Virchow's extensive study of over 10,000 German schoolchildren published in 1886 was accurate, they were also indistinguishable in terms of skin, hair, and eye color from the greater masses of those who lived in Germany.[20] Virchow's statistics sought to show that where a greater percentage of the overall population had lighter skin or bluer eyes or blonder hair, a greater percentage of Jews had lighter skin or bluer eyes or blonder hair. Later this tendency was explained by Felix von Luschan as a social phenomenon, rather than as one of adaptation or biological mimicry. He suggested that Jews select those mates who mirror the ideal types present in those societies in which they live. Thus they select for precisely those qualities which would make them most like the majority culture.[21] Unlike skin or hair or eye color, the male Jewish body was marked as different. The debates about the meaning of circumcision in the nineteenth century must be understood in the context of this specifically European recognition of circumcision as the most evident sign of the racial difference of the Jew.[22]

But to say that it was assumed that Jews bore the stigmata of circumcision as a sign of the difference is much too vague. It is clear that there has been a wide range of meanings associated with the act of circumcision in the West. Circumcision has been read to be a sign of everything from sexual hygiene, to cosmetic appearance, to tribal identity or a mark of adulthood, to either diminished or enhanced sexual desire, to increased or decreased fertility, to patriarchal subjugation, to enhanced purity, to the improvement of sexual endurance, to a form of attenuated castration, to menstrual envy, to a substitute for human sacrifice. But there are four "traditional" perspectives on the "meaning" of circumcision in connection with the Jews which have dominated Western thought since the rise of Christianity.[23] Following the writings of Paul, the first perspective treated circumcision as inherently symbolic and therefore no longer valid after the rise of Christianity. This view was espoused by the Church Fathers, Eusebius and Origen, and it continued through the Renaissance (Erasmus) and through the Reformation (Luther). It forms the theological basis for the distinction which Christians were able to make between their bodies and the bodies of the Jews.[24]

The second "traditional" perspective held that circumcision was a sign of a political or group identity. The rhetoric in which the accepted science of the late nineteenth century clothed its rejection of circumcision is of importance. It was intense and virulent, as has been remarked, and never free from negative value judgments. One central example should suffice. Paolo Mantegazza (1831–1901) was one of the standard "ethnological" sources for the late nineteenth century for the nature of human sexuality. The controversial centerpiece of Mantegazza's work is his trilogy on love and sex: *Physiology of Love* (1872), *Hygiene of Love* (1877), and *On*

Human Love (1885).[25] Cited widely by sexologists from Cesare Lombroso, Richard Krafft-Ebing, Havelock Ellis, and Iwan Bloch to Magnus Hirschfeld, Mantegazza remained one of the accessible, "popular" sources for "scientific" knowledge (and misinformation) to the educated public at the turn of the century.[26] One of a group of physician-anthropologists that included Cesare Lombroso, Mantegazza had pioneered the introduction of the study (and enjoyment) of *Erthroxylon coca* and its derivative, cocaine, in the late 1850s. Following the publication of Darwin's *Descent of Man*, Mantegazza became one of Darwin's most avid correspondents (and sources), supplying Darwin with a series of "anthropological" photographs which Darwin used for his later work.

If we turn to the chapter in Mantegazza's study of the anthropology of sexual practices after the one on "perversions," we come to a detailed discussion of the "mutilation of the genitals" which recounts the history of these practices among "savage tribes" including the Jews.[27] Indeed, it is only in Mantegazza's discussion of the Jews that the text turns from a titillating account of "unnatural practices" into a polemic (echoing Spinoza's often cited comments on the centrality of circumcision for the definition of the Jew)[28] against the perverse practices of that people out of their correct "space" and "time"—the Jews:

> Circumcision is a shame and an infamy; and I, who am not in the least anti-Semitic, who indeed have much esteem for the Israelites, I who demand of no living soul a profession of religious faith, insisting only upon the brotherhood of soap and water and of honesty, I shout and shall continue to shout at the Hebrews, until my last breath: Cease mutilating yourselves: cease imprinting upon your flesh an odious brand to distinguish you from other men; until you do this, you cannot pretend to be our equal. As it is, you, of your own accord, with the branding iron, from the first days of your lives, proceed to proclaim yourselves a race apart, one that cannot, and does not care to, mix with ours.[29]

This was not his view alone. Edvard Westermarck, the creator of the sociology of marriage, simply labeled circumcision as "the mutilation of the sexual organ."[30]

Mantegazza introduces his discussion of the sexual exclusivity of the Jews with the following passage:

> It is altogether likely that the most important reason which has led men of various ages and of varying civilizations to adopt the custom of cutting off the prepuce has been that it was felt to be necessary to imprint upon the human body a clear and indelible sign which would serve to distinguish one people from another and, by putting a seal of consecration upon nationality, would tend to impede the mixture of races. A woman, before accepting the embraces of a man, must first make sure, with her eyes and with her hands, as to whether he was of the circumcised or the uncircumcised; nor would she be able to find any excuse for mingling her own blood-stream with that of the foreigner. It had, however, not occurred to the legislator that this same indelible characteristic would inspire in the woman a curiosity to see and to handle men of a different sort.[31]

The seduction of the Jewish woman by the Other—here the non-Jew—is the result of the "seeing" of the difference in the form of the genitalia. The need to "see" and "touch" the Other is the fault of the circumcised (male) Jew whose very physical form tempts the female to explore the Other. Here we have another form of the displacement of the act of touching (sexual contact) with the permitted (indeed, necessary) act of seeing, but here it is given a pathological interpretation.

Mantegazza notes that "the hygienic value of circumcision has been exaggerated by the historians of Judaism. It is true enough that the circumcised are a little less disposed to masturbation and to venereal infection; but every day, we do have Jewish masturbators and Jewish syphilitics. Circumcision is a mark of racial distinction . . . it is a sanguinary protest against universal brotherhood; and if it be true that Christ was circumcised, it is likewise true that he protested on the cross against any symbol which would tend to part men asunder."[32] This view is clearly antithetical to the view of scholars such as the sociologist Edvard Westermarck and the sexologist August Forel, who link "the intention of exciting the sexual appetite" through circumcision with "the hygienic advantage of circumcision [which] took a part in its transformation into a rite."[33] "We may go to Moses for instruction in some of the best methods in hygiene," according to William Osler in 1914, even though the Jew is less adept in the world of "intellect and science."[34] Ernest Crawley's marriage study, where he reported that the "Jews considered circumcision as a 'cleansing.'"[35] echoed the traditional view. Mantegazza's rhetoric sets the

Jew apart and makes out of his body a mark of his pariahdom.

The third reading of circumcision saw it as a remnant of the early Jewish idol or phallus worship. Thus J.H.F. Autenrieth saw circumcision as but a primitive act practiced by culturally inferior peoples such as Jews and African blacks. Autenrieth, by 1829 the chancellor of the University of Tübingen, entered the discussion on the meaning of circumcision with a public lecture on its history. For him, as for others, circumcision was a surrogate for human sacrifice.[36] John Lubbock saw the rite of sacrifice as a "stage through which, in any natural process of development, religion must pass."[37] But the Jews also sacrificed their animals at the Temple as "symbols of human sacrifice...[which] were at one time habitual among the Jews."[38] Circumcision was a sign of "the inherent barbarism of this people," a view seconded by a Dr. Hacker in a medical journal in 1843.[39] Here again the medical discussion of a social practice becomes contaminated by the racial context into which it is placed. Indeed, this view dominates the ethnopsychological discussion about the meaning of circumcision into the late nineteenth and early twentieth centuries. The experimentalist Wilhelm Wundt sees circumcision as "of the nature of sacrifice. Along with the offering of hair in the cult of the dead and with the pouring out of blood in connection with deity worship, it belongs to that form of sacrifice in which the sacrificial object gains its unique value by virtue of its being the vehicle of the soul. Thus the object of sacrifice, in the case of circumcision, may perhaps be interpreted as a substitute for such internal organs as the kidneys or testicles, which are particularly prized as vehicles of the soul but which can either not be offered at all, on the part of the living, or whose sacrifice involves serious difficulties."[40] For Wundt, politically a liberal in his time, Judaism is "but one of those vanquished cults which struggled for supremacy in the pre-Constantinian period of the Roman World Empire."[41] And the practice of this substitute for ritual sacrifice is a sign of the barbarism and marginality of the Jew.

The fourth reading of circumcision saw it as a form of medical prophylaxis. This seems to be first claimed in the writing of Philo, who was writing in a strongly Hellenistic culture which found any mutilation of the body abhorrent.[42] He claimed that it was a prophylaxis against diseases of the penis but also promoted the well-being of the individual and assured fertility. But the hygienic rationale was also evoked, as we have seen, in the work of Johann David Michaelis, the central German commentator on this practice in the eighteenth century. It is only in the middle of the nineteenth century that the debate about the medical meaning of circumcision impacts upon the Jewish community in Central Europe. Prior to this the discussions concerning the meaning of circumcision in the Christian community remained separate from Jewish concern in Europe. While the image of the circumcised Jew was raised as a central metaphor for Jewish difference in Great Britain with the presentation of the Jewish Naturalization Act in 1753,[43] it only becomes of importance with the gradual acculturation of the Jews in Germany and Austria toward the middle of the nineteenth century. The debates within and outside the Jewish communities concerning the nature and implication of circumcision surfaced in Germany during the 1840s. German Jews had become acculturated to German middle-class values and had come to question the quasi-sacramental requirement of circumcision as a prerequisite of their Jewish identity.

On July 15, 1843, a position paper by the "Friends of Reform" was published in the *Frankfurter Journal* in which the platform for a new, "reformed" Judaism was put forth. The abolition of circumcision was one of the keystones of that program. Led by the radical reform rabbi Samuel Holdheim, it responded not only to a Christian (both Catholic and Protestant) tradition which denigrated circumcision as a sign of inferiority, but also to the growing charge that it was an "unhealthy" practice.[44] Holdheim held that circumcision was a ritual which was not binding upon Jews, any more than the rabbinic laws concerning the many other rituals.[45] Holdheim saw circumcision as having a purely religious function as a sign of the membership of the community. The sign of the covenant was understood symbolically and internally rather than incised upon the body. He does not see it as a necessity any more than the abandoned sacrifice of the paschal lamb. Holdheim's position was the most radical in the Jewish community of his day. While Holdheim did not evoke the medical opposition to circumcision, it was already quite vocal in Germany.

In 1844 a Berlin physician, J. Bergson, a Jewish advocate of circumcision, responded to Holdheim's call of the abolition of infant male circumcision by advocating medical reforms which would enable the procedure to become safe.[46] He shifts the debate from its religious necessity to its medical implications. Already in 1825 a Dr. Wolfers, a physician and "male-midwife" from Lemförde, had argued that circumcision was a dangerous procedure and should be placed under the supervision of the "medical police."[47] He discusses the poor preparation of the ritual circumcisers, the *mohelim*, and the destructive results of their incompetence. Beginning in 1819 the Berlin Jewish community had insisted on a medical presence at the *bris* (ritual circumcision).[48] This remained a concern well into mid-century. A Dr. Klein in Ratibor suggested in 1853 that such a public health control was in no way a violation of freedom of religious practice but solely a public health question.[49] This view became one of the leading proposals that formed the background to Holdheim's suggestion. For if the procedure were dangerous then it must be abolished. But the political implications of abolition must not have been clear to Holdheim. For in Prussian and Austrian state law, at least, if a child were not circumcised, he had to be baptized. Indeed, in a case in Brunswick in 1847 the parents, after refusing to have their child circumcised for medical reasons, were ordered to have him either circumcised or baptized within fourteen days.[50] Here the echo of the discussion of the inheritability of the act of circumcision comes into play. Can Jews truly abandon circumcision as a sign of their religious identity? Or is that as useless as trying to abandon their racial identity? The choice between circumcision or baptism meant, given the marginal status of baptized Jews within German culture, in practice remaining a Jew, baptized or not. The inner sign of circumcision remains and can be spontaneously written upon the body through the somatic inheritance of acquired characteristics.

The Internalization of the Meaning of the Jewish Body after the Shoah in the Writing of Jewish Women

The implications of circumcision as a sign of the body of the Jew seems to be missing in much of the writing by contemporary

Jewish women who write in German such as Lea Fleischmann or Barbara Honigmann, whose works reflect on many of the same conflicts of identity as those found in the writings of their male counterparts.[51] Much of this self-consciously feminist writing, however, shares this sense of the difference of the Jew's body with the Jewish male, but on a metaphoric level. In these texts an awareness of the difference of the Jewish body is linked to its symbolic representation, usually through the evocation of the Star of David and its historical function as the Nazi marker of the Jewish body. For example, Esther Dischereit presents an aspect of the gendered distinction between the writing of a self-labeled Jewish woman in German culture and that of a Jewish masculine sensibility. In her novel about survival and identity formation in pre- and postwar Germany, *Joëmis Table* (1988), she evokes a string of associations with being Jewish, at least being Jewish as evoked by seeing the Jewish cemetery at Fez with its new graves: "Where death is, there is also mumbling, kaddish, Passover and circumcision. In my Frankfurt—there is no death."[52] There is no death, for all have already died and died without the ceremony of remembrance. Circumcision is central to her definition of being a Jew. There seems to be no pejorative association at all. Yet she imagines her own body, the body of the Jew, inscribed with the "inherited mark of Cain, forgotten under the water of Socialism, [which] shimmers through onto [her] skin" (9). This mark of Cain (historically a common association with circumcision) is represented by Dischereit in a way very different from the circumcised male Jewish body. She fantasizes that her body is transparent as she crosses the German border: "But if they demand that I should disrobe—why should they demand that—if they demand that I should disrobe, and I would undress. And one would see the star through the clothes—one does not see it—through the clothes, burned into my skin—it is not burnt, I wasn't ever there—burned into my skin, and the dogs would come to me." (35) The Nazi's "Jewish Star" is inscribed on her sense of her own body—it is burned into her living soul since she survived the actual burning of the body in the camps. Here the internalization of the mark upon the body, the mark of Cain usually associated with the act of male circumcision, is replaced with a metaphor of Jewish difference. But the context remains the same—it is the act of disrobing, of revealing the body that reveals the nature of the Jew. This theme is reflected in the powerful film *Hitlerjunge Salomon* (1991) (released in English as *Europa, Europa*) in which the circumcised body of the Jewish protagonist can never be revealed, as it would betray him to the Nazis among whom he is hiding. The Polish-Jewish director, Agnieszka Holland, struggles with this theme taken from the real life experiences of Salomon Perel, a survivor of the Shoah. Unlike Dischereit, she refuses to allow the theme to become solely a metaphor. But her image is bound by respect for the life experiences of a Jewish male in Germany though seen through the lens of a Polish-Jewish woman director. What Holland reflects, Dischereit internalizes.

An interesting problem in the discussion of the representation of the Jewish male body in German culture can be found in the work of three American female writers who confront the Jewish question in Germany in very different ways, each of which frames the problem of a male Jewish voice in a radically different manner. Irene Dische, of German-Jewish ancestry but raised Catholic, moved to Germany from the United States in the 1980s. Her short stories (first available in German translation) present the body of the Jewish male as unremarkable. In her major short story, "A Jewess for Charles Allen," an American Catholic man of Jewish ancestry rapes a German woman who had Nazi parents but here plays the Jewish role. Dische does not represent the Jewish male body as different.[53] Coming from a society in which circumcision is nearly universal, but from a cultural-religious background in which it plays no defining role, Irene Dische is impervious to any sense of the difference of the male Jew's body. Her Jewish male (who by his religious education is a Catholic) seems to possess no identifiable physical characteristics while her Jewish female (who is in reality a non-Jewish German) publicly represents her Jewish identity by the "silver Star of David" she wears about her neck (13). Our reading of her dark physiognomy is immediately shaped by this article of jewelry—as is the male protagonist's reading of her. She becomes for him (and for us) the essential Jewish female. The symbolic representation of the Jew's body is the Star of David. In Dische's account, her protagonist is shown to be merely a repressed male, repressed in his identity as well as his sexuality, who lashes out at his female tormentor the only way he knows how—through sexual assault. Dische's own evocation of the anti-Semitic trope of the Jewish male desiring to possess the body of the non-Jewish woman, which underlies this masquerade of identities, provides a model for her understanding of the Jewish male and his sexuality. For in the end it is the Jewish male (whose circumcised state is implied though never stated) who rapes the German female. The power of the trope transcends all of the masquerades in this novel. The "Jewish Star" now marks the body of the female victim of the male Jew's anger and lust.

Dische's work is paralleled in an autobiographical vein by Jane E. Gilbert, born in the United States of Eastern European Jewish parents, who immigrated in the 1970s to the Federal Republic of Germany, where she took German citizenship and still resides. Her experiences in learning to deal with Germans as individuals rather than as a stereotyped collective is the theme of her autobiography. Within this autobiography, however, there is a striking moment in which she seems to characterize the anti-Zionist feelings that came to replace overt anti-Semitism among the members of the German Left during the 1970s. She tells the story of a Jewish male friend of hers, who met a young German woman at a bar and goes home with her. She flees, according to Gilbert, when she spies his Star of David pendant as he undresses for bed, cursing him as a "Zionist." Here the pendant (echoing the Nazi's use of the "Jewish Star" as a marker of the Jew) overtly replaces the circumcised penis, which is the most evident sign of the Jew which can be seen when the Jewish male undresses.[54] Whether this is the result of the self-censorship of the author or her acquaintance is not at all clear. But the Star of David comes, as it does in the work of Dische and Dischereit, to represent the idea of difference present in the *body* of the Jew—as understood in a symbolic mode in German culture. It is evident from her text that Gilbert is aware of the significance of the act of circumcision in Germany. An earlier anecdote reveals that a male friend of hers exposed a petty criminal posing as a Jew in Berlin through the "fact" that he was uncircumcised (176). For in this context circumcision is the mark of authenticity. In the anecdote about the conflation of "Jew" and "Israeli," Gilbert does not make the evident connection. She is appalled that these two categories are conflated. They meet in the image of the male Jewish body, whose circumcision signifies his inherent difference from the German.

Radically different is the representation of the Jewish male body in the autobiographical work by Susan Neiman. An American of Eastern European Jewish ancestry, she went to Berlin in the mid-1980s as a student. She becomes a critical commentator as well as a participant in the daily life of the city. It is there that she develops a sense of what being Jewish in Germany meant—at least for her. One of her non-Jewish lovers shocked her by commenting, "'Every time I see you I think of Dachau . . . baby."[55] But their uncircumcised bodies do not seem remarkable for her. When she finally meets Michael, the man she is to marry, she discovers that he has a Jewish mother (though his father was a member of the Wehrmacht). But even with Michael, there is no comment on the nature of the adult male's body. This question only arises with her representation of the body of the Jewish male child. When the child of a Jewish couple they know had been put into day-care, the question of the child's circumcision becomes central to Neiman's representation of the child's difference: "'Have they ever asked why he's circumcised?' asked Jesse one night. 'I know,' Sarah answered. 'It really stands out when the kids are naked. No. They haven't.' 'Afraid to ask.' 'I don't think it occurs to them'" (190). This sign marks the inherent difference of the Jew. It is internalized by his parents, who note it and suppress its implications. The non-Jewish day-care workers understand that the child is "really" different from the other children. When Susan and Michael's child, Benjamin, is circumcised, the image of the *bri't milah* is one of the most ironic yet moving chapters of her memoir (209–13). The act of circumcision comes to represent the revitalization of Jewish life in Germany. Jacob Taubes, the late and lamented professor of philosophy at the Free University (Berlin), serves as the child's godfather and the event serves as a microcosm of the tensions in the new and growing Jewish community—a community that now shows its fissures as a sign of its health. Neiman, unlike Dische, understands the difference that the Germans attribute to the marking of the Jewish body. For her, the ritual importance of the covenant for her own child is to no small degree determined by her sense of her own difference in German society. Her memoir chronicles how she became aware of her own Jewish identity through her exposure to the repression of Jewish identity in German culture during the 1980s. But the constant foreboding that this active forgetting caused her also brought a heightened sense of her own Jewish identity.

The circumcised adult Jew is thus missing from the world of most of these Jewish women. His absence is a sign of the extraordinary complexity of meaning associated with the image of the circumcised male for Jewish women. For non-Jewish women, even placed in a different cultural context, this association seems to be equally pejorative. The director and author Doris Dörrie, in her story "Straight to the Heart," recounts the kidnapping of a Turkish baby by a young German woman desperate for a child. Changing the baby's name from "Kenan" to "Jan" she brings the baby home to her husband, who believes the child to be theirs:" He wanted to change Jan's diaper. Anna had to show him how. Thrilled, Armin felt Jan's arms and legs, the feet the size of his thumb, the plump belly with its umbilical knot. Good heavens, could it be Kenan had been circumcised. . . . She noticed how her face was twitching. She would have liked to shove Armin aside. It was her baby. Hers alone."[56] Her fear was that the baby's body would be marked by the sign of its difference, revealing it to be not her own. The very concept that circumcision reveals difference is embodied here in the text. This sense of difference is played out to no little degree in her representation of the meaning and complexity of the male body as the different body. But here an added aspect is introduced—it is the marked *male* body that reveals difference.

The Internalization of the Meaning of the Jewish Body after the Shoah in the Writing of Jewish Men

Recent German prose by a new generation of male Jewish writers in Germany reflect on this problem in the most recent Jewish writing in German. These texts present the problem of the new Jewish literary sensibility in German culture within a continuation of the debate about the meaning of circumcision begun by St. Paul.

Jurek Becker's novel, *Bronstein's Children* (1986), was his first return to a "Jewish" theme since his immigration to West Berlin in 1977.[57] Becker, a child-survivor of the Lodz ghetto, came to East Berlin with his father immediately after the war and was raised in the German Democratic Republic. Expelled following the Wolf Biermann controversy, Becker moved to West Berlin. *Bronstein's Children* is without a doubt the most successful work Becker has written in the West. Originally intended to be titled "How I Became A German," the novel traces two years in the formation of a young Jew in the German Democratic Republic from the perspective of his growing sense of his own conflicts of identity. The plot deals with a family—a father, his eighteen-year-old son, and grown daughter—and their lives in 1973 and 1974 in East Berlin.

The "hero" or at least narrator of the novel is the son, Hans, who tells the story a year after his father Arno's death in 1973. He attempts to reconstruct the events leading to his father's death and to understand how he has been constructing his life following that event. Becker provided a representation of the development of a Jewish identity in Germany (here the GDR) in those individuals who had no firsthand experience of the Shoah but whose parents (or here, a sibling) survived.

This generation's experience is the focus of this novel as well as Rafael Seligmann's *Rubinstein's Auction*, published in 1989, and the short stories of Maxim Biller, published in 1990.[58] Seligmann, born in Israel in 1947, emigrated with his parents to Munich as a ten-year-old. His novel represents the analogous experience, covering the same development (though set in the late 1960s rather than the early 1970s) within the Federal Republic. All of these present the complexities of dealing with an identity formed by the history of the Shoah but without any personal memory or experience of these events.

Central to all of these texts is the question of male sexuality and the representation of the male Jewish body. Both novels are indeed tales of adolescence, adolescent rebellion, and the discovery of the sexual. But more important, both novels focus on the perceived or real difference of the Jewish body and the internalization of that difference in the structuring of the male protagonist's sense of insecurity. The alienation experienced by the adolescent male as represented in modern fiction by, for example, J. D. Salinger's Holden Caulfield, is heightened by the sense of insecurity felt by males understood to be Jewish in German post-Shoah culture. These texts come to be as much about the meaning of the Jewish body as any other single question. The body of the Jew, with all of its implications, itself becomes an icon for the perceived and internalized differences of the sexuality of the Jewish male.

Jurek Becker's description of the narrator Hans as an athlete at the very beginning of the novel forms an epiphany that illuminates the rest of the text, in a manner uncomprehended by the narrator until the conclusion of the work. Hans must complete the swimming test in order to graduate from high school, and his disinterest in doing so reflects one of the images of the Jew in German fiction—the Jew who avoids any physical exertion. One is reminded of the Zionist leader Max Nordau's fin-de-siècle call for Jews to reform their bodies and become "New Muscle Jews" in order to become the physical equal of the Aryans. And yet Becker plays with this standard theme much more consciously than he did in any of his earlier "Jewish" novels.

The scene is set. Hans must take his swimming test and is ordered by one of his schoolmates, in a Prussian schoolboy's tone, to take off his swimsuit and shower before entering the pool. Hans's answer is to punch him in the nose, to which the boy responds, after he gets up, that "he's crazy" (43). The reader is led into the resulting uproar by the teachers who flood into the locker room. Their apparent explanation, which Hans imagines a teacher whispering to the victim, is that he's a Jew: "There are slight sensitivities, which we cannot so easily comprehend" (47). The implication is that Hans did not want to remove his swimsuit because of his physical difference, because of his circumcised penis. But the chapter ends with the revelation, in the narrator's interior monologue, that he is not circumcised. He had no hidden

"Jewish" motivation (in his own understanding of this) to hit his schoolmate, only an objection to his schoolmate's pedantic, Prussian tone. Jews, according to Hans's account of Arno's view, are an invention of those who wish to victimize those labeled as Jews. This powerful scene reveals the reactive moment in Becker's characters; their Jewishness is revealed only in their response to the corrupt world about them. Or so we are led to believe by Hans.

The question of the politics of circumcision among Jews in Germany is accentuated in the recent work of Maxim Biller. Biller, born in 1960 in Prague, emigrated to the Federal Republic in 1970. His volume of short stories on the experience of Jewish life in the contemporary Germany of 1990 contains reflections on this ambiguity associated with making the Jew's body. Biller sees himself (or at least constructs his literary persona) after the model of Joseph Heller, with whom he fantasizes talking about "literature, sex, and Judaism."[59] Thus the definition of the cultural Jew is linked by his imagination (or at least the imagination of his literary voice) with the sexuality of the Jew. In his short story "Betrayal," Biller presents the central problem of Jurek Becker's work: "How can you make a Jew?" or perhaps better stated as "How does the world make Jews?" Like Becker, Biller sees the construction of the Jew's body and his sexual identity as central to his argument. Biller's story stands in a literary tradition that reflects the fascination of fin-de-siècle Jewish writers, such as Mynona (Salomo Friedländer), with the "operated Goy," or how can one make a Jewish body out of that of a non-Jew.[60] Central to both undertakings is circumcision—circumcision not only of the penis but of the heart (following the Christian model of internalization of circumcision).

The protagonist of Biller's tale "Betrayal," Hugo Niehouß, a young journalist, discovers the meaning of his own, uncircumcised body during his first homosexual encounter. He asks his partner, whose penis is circumcised, whether he is Jewish. (He comments that "this was, without a doubt, a very intense form of projection" [188].) His partner replied that "naturally" he wasn't a Jew, rather he had had himself circumcised for medical reasons. "Niehouß heard in his answer a sense of embarrassment. At that point he still had his foreskin, and that was exactly the reason why he suddenly felt so subordinate to this SS hunk—he had, if you want, seen the dead end." Niehouß articulates his anxiety about his difference in terms of the essential model of difference in the world in which he lives—after the Shoah it is the Jew who is the icon of difference. The anxiety about being seen as Jewish is heightened by the sense of self-awareness of the Jew's body. If one feels like a Jew, one's body must be marked, must be different—especially inasmuch as it reveals the Jew within. Once Niehouß discovers that his mother, Lea Sonnenson, was a Jewish survivor, he is suddenly able to articulate his sense of difference, an essential difference that he feels had been the root of his generalized alienation from the world in which he lived. Five weeks after he is told of his mother's Jewish identity by his father, he has himself circumcised by a *mohel* (ritual circumciser) at the Jewish Hospital (191). This change of the body only focused the existing sense of difference, which Niehouß had always sensed within himself. Now it had a focus, a meaning beyond himself. He suffers from "Jewish self-hatred" as diagnosed by the story's narrative voice. His is now not an undifferentiated neurotic self-loathing; it now has a basis in the world in which he lives, the world of the Jew in Germany after the *Churban*, the destruction of the Jews of Europe. Niehouß rejects his Jewishness in becoming a Jew, casting his Jewish survivor mother totally out of his life. For unlike the Jew within, this Jew without could be exorcised and kept at a distance. The story ends when mother and son see one another on a Munich street after a four-year separation, and each ignores the other's presence. He has become, in his mother's and his own estimation, a "smart-mouthed, self-assured Jew" (198). But this leads only to a neurotic self-loathing on his part.

In a later tale, "Glasses, Lara, and the Bells of St. Ursula," Biller incorporates a similar moment. When the Jewish protagonist's non-Jewish girlfriend speaks to him about his "circumcised member" while stroking him, his response, instead of being erotic, is to turn away from her. And her eyes "suddenly turn in upon themselves" (214) when she realizes that his circumcised penis now reflects his self-doubt. The centrality of the act of circumcision in Biller's world can be seen when he constructs the voice of a Jewish woman in his tale of the seemingly hypochondriacal "Cilly," whose Russian boyfriend's uncircumcised "elephant trunk" (145–158) leads directly to her death from heart failure. (She makes love with him even after having been warned against such intense actions by her physician.) It is the Jewish woman's attraction to the uncircumcised member that marks her awareness of the meaning of circumcision as a sign of the undesirability of the Jewish male as a sexual partner. It stresses the Russian's difference, the animal-like sexuality represented by his uncircumcised penis. Throughout Biller's world, circumcision defines identity, but it also defines pathology. It comes to be a sign of the nature of the soul inscribed on the body. It is, however, not incidental that all of Biller's Jewish protagonists are teenagers or young adults. For it is precisely here that the confusion between the essential ambivalence of the sense of self and the impact of an awareness of the meaning of the Jewish body is greatest.

Biller establishes an image of the gay male body that draws upon the internalized sense of difference of the uncircumcised Jew. It is striking to an American reader that it is the circumcised penis that is attractive because it is "exotic" in the German gay community, since it is the "uncut" male who is often deemed attractive in the circumcised world of the American gay community. The autobiography of Andreas Sinakowski, *The Interrogation* (1991), is one of the few contemporary German texts that links Jewish and gay identities.[61] Born in East Berlin in 1960, he was a member of the Secret Police (Stasi) of the former German Democratic Republic from 1979 to 1985, when he received official permission to leave for West Berlin. Sinakowski's volume is one of a spate of recent self-revelatory autobiographies by citizens of German Democratic Republic including the former head of the Stasi, Markus Wolf. Sinakowski left the GDR prior to its collapse, and his text is a self-declared attempt to establish himself in the world of contemporary pan-German gay literature as a double victim of a repressive system, a system which permitted him little choice but to be an internal (and quite "official") spy.

It is fascinating that the "Jewish" aspect of Sinakowski's identity is marginalized in his autobiographic account, yet it constantly reappears to underscore his self-definition as a victim. He sees himself (at least in 1991) as a gay writer who happens to be

Jewish. And yet these images merge in his image of the victim. Sinakowski lives "in the beautiful land of burned flesh" populated by old Nazis (18). It is a world that "praised Hitler yesterday" (63). But the world of Hitler is specifically the world "which banned all Jews out of its realm of power." (87) It is not the image of the gay which marks the victim of the Nazis, but the image of the Jew. Sinakowski's irony aims at the specific denial of the Shoah, a Shoah defined in terms of the murder of the Jews: "Privately fifty percent were always against it. Privately after the war about twenty million Germans had hidden 2.5 Jews. . . . Privately Maria Rōkk has always been against the persecution of the Jews. Privately my friends always knew about 'it.' Privately they never knew anything about it" (97–98). What is missing in Sinakowski's account of his life, especially in his detailed account of his sexual experiences, is anything which differentiates his own body from that of the other gay men he meets and with whom he sleeps. His body is a gay body, not a Jewish body. His solidarity is as a gay East German, even though, given the antifascist rhetoric of the GDR, he uses the images of the persecution of the Jews as his metaphoric frame. He presents himself as the gay victim of the Stasi, just as the Jews were the victims of the Nazis. The two worlds remain separate as Sinakowski's focus remains on establishing his credentials as a gay writer in the new Germany.

Rafael Seligmann's novel, *Rubinstein's Auction*, begins with the incident that gives the novel its name. The eponymous protagonist Jonathan Rubinstein, in his final year in high school, is asked by his attractive Aryan teacher Ms. Taucher, to sit next to her in the classroom. In a manner typical of the counter-culture 1960s in West Germany, she has reorganized the classroom, moving the chairs into a circle so as to intentionally undermine the authoritarian structure of the class. One of the seats next to her is finally taken by Rubinstein, after it was left empty by the rest of the class. She rewards Rubinstein, who is secretly attracted to the teacher in a pubescent manner, by holding his hand. Suddenly all of the male students want to sit next to her, and Rubinstein, flustered by the attention given to him by her and his classmates, is inspired to hold an auction for the seat to give everyone in the class a chance. Eventually one of the students bids a hundred marks and

Rubinstein, still confused by the teacher's actions, gives up his seat to him. The victor's response is to comment: "No sooner does a German woman hold his hand, then Rubinstein auctions her off to the one who offers the most money. Now I understand how you get your money" (9). Rubinstein is taken aback as his offer to share the teacher's attention is read as a typically Jewish act. His own sexuality, torn between his unacceptable attraction for his teacher, who is both an authority figure and a non-Jew, is exposed as "Jewish." He quickly offers to donate the money to a good cause. His tormentor suggests giving it to the synagogue fund.

The central theme in Seligmann's novel is the confusing juxtaposition of Jewishness and male sexuality—each coming to represent the other. Rubinstein's impotence in the face of non-Jewish women; his complex, sexualized, but unrealized relationship with Jewish women; even his attempted seduction by his teacher and his eventual relationship with the daughter of a former member of the SS all relate to this confusion between sexual identity and the essence of Jewishness. And, as with Becker, at its core lies the very body of the Jew. In one of the central passages of the novel, Rubinstein, like the protagonist of Becker's earlier novel *The Boxer*, tries to understand what exactly makes him different, what exactly makes him a Jew. It is Sabbath morning and Rubinstein is sitting in the Reichenbach Synagogue in Munich:

> Why do I even come here? What do I have in common with these people? That we are all members of the covenant with the Lord? What does that really mean? Our forefathers had their religion, their teaching, and tradition. And we? What do we have? The "covenant" has become degraded to a community of the circumcised. German-Jewry so to say has come down to the prick. The covenant with the Lord now consists of a long chain of sacrificed foreskins. And what do I have from these sacrifices? A more sensitive prick, nothing else. Maybe that's the reason I spend the whole day thinking about nothing but my cock. The other guys in my class do the same thing. And in spite of that I am different. Only because my foreskin is missing? That's where it begins. The goyim supply the rest. (89–90)

Here too, it is circumcision that marks the Jewish male body as different, which provides a different relationship to the female, both Jewish and non-Jewish, and marks the Jew's psyche as different as well.

Among Seligmann's contemporaries, none is more brittle in regard to the representation of the "negative symbiosis" of Jews into contemporary "German" society than the Viennese poet-novelist Robert Schindel. Schindel was born in 1944 and was hidden in occupied Vienna after his parents were sent to Auschwitz. In the early 1990s the Austrian situation, with Kurt Waldheim as President, became emblematic for a world which is so tolerant of the past as to make the present life of Jews in Austria untenable. Even Sinakowski evokes this in his autobiography (108). In Schindel's best-selling novel *Born* (1992), he depicts the lives of two men who are "born" into specific roles—the sons of a survivor and a high Nazi functionary.[62] Like Seligmann, Schindel places the male Jewish body central to his understanding of the necessary contortions Jewish males must make to function in a contemporary Austria in which the old, anti-Semitic rhetoric is ubiquitous. He notes, for example, the memory of his Jewish protagonist's non-Jewish girlfriend: "He remembered that Käthe, during her first night in Vienna, said that the thing about him that pleased her best was his racial sign (*Rassenmerkmal*). He had laughed and thought about his circumcised penis, but she brushed her finger teasingly over his nose. Then he embraced her and explained to her, while kissing her, that it wasn't a racial sign and that the Jews weren't a race and so on" (137). But the Jews are a "race" in the eyes of the Austrians in that they are seen as distant and different.

For the Jewish writer this difference becomes part of the literary sensitivity of the Jew, part of his manner of representing the world in which he lives. For this difference is experienced by "blonde mother's son" as "sedimentary bone-Hebrew" (*sedimentiertes Knochenhebräisch*) (14). It is in the language of the Jew that this difference is inscribed by the culture. The Jews speak differently; they have a "special relationship to language." This difference, like their internalization of the meaning of circumcision, shapes the way they see the world. When Jews are among themselves, they mock those Jews who are "Judeocentric" by "contorting their mouths and speaking with a Jewish accent (*mauschelnd*)" (142). Despite the protagonist's pure German, the

German which is the novelist's tool, he is given to understand that his language, too, is different: "'What does that mean, that my language has something Jewish in it? I write a perfect German.' 'That's how you are different from the Germans. In contrast to them, you have to prove it'" (275). The internalized sense of the difference of the Jew's circumcised body becomes the difference of the writer.

The topos of circumcision as the sign of the problem of Central European Jewry after the Shoah appears within other literary contexts. Simon Louvish, the brilliant Anglo-Israeli novelist, presented the self-image of the "mad" Hungarian Jew, Yerachmiel Farkash-Fenschechter, whose life as "Friedrich Nietzsche" in a Jerusalem asylum is one of the focuses of the first volume of his Avrom Blok trilogy written in the late 1980s. This self-representation is historically associated with the act of circumcision: "By the time the Kecskemét mohel was cutting into the poor babe's ding dong the old order in Europe had crumbled." As an ironic side-bar, Louvish offers his micro-history of the meanings ascribed to circumcision as seen from an Israeli perspective:

[Circumcision] was widespread in Pharaonic Egypt, they say. The Lord said to Abraham: "And ye shall circumcise the flesh of your foreskin, and it shall be a token of the covenant between me and you." "Sure, sure, Boss," said Abe, who had been promised a profusion of goodies. Siggy Freud, on the other hand, laid the blame on Moses, and blew the gaffe on the whole damn schmeer: "Circumcision," said he, "is the symbolic substitute for the castration which the primal father once inflicted upon his sons in the plenitude of his absolute power, and whoever accepted that symbol was showing by it that he was prepared to submit to the father's will, even if it imposed the most painful sacrifice on him." But some anthropologists said it derived from the clipping of the vine, without which it would bear no fruit. A wag in Jerusalem's Ta'amon Café, though, had the last word on the issue, claiming Jewish boys were circumcised so that their foreskins should not get caught in their zips.[63]

This theological-historical discourse about circumcision, as mirrored in Louvish's micro-history, is of course ironic. His answer to it is to dismiss it as trivial— circumcision is a practical social necessity given the "modern" replacement of buttons with zippers. For Louvish, neither Abraham nor Sigmund Freud can explain the centrality of Jewish male sexuality to the Jewish male self-image (here the "mad" Jew has so internalized the world which tried to destroy him in the Shoah that he became "Friedrich Nietzsche," the very philosopher claimed by his tormentors). But Louvish understands the importance of the act of circumcision for Central European Jewish males—it made them into Jews and stressed the difference in their sexuality. The Jew in Europe, of course, was traditionally seen as sexually deviant.

Louvish's image reflects a European tradition according to which Jewish sexuality is corrupt and corrupting. The definition of the Jew as the member of the convenant—one who is circumcised—places the focus on the nature of Jewish male sexuality in a unique manner. The Jewish male's psyche, like that of his body, is different. This is an ancient topos that harks back to Tacitus's description of the Jews as the "projectissima ad libidinem gens"—the most sensual of peoples. By the close of the nineteenth century it had become part of the German medical-forensic literature. A standard forensic study of the time described the nature of the Jew thus: "Further it must be noted that the sexuality of the Semitic race is in general powerful, yes, often greatly exaggerated."[64] Or as John S. Billings, the leading American student of Jewish illness and the head of the Surgeon General's Library in Washington, noted, that when Jewish males are integrated into Western culture they "are probably more addicted to . . . sexual excesses than their ancestors were."[65] The physiognomy of the "sexual" male, like that of the representation of the Jew within modern culture, is "dark" (Biérent), or has a "dark complexion" (Bouchereau), or has "brown skin" and "long noses" (Mantegazza).[66] Jewish physicians of the period understood the implications of this charge. The Viennese Jewish physician Hanns Sachs, who was involved in the earliest development of psychoanalysis, commented in his memoirs on this version of the "timeworn prejudice that the Jewish...mind was abnormally preoccupied with matters of a sexual nature."[67] Some Jewish scientists of the fin-de-siècle, such as the Munich neurologist Leopold Löwenfeld, were forced to confront this charge and were unable to dismiss it. He argued, in a study of sexual constitution published in 1911, that the role of racial predisposition in structuring the sexual drives could be confused by the mediating role that climate, nutrition, or culture can play.[68] But he, and his Jewish contemporaries such as Iwan Bloch, have no doubt that racial identity does play some role in structuring sexual constitution. Others, like one of the original founders of the Vienna Psychoanalytic Association and Sigmund Freud's Jewish lodge brother Eduard Hitschmann, believed that "neuroses, psychoses, suicides, etc., play a more important role among the Jews . . . they have many more sexual experiences than others and—a fact that must be particularly emphasized—take them much more seriously."[69] The Jews' mental states, specifically the psychopathologies associated with the Jews, are closely linked to their intense sexuality.

The Jew as Child Abuser and Circumcision as Child Abuse

The psychopathologies associated with the Jews differ from culture to culture over time. With the near universality of surgical circumcision in post-Shoah America, the circumcised penis is no longer an absolute mark of Jewish difference.[70] In post-Shoah Germany (both East and West and together) it still remains a sign of the male Jewish body.[71] (The exoticism of the circumcised gay male is simply a romantic reversal of this image within a highly marginalized social group.) Indeed, Great Britain, where Simon Louvish now lives and works, is in an intermediate position concerning the ubiquitousness of infant male circumcision. The British circumcise their male infants more frequently than do the Germans, but less frequently than do the Americans. Post-Shoah Germany remains a culture where circumcision is not only a mark of difference but one that continues to be associated with the older, negative tradition of the perverse sexuality of the Jews.

This can be seen in the discourse about circumcision, for example, in the most recent book by the widely read and widely respected German psychoanalyst Alice Miller. Miller, long a resident of Switzerland, broke with traditional psychoanalysis over the issue of the reality of trauma as the origin of neurosis. Like Sándor Ferenczi at the end of his life, she argued that Freud was wrong in having abandoned the seduction theory. In her 1988 book *Banished Knowledge: Facing Childhood Injuries,* she argues that "*crimes against children represent the most frequent of all types of crime*" (her emphasis). However, "child abuse" is not only the physical and psychological maltreatment of children. For Miller it extends into the realm of the adult's treatment of the child's body, "the actual physical mutilation of small children," and thus into a devastating critique of "the cruel mutilation of children's sexual organs."[72] Over three pages, she cites the American anthropologist Desmond Morris's attack on male infant circumcision.[73] He traces the tradition of circumcision from its religious roots, through its medicalization as a therapy against masturbatory insanity and the predisposition of the uncircumcised penis to cancer of the penis. Alice Miller sees this as a form of torture: "What eventually happens to the person who was mutilated as a child? When a small child is tortured by ignorant adults, won't he have to take his revenge later in life?" The form of this revenge is very specific for Alice Miller.

For Miller it is a "fictitious claim that circumcision is performed in the interests of the child."[74] This is the medical profession's standard defense of the large-scale practice of infant male circumcision. But for Miller it "constitutes a cruelty that will later encourage the adult to indulge in similar, also denied, cruelties and will invest his deeds with the legitimacy of a clear conscience." Here the attack on surgical circumcision is made an attack on the psychological results of the practice for every circumcised male child. Circumcision is "outlandish behavior" which "mutilates" children. Even when circumcision is a religious obligation, it remains a "cruelty . . . because of the ignorance of the priests." What happens to these "mutilated" male children in society? "He is bound to avenge himself." This revenge is inflicted on the children of the "abused" individual in the form of the repetition of the act, but even more so these "victims" can also become "criminals." For Alice Miller all criminals were once victims. Only the individual who can "confront his own past" will avoid such asocial actions.

Now Miller's rhetoric about circumcision has its own tradition within modern psychology. In 1950 Erik H. Erikson, the German-

Jewish psychoanalyst, saw the ritual of circumcision among the Jews as the way the Jew "'asked for it.'"[75] "It" in this context is the unwanted attention from anti-Semites which lead to the Shoah. This view has its obscure roots in Sigmund Freud's own association of circumcision with the continuity of anti-Semitism in his 1938 study of *Moses and Monotheism*.[76] But in a post-Shoah Germany, any such direct labeling of circumcision as a Jewish problem would be taboo. Rather, Miller's view is very similar to the radical feminist critique of Judaism, found in Germany during the 1980s, as the ultimate patriarchal religion.[77] The Jew is rarely mentioned, but all of the associations of the older, anti-Semitic representation of the Jew are attributed to "religious patriarchy." This representation is continuous with German images past and present of the Jews as the font of all evil. In a famous case of media censorship in 1979, the West German television authorities were forbidden to broadcast a program on anti-Semitism in the Black Forest in which one of those interviewed globally referred to Jews as "circumcised fools."[78] In Miller's text, too, the discourse about the Jewish male body as the representation of all "evil, destructiveness, and perversion" represents a continuity with the past. For not all males are thought to be circumcised, but all Jewish males are. The social category of the Jewish male is the one that exclusively consists of damaged and abused individuals, who themselves damage and abuse. German-speaking Jewish males confront this attitude toward their own body, and therefore, their own psyche, at every turn in German culture. They are different, and this difference is embedded in their sexuality.

All circumcised males are abused children. In the European context, it is the male Jew who is thus labeled as inherently different and corrupted. As we have seen within the two novels, circumcision defines the Jewish male—even within his own fantasy. The central image is that all male Jews (whether they are or are not circumcised) are abused children and therefore abusing adults. This abuse is played out in two of the novels under discussion through the representation of the conflicts between the generations, between Becker's and Seligmann's teenaged males and their parents. This conflict is understood to be an essential part of the development of the child, but it is placed within these texts as a reflex of the Jewish identity of these children. Becker's father figure, with his link to the Shoah and his revengeful nature, and the German-Jewish parents in Seligmann's novel are exemplars of the focus of any child's Oedipal fantasies. But here they are also Jews who have themselves been abused. In the text this abuse is at the hands of the entire society in which they dwell. They are damaged because of their historical experience as victims and survivors. Miller can argue only on the level of the individual, so circumcision becomes the mark of the Jews' abuse of the Jews. It is clear that there are analogous discussions of male sexuality in the work of North American writers such as Philip Roth and Mordechai Richler. But the obsessive focus on the physical difference of the male Jew as the icon of the sexual difference ascribed to him is missing. Alexander Portnoy's masturbatory fantasies and Joshua Shapiro's sexual difficulties are parodies of the sexual taboos associated with the representation of the Jew. (In Bernard Malamud's *The Assistant* [1957] the relationship between the lack of circumcision and the brutal sexuality of the non-Jew arises in the context of the rape of a Jewish woman by her father's non-Jewish "assistant." And it is resolved by the rapist's expiation of his act in having himself circumcised and converting to Judaism.) These representations, like Seligmann's image, represent the endogenous sexual selectivity associated with the Jew in Jewish religious practice. For Anglo-Jewish writers the image of circumcision as the keystone to the nature of the Jewish body seems to vanish. The Anglo-Jewish writer Clive Sinclair, in his short story "The Promised Land," employs the metaphor of circumcision to contrast his own sense of Diaspora identity and the "true" Jewish identity of the Israeli:

> "'Slicha, efor Rehov Gruniman?' I say to the locals, but cannot understand the reply. I don't blame Rivka, she didn't write the textbook after all, but outside the supermarkets my vocabulary is useless. There's one version of the Bible in which Moses attempts to extricate himself from God's command by stammering that his tongue is not circumcised. Well, that's exactly how I feel in Israel: I am Jewish, but my tongue is not circumcised. "Ani lo mdaber ivrit." I say. I do not speak Hebrew."[79]

The internalization of the circumcised Jew as the image of the true Jew ironically presented by Clive Sinclair reflects the European tradition that circumcision represents the essence of Jewish identity. This image, one which is of such great power within German culture that even Friedrich Schiller could evoke the image of the male Jew as having been born circumcised, reflects the need to make an absolute distinction between the nature of the Jew and that of the Aryan.[80] In a recent Jewish context in German, parallel images are to be found in Robert Schindel's novel *Born* as well as in the short story "Betrayal" by Maxim Biller discussed above. Biller's central character undergoes circumcision once he discovers himself to be the son of a Jewish mother and, as a result, he begins to speak more and more markedly Jewish ("Jiddeln") (192). Biller's protagonists tongue is circumcised through the act of circumcision. Biller in no way evokes a simple biological reflex. Rather, the sign of circumcision reflected his protagonist's sudden awareness of the Jewishness projected onto his character, even to his use of language.

The meaningful distinction between Jew and non-Jew based on the practice of infant male circumcision becomes less and less possible as the practice becomes more and more widespread. Among Jews in Central Europe, as can be seen in the images evoked by Becker and Biller, the debate about circumcision reaches back into the 1840s, and the practice among Jews is by no means universal at the beginning of the twentieth century. Indeed, Samuel Holdheim, the most radical exponent of reformed Judaism, argued that circumcision was in no way to be understood as a necessity of male Jewish identity. This ambivalence became a touchstone for the establishment of the internalized sense of the Jewish male body. The primary means of avoiding these confrontations was to understate the significance of circumcision.

For the post-Shoah generation, circumcision becomes an external mark of difference which defines the Jewish body within the body politic. Authors such as Becker, Biller, and Seligmann can evoke this difference without any hesitation as the mark of the characters' sense of isolation and distance from the Aryan body. The culture in which they live remains permeated with an intense sense of the difference of the Jew. Indeed, a recent survey established that every eighth German holds anti-Semitic attitudes.[81] But in evoking this anxiety about their own identity, they also draw its validity as a marker of their own identity into question. Through their projection of the image of the damaged body of the Jew into their fictive creation, they enable the reader to see this difference (and to judge its internalization). The readers' judgment—like the authors'—draws the self-doubt of the Jewish male into question—or at least frames it within the tradition of the narrative of adolescent development. Biller, Becker, and Seligmann argue for acculturation. They see the creation of a new sense of Jewish identity in the new Germany not as desirable but as necessary. Unlike Henryk Broder, they do not advocate a removal of the Jew from German culture. Whether Jews in the United States or Israel approve of this development or not, whether non-Jewish Germans are aware of it or not, there is a new sense of diaspora-Jewish identity evolving in Germany. Thus Jewish writers, especially male writers, need to draw the Jew's difference, as Alice Miller's work represents it, into question. This difference is what these authors inscribe on the bodies of their fictive characters so as to foreground the implications of the Jewish male body—their own bodies—in the struggle for a male Jewish identity in contemporary Germany.

Notes

1. A recent conference in Munich was devoted to the topic of the new role of young Jews in Germany and the problems they face in defining a Diaspora experience in the new Germany. *Junge Juden in Deutschland: Protokoll einer Tagung* (Munich: Jugend und Kulturzentrum der israelitischen Kultusgemeinde München, 1991).
2. See my *The Jew's Body* (New York: Routledge, 1991).
3. Jacob Wassermann, *My Life as German and Jew* (London: George Allen & Unwin, 1933), 156.
4. Wassermann, *My Life*, 156.
5. On the cultural background for this concept, see Jacob Katz, *Out of the Ghetto: The Social Background of Jewish Emancipation 1770–1870* (Cambridge, Mass.: Harvard University Press, 1973), and Rainer Erb and Werner Bergmann, *Die Nachtseite der Judenemanzipation: Der Widerstand gegen die Integration der Juden in Deutschland 1780–1860* (Berlin: Metropol, 1989).

6. Albert Drach, *Das große Protokoll gegen Zwetschkenbaum* (Munich: Carl Hanser, 1989), 20.
7. *Herr Moritz Deutschösterreicher: Eine jüdische Erzählung zwischen Assimilation und Exil*, ed. Jürgen Egyptien (Vienna: Droschl, 1988), 5.
8. Susann Heenen-Wolff, *Im Haus des Henkers: Gespräche in Deutschland* (Frankfurt /Main: Dvorah, 1992), 68–69.
9. Jacob R. Marcus, *The Colonial American Jew, 1492–1776*. 3 vols. (Detroit: Wayne State University Press, 1970), 2: 984. On the American tradition, see Jay Brodbar-Nemzer, Peter Conrad, and Shelly Tenenbaum, "American Circumcision Practices and Social Reality," *Sociology and Social Research* 71 (1987): 275–79.
10. Richard Andree, *Zur Volkskunde der Juden* (Leipzig: Velhagen & Klasing, 1881), 157.
11. Humphrey Carpenter, *A Serious Character: The Life of Ezra Pound* (Boston: Houghton Mifflin, 1988), 362.
12. Richard Burton, *Love, War and Fancy: The Customs and Manners of the East from the Writings on 'The Arabian Nights,'* ed. Kenneth Walker (London: W. Kimber, 1964), 106.
13. See the exemplary use of the discussion of the Jews as a race in Richard Weinberg, "Zur Theorie einer anatomischen Rassensystematik," *Archiv für Rassen- und Gesellschafts-Biologie* 2 (1905): 198–214, especially 205–6. Weinberg notes ten different physical characteristics that determine the definition of racial difference.
14. A summary of the German-Jewish views on the meaning of this practice in the 1920s can be found in the essay on "Berit mila" in the *Jüdisches Lexikon*, ed. Georg Herlitz and Bruno Kirschner, 4 vols. in 5 (Berlin: Jüdischer Verlag, 1927–30), 1: 861–66. This essay stresses seven different readings of infant circumcision: as a hygienic practice, as the remains of older practices of castration, as the mark of stigmatization, as a sign of tribal membership, as a test of the child, as a sanctification of the penis, as a prophylaxis against incest. For the latter, psychoanalytic theory is invoked. On the Jewish views of the meaning and function of this practice see J. David Bleich, *Judaism and Healing: Halakhic Perspectives* (New York: KTAV, 1981), 47–50. On the history of the Jewish tradition see Julius Preuss, *Biblisch-talmudische Medizin: Beiträge zur Geschichte der Heilkunde und der Kultur überhaupt* (Berlin: S. Karger, 1927), 279. Compare John J. Collins, "A Symbol of Otherness: Circumcision and Salvation in the First Century," in Jacob Neusner and Ernest S. Frerichs, eds., *"To See Ourselves as Others See Us": Christians, Jews, "Others," in Late Antiquity* (Chico, Calif.: Scholars Press, 1985), 163–85 and Nigel Allan, "A Polish Rabbi's Circumcision Manual," *Medical History* 33 (1989): 247–54.
15. Anonymous, "Die rituelle Beschneidung bei den Juden und ihre Gefahren," *Journal für Kinderkrankheiten* 59 (1872): 367–72.

16. G. S. Thompson, "Circumcision—A Barbarous and Unnecessary Mutilation," *The British Medical Journal* 1 (1920): 437.
17. See in this context the most recent and most extensive American presentation of this argument: Rosemary Romberg, ed., *Circumcision: The Painful Dilemma* (South Hadley, Mass.: Bergin & Garvey, 1985), which was published in conjunction with INTACT Educational Foundation. The most recent debate about the medical implications in the United States of this widespread practice was begun by E. N. Preston, "Wither the Foreskin? A Consideration of Routine Neonatal Circumcision," *Journal of the American Medical Association* 216 (1970): 1853–58. In this vein see also Edward Wallerstein, "Circumcision: The Uniquely American Medical Enigma," *The Urologic Clinics of North America* 12 (1985): 123–32, which discusses the debates about infection in the context of an attack on the practice. In this context see Moisés Trachtenberg and Philip Slotkin, "Circumcision, Crucifixion, and Anti-Semitism: The Antithetical Character of Ideologies and Their Symbol Which Contain Crossed Lines," *International Review of Psycho-Analysis* 16 (1989): 459–71; E. A. Grossman and N. A. Posner, "The Circumcision Controversy: An Update," *Obstetrics and Gynecological Annual* 13 (1984): 181–95; E. Grossman and N. A. Posner, "Surgical Circumcision of Neonates: A History of its Development," *Obstetrics and Gynecology* 58 (1981): 241–46; S. J. Waszak, "The Historic Significance of Circumcision," *Obstetrics and Gynecology* 51 (1978): 499–501.

    The anthropological literature on this topic is often critical and superficial, see Desmond Morris, *Bodywatching* (London: Jonathan Cape, 1985), 218–20. By far the best anthropological discussion of what the difference of the circumcised body means is to be found in the published work of James Boon, *Other Tribes, Other Scribes* (New York: Cambridge University Press, 1982), 162–68; *Affinities and Extremes* (Chicago: University of Chicago Press, 1990), 55–60; see also his unpublished paper "Circumscribing Circumcision / Uncircumcision" (1990), in which the meaning of the act of circumcision is most intelligently and most sophisticatedly drawn into question. The reading of the Jewish practice in the light of the history of nineteenth-century anthropology is extraordinarily well documented in Howard Eilberg-Schwartz, *The Savage in Judaism: An Anthropology of Israelite Religion and Ancient Judaism* (Bloomington: Indiana University Press, 1990), 141–76. See also Moisés Trachtenberg, *Psicanálise da circuncisão* (Porto Alegre: Sagra, 1990), and Claude Lévi-Strauss, "Exode sur Exode," *Homme* 28 (1988): 106–7.
18. See my essays "Jewish Writers and German Letters: Anti-Semitism and the Hidden Language of the Jews," *The Jewish Quarterly Review* 77 (1986–87): 119–48.
19. Jakov Lind, the Viennese-Jewish novelist, long a resident of Great Britain, stated it most clearly in his autobiography:

All he needed was a foreskin,
otherwise he felt all right.
He lived it up like a Duke on his castle,
with pheasant shooting and old paintings,
all he needed was a little foreskin,
otherwise he was all right.

He lived it up like the Roi de Soleil
on Trianon, they feed him oysters with a spoon,
all he needed was a bit of skin,
otherwise he was all right.

He lived it up like Zeus in the Parthenon,
makes it only with Goddesses,
all he needs is a bit more skin
and everything will be fine.

Jakov Lind, *Counting My Steps: An Autobiography* (London: Macmillan, 1969), 135–36.

20. Rudolf Virchow, "Gesamtbericht über die Farbe der Haut, der Haare und der Augen der Schulkinder in Deutschland," *Archiv für Anthropologie* 16 (1886): 275–475.
21. Felix von Luschan, *Völker, Rasse und Sprachen* (Berlin: Welt Verlag, 1922), 169.
22. On the colonial implications of the debate about circumcision in Great Britain and its association with Islam as well as the Jews see Ronald Hyam, *Empire and Sexuality: The British Experience* (Manchester: Manchester University Press, 1990), 76–79.
23. There is no comprehensive study of the German debates on circumcision. See Julius Preuss, "Die Beschneidung nach Bibel und Talmud," *Wiener klinische Rundschau* 11 (1897): 708–9, 724–27; J. Alkvist, "Geschichte der Circumcision," *Janus* 30 (1926): 86–104, 152–71, as well as Samuel Krauss, *Geschichte der jüdischen Ärzte vom frühsten Mittelalter bis zur Gleichberechtigung* (Vienna: A. S. Bettelheim-Stiftung, 1930), 157–58.
24. One can note that at least one Jewish convert to Christianity in the sixteenth century, Antonius Margaritha, while stressing the evident pain of the infant, does not condemn the ritual practice. See his *Der gantz Jüdisch glaub* (Augsburg: Heinrich Steyner, 1530), H1v–H2r. On Margaritha see my *Jewish Self-Hatred: Anti-Semitism and the Hidden Language of the Jews* (Baltimore: The Johns Hopkins University Press, 1986), 62–66.
25. The authorized German editions of Mantegazza are *Die Physiologie der Liebe*, trans. Eduard Engel (Jena: Hermann Costenoble, 1877); *Die Hygiene der Liebe*, trans. R. Teutscher (Jena: Hermann Costenoble [1877]); *Anthropologisch-kulturhistorische Studien über die Geschlechts-*

verhältnisse des Menschen (Jena: Hermann Costenoble [1891]).

26. On Mantegazza, see Giovanni Landucci, *Darwinismo a Firenze: Tra scienza e ideologia (1860–1900),* (Florence: Leo S. Olschki, 1977), 107–28.
27. The relevant passages in the German edition, *Anthropologisch-kulturhistorische Studien über die Geschlechtsverhältnisse des Menschen* (op. cit.), are on 132–37. All of the quotations from Mantegazza are to the English translation: Paolo Mantegazza, *The Sexual Relations of Mankind,* trans. Samuel Putnam (New York: Eugenics Publishing., 1938).
28. Spinoza's text, often cited and often commented on in the nineteenth century, labels circumcision as the primary reason for the survival of the Jews as "they have incurred universal hatred by cutting themselves off completely from all other peoples." It also made them "effeminate" and thus unlikely to assume a political role in the future. Benedict Spinoza, *The Political Works,* trans. A. G. Wernham (Oxford: Oxford University Press, 1958), 63.
29. Mantegazza, *Sexual Relations,* 99.
30. Edvard Westermarck, *The History of Marriage,* 3 vols. (London: Macmillan, 1921), 1: 561.
31. Mantegazza, *Sexual Relations,* 98.
32. Mantegazza, *Sexual Relations,* 98–99.
33. August Forel, *Die sexuelle Frage* (Munich: Ernst Reinhardt, 1906), 172; *The Sexual Question,* trans. C. F. Marshall (New York: Medical Art Agency, 1922), 158. Forel cites Edward Westermarck as his authority.
34. William Osler, "Israel and Medicine" (1914), in William Osler, *Men and Books,* ed. Earl F. Nation (Pasadena, Calif.: Castle Press, 1959), 56.
35. Ernest Crawley, *The Mystic Rose: A Study of Primitive Marriage* (London: Macmillan, 1902), 138.
36. J.H.F. Autenrieth, *Abbhandlung über den Ursprung der Beschneidung* (Tübingen: Heinrich Laupp, 1829).
37. John Lubbock, *The Origin of Civilization and the Primitive Condition of Man* (1870; Chicago: University of Chicago Press, 1978), 237.
38. Lubbock, *The Origin,* 243.
39. Dr. Hacker, "Die Bescheidung der Juden, ein Ueberrest der Barbarei dieses Volkes, und ein Ersatz für seine früheren Menschenopfer," *Medicinischer Argos* 5 (1843): 375–79.
40. Wilhelm Wundt, *Elements of Folk Psychology: Outlines of a Psychological History of the Development of Mankind,* trans. Edward Leroy Schaub (London: George Allen & Unwin, 1916), 445.
41. Wundt, *Elements,* 498.
42. *Philo,* trans. F. H. Colson, 12 vols. (Cambridge, Mass.: Harvard University Press, 1953–63), 7: 103–5 (*De specialibus legibus,* 1: 4–7). See Theodore James, "Philo on Circumcision," *South African Medical Journal* 50 (1976): 1409–12.
43. Roy S. Wolper, "Circumcision as Polemic in the Jew Bill of 1753: The Cutter Cut?" *Eighteenth-Century Life* 7 (1982): 28–36.

44. See my *Sexuality: An Illustrated History* (New York: Wiley, 1989).
45. Samuel Holdheim, *Über die Beschneidung zunächst in religiös-dogmatischer Beziehung* (Schwerin: C. Kürschner, 1844).
46. J. Bergson, *Die Beschneidung vom historischen, kritischen und medizinischen Standpunkt* (Berlin: Th. Scherk/Athenaeum, 1844).
47. Dr. Wolfers, "Ueber die Beschneidung der Judenkinder," *Zeitschrift für Staatsarzneikunde* 9 (1825): 205–9.
48. See the discussion in M. G. Salomon, *Die Beschneidung, historisch und medizinische beleuchtet* (Braunschweig: Vieweg, 1844).
49. Dr. Klein, "Die rituelle Circumcision, eine sanitätspolizeiliche Frage," *Allgemeine Medizinische Zentral-Zeitung* 22 (1853): 368–69.
50. S. Arnhold, *Die Beschneidung und ihre Reform* (Leipzig: n. p., 1847), 50–51.
51. Lea Fleischmann's work provides an account of growing up as a Jewish girl and woman in Germany: *Dies is nicht mein Land: Eine Jüdin verlässt die Bundesrepublik* (Hamburg: Hoffman and Campe, 1980); her account of her early life in Israel (as an adult), *Ich bin Israelin: Erfahrung in einem orientalischen Land* (Hamburg: Hoffman and Campe, 1982); as well as her two volumes of short stories, *Nichts ist so, wie es uns scheint: Jüdische Geschichten* (Hamburg: Rasch und Röhring, 1985), and *Abrahams Heimkehr: Geschichten zu den jüdischen Feiertage* (Hamburg: Rasch und Röhring, 1989). In all of these contexts male writers evoke the question of their sexual identity. Barbara Honigmann's *Roman von einem Kind* (Frankfurt/Main: Luchterhand, 1989), which is actually six interconnected tales, also represents early childhood awareness without an analogous attention to the politics of the body.
52. Esther Dischereit, *Joëmis Tisch. Eine jüdische Geschichte* (Frankfurt/Main: Suhrkamp, 1988), 11.
53. Irene Dische, *Fromme Lügen*, trans. Otto Bayer and Monika Elwenspoek (Frankfurt/Main: Eichborn, 1989), 5–75. See also her recent *Der Doktor braucht ein Heim*, trans. Reinhard Kaiser (Frankfurt/Main: Suhrkamp, 1990).
54. Jane E. Gilbert, *Ich Musste Mich vom Hass befreien: Eine Jüdin emigriert nach Deutschland* (Bern: Scherz, 1989), 204.
55. Susan Neiman, *Slow Fire: Jewish Notes from Berlin* (New York: Schocken, 1992), ix. The references are to the uncorrected galleys.
56. Dories Dörrie, *Love, Pain and Whole Damn Thing*, trans. John E. Woods (New York: Viking, 1989), 35–6. The original is *Liebe, Schmerz und das ganze verdammte Zeug* (Zurich: Diogenes, 1987).
57. All references are to *Bronsteins Kinder* (Frankfurt/Main: Suhrkamp, 1986). Unless noted, all translations are mine.
58. All references are to Rafael Seligmann, *Rubinsteins Versteigerung* (Frankfurt/Main: Eichborn, 1989). For the prior publishing history of the novel, see Henryk M. Broder, "Rubinsteins Beschwerden," *Die Zeit*, 18 August 1989, 13.

59. Maxim Biller, *Wenn ich einmal reich und tot bin* (Cologne: Kiepenheuer und Witsch, 1990), 18.
60. *The Jew's Body*, 205–7.
61. Andreas Sinakowski, *Das Verhör* (Berlin: Basisdruck, 1991).
62. Robert Schindel, *Gebürtig* (Frankfurt/Main: Suhrkamp, 1992).
63. Simon Louvish, *The Therapy of Avram Blok: A Phantasm of Israel among the Nations* (London: Flamingo, 1990), 143. Unexpurgated version of the original novel, published in 1985.
64. Erich Wulffen, *Der Sexualverbrecher* (Berlin: P. Langenscheidt, 1910), 302. This was considered to be one of the major innovative contributions to criminology of the day. See the review in the *Jahrbuch für sexuelle Zwischenstufen* NF 3 (1911): 376–78.
65. John S. Billings, "Vital Statistics of the Jews," *North American Review* 153 (1891): 70–84.
66. All of these fin-de-siècle sources are cited by Havelock Ellis, *Studies in the Psychology of Sex*, 7 vols. (Philadelphia: F. A. Davis, 1900–1928), 5: 185–86.
67. Hanns Sachs, *Freud: Master and Friend* (Cambridge, Mass.: Harvard University Press, 1946), 19.
68. Leopold Löwenfeld, *Über die sexuelle Konstitution und andere Sexualprobleme* (Wiesbaden: J. F. Bergmann, 1911), 75–76.
69. *Protokolle der Wiener Psychoanalytischen Vereinigung*, ed. Herman Nunberg and Ernst Federn, 4 vols. (Frankfurt/Main: Fischer, 1976–81), 2: 41; translation from *Minutes of the Vienna Psychoanalytic Society*, trans. M. Nunberg, 4 vols. (New York: International Universities Press, 1962–75), 2: 45.
70. On the American tradition, see Jay Brodbar-Nemzer, Peter Conrad, and Shelly Tenenbaum, "American Circumcision Practices and Social Reality," *Sociology and Social Research* 71 (1987): 275–79.
71. See note 23.
72. Alice Miller, *Banished Knowledge: Facing Childhood Injuries*, trans. Leila Vennewitz (New York: Doubleday, 1990), 135–39. See Lawrence Birken, "From Seduction Theory to Oedipus Complex: A Historical Analysis," *New German Critique* 43 (1988): 83–96.
73. Desmond Morris, *Bodywatching* (London: Jonathan Cape, 1985), 218–20.
74. All of the following quotations are taken from Miller, *Banished Knowledge*, 135–43.
75. See the discussion of Erikson in my *Difference and Pathology: Stereotypes of Sexuality, Race, and Madness* (Ithaca, N.Y.: Cornell University Press, 1985), 31–32.
76. See in this context: Susann Heenen-Wolff, "Les travaux de Freud sur Moïse et sa relation au judaïsme et à l'antisémitisme," *Le Coq-Héron* 120 (1991): 9–17; David Bakan, "A Note on Freud's Idea that Moses Was an Egyptian as Scriptural and Traditional," *Journal of the History of the*

Behavioral Sciences (1989): 163–64; Ritchie Robertson, "Freud's Testament: *Moses and Monotheism*," in Edward Timms and Naomi Segal, eds., *Freud in Exile* (New Haven, Conn.: Yale University Press, 1988), 80–89; Michael P. Carroll, "*Moses and Monotheism* and the Psychoanalytic Study of Early Christian Mythology," *Journal of Psychohistory* 15 (1988): 295–310; Philip Rieff, "Intimations of Therapeutic Truth: Decoding Appendix G in *Moses and Monotheism*," *Humanities in Society* 4 (1981): 197–201; Jean Jofen, "A Freudian Interpretation of Freud's *Moses and Monotheism*," *Michigan Academician* 12 (1979–80): 231–40; Edwin R. Wallace IV, "The Psychodynamic Determinants of *Moses and Monotheism*," *Psychiatry* 40 (1977): 79–87; M. S. Bergmann, "Moses and the Evolution of Freud's Jewish Identity," *Israeli Annals of Psychiatry* 14 (1976): 3–26.

77. Susannah Heschel, "Jüdisch-feministische Theologie und Antijudaismus in christlich-feministischer Theologie," in Leonore Siegele-Wenschkewitz, ed., *Verdrängte Vergangenheit, die uns bedrängt: Feministische Theologie in der Verantwortung für die Geschichte* (Munich: Chr. Kaiser, 1988), 54–103.
78. "Völkische Stimmen," *Der Spiegel* 29 (16 July 1979): 46.
79. Clive Sinclair, "The Promised Land," *Hearts of Gold* (London: Allison & Busby, 1979), 27.
80. See my essay, "The Indelibility of Circumcision," *Koroth* (Jerusalem), 9 (1991): 23–41.
81. *Der Spiegel* 4 (1992): 41–50.

PART FOUR

Concluding Voices

11. In Defense of Ambiguity

Susan Neiman

I was asked not to write a scholarly paper for this conference, and fortunately or not, I'm in no position to do so. What I offer instead is a record of my own *Zerrissenheit:* of the fact that no day goes by without wondering whether my decision to leave Berlin four years ago was a terrible mistake. The seven years I spent there were the most intensely lived ones I've ever known. In November 1988, despite them, I packed what I owned and shipped it back to America, convinced that nothing resembling a sane Jewish life was possible on German ground.

Last August I returned from Berlin in rapture. I mention this from the start, for my sense of historical timing, among other things, has taken a beating recently. It was my first visit since reunification to the city which I, like many—and many Jews—had loved the way one does a lover: urgent, uneasy, only partially explicable. To this day the thought of certain street corners, the slant of a roof, the weight of an old double door key can leave me almost breathless. I'd gone with apprehension: Berlin friends and newspapers had reported but the bleakest of tidings. An era had ended; the Berlin we knew had given way to the sullen struggle for consumer goods. "Dann bin ich wenigstens meine Sehnsucht los," I had muttered, but it didn't happen. I returned full of conversations that went on until morning and began again the next afternoon, punctuated by midnight swims unspoiled by the slimyness of the Krumme Lanke; by hours spent reading aloud between five languages, or examining a friend's paintings; by the chutzpah—call it *Frechheit*—of the children on the street and the baker at the market. Nothing crucial seemed changed: the city still shone its extraordinary mixture of provinciality and sophistication, still forced significance out of every encounter; where everything *matters,* but carefully. The whole world may be present in a single *Kneipe,* and still be at ease.

I scoffed at my friends' grumbling. (If you call this Americanization, you should see the real thing.) Nothing *really* crucial had changed. Or if it had, it had changed for the better. With an eye to returning, I sought signs of a revival of Jewish life. Three years earlier, buying matzah for Pesach hadn't quite been a private act, but it surely wasn't a public one. There was one sidestreet store where you could do it, its name and contents disguised by a sign advertising oriental specialties. Now Shalom had competitors in the business of kosher food, mezzuzot, and yarmulkes; a second Jewish school was underway in the East, and alternatives to the official Gemeinde were beginning to grow. ("Alles Gauner, oder Stasi," said my Jewish friends, but this reaction too seemed so very Berlin—Jewish Berlin—that I found it delightful.)

Even more striking was another set of rooms. In a city where so much life takes place in public, the presence of not one but two Jewish *Kneipen* on what was now the main drag seemed positively astonishing. For years the city ceremonially honored the dead but extinguished every sign of the presence of living Jews. I had learned to live in semi-hiding, with a glance and an ear for the others. After all of that, to sit in a bright room eating borscht, listening to Israeli music, and leafing through the *Jüdische Allgemeine,* G-d help me, instead of the *taz,* was nothing short of exhilarating. Ach Berlin, I sighed, feeling sure that we had given up too soon. Even the remembered remarks at our son's daycare center—"If I'd known you were Jewish, I wouldn't have taken him"—seemed less chilling.

Passion blinds, notoriously, but I wasn't incapable of seeing the downside. Acquaintances in the East and friends in the West told much the same tale: the differences lay in the degree of wryness with which they spoke of unification as colonization. A botched attempt at business as usual had taken the place of what might have been, and worse was sure to come. Even I couldn't overlook the mutual resentment, the cracks, the solutions so provisional as to be none at all. Nor were the flaws confined to the new tensions produced by reunification. At five o'clock one morning, as I stumbled away from a kitchen table in Steglitz where I'd hotly defended the city's virtues, a cab driver presented me with a splendid example of that *stumpfe Borniertheit* which can seem so typically Berlinerish as to be untranslatable. I told the story the next day, laughing, for all in all I felt wonderful.

My German Jewish husband, who had chosen to stay in Connecticut, did interrupt my glowing reports with the reminder: you were with *Chileans.* And *Croatians.* And a couple of Jews. It is true that hardly a close friend would count as a full-blooded Aryan, but that *was* my Berlin, anyway. We began, once again, to discuss possibilities of return.

The first chill came with a phone call from an elderly German artist with whom I'd struck up the friendship of those who feel marooned, one way or another, in New Haven. She was hungry for impressions: had Berlin changed terribly since reunification? "Surprisingly little," I assured her, and the artist sighed relief. "For my friends all complain that reunification has ruined Berlin."

"So do mine," I continued, "But—"

"Crowded, expensive, overflooded with foreigners—"

"Oh," I said dully. "Most of my friends in Berlin *are* foreigners, and we see every addition as an improvement."

"Well," she said, with stiff brightness, "*That's* a different perspective."

The next week was Rostock.

My own fears are marked not only by skinheads lurking in subways, and rock bands singing "*Deutschland erwache,*" and the desecration of monuments whose false piety I once despised. Nor is it only—*only?*—the deaths and death threats, whose number will undoubtedly increase before this piece is printed. Nor is it even—*even?*—the spectacle of politicians cowering before the right on the one hand, and *das Ausland* on the other, unable to provide the smallest hope of a response to the terror that would be a hope from, and for, a truly new Germany. Nor is it my own favorite, as it were—the note from an anonymous schoolboy printed in *Der Spiegel,* proposing to gas all the "Ossies" the way Hitler did it to the Jews.

Thinking of these I think, each time, of the conversation with the elderly German in August. Her condemnation of the firebombings and swastikas is loud, energetic, and completely sincere. Her friends are among those who have joined hands and held candles by the thousands in protest against racism and government inaction. And that, precisely, is what frightens me most. Much has been written in an attempt to understand the new expressions of Nazism resulting from the difficult conditions in what used to be called the East, but the older and quieter western phenomena remain. The aristocratic xenophobia of the established intelligentsia, the thoughtless anti-Semitism of the *Szene,* are the backdrops for Rostock and Hoyersweda and Mölln. Here we see the connections. There, with the best of all possible wills, they don't.

Would I have forgotten her remarks if it hadn't been for what followed? Quite probably, given the mood in which I returned from Berlin. But now I cannot, caught by surprise, for the second time in a couple of years—and how. My nightmares had been subtler. More frightening, perhaps, and harder to handle: the overblown obeisance to the victims which can come to seem like a deathcult. Suffocating, and crazy, but subtler. I could have imagined many things, maybe newer, even wilder, but not *this.* Speechlessness is always an option. Like all of us, I suppose, I accepted the invitation to speak at a conference on the reemergence of German Jewish culture under very different circumstances. American Jews to whom I mention the task in passing stare in sheer disbelief. For the events of the fall of 1992 seem to confirm the common view with a vengeance. Even those few remaining blockheads (nostalgics? *Jeckes*? traitors?) who still needed convincing must see, by now, that Jewish life in Germany is thoroughly and definitely impossible.

My attempt to answer them is filled with the sense that I may be deeply wrong, perhaps as wrong as Hermann Cohen was when he wrote, in 1915, of the essential relatedness of the German and Jewish peoples. A philosopher whom I cherish for his belief that being a Kantian, a socialist, and a committed Jew are not only mutually compatible, but practically inevitable, Cohen has been virtually ignored for half a century. That essay did him in. "*Deutschtum und Judentum*" seemed, to most everyone, the pitiful swansong of the ultimate *Jecke,* who was lucky enough to die before he could learn how mistaken he had been. And there's no denying that he was mistaken, somehow, about Germany. So that any attempt to defend Hermann Cohen must begin somewhere else.

In America, perhaps. If I begin by describing what I miss here, I will leave out the matters we know: the *Sozialstaat,* the public spaces, the altered sense of time. Important as they are, they are differences between America and Europe; nothing particularly German, or German Jewish, depends on them. What has come close to driving me wild with longing is something stranger. If I left Berlin in order to leave what had become a daily confrontation with the Holocaust, the departure was a failure. For that confrontation is hardly less present in the American Jewish community, and the manner of its presence produces a permanent cringe.

For those of you who weren't on the mailing list for the Holocaust Museum's fund-raising drive, a small sample will be (more than) enough. This particular letter begins with the promise to tell the reader why becoming a donor "will be such a rewarding experience for you," after first explaining "why building the U.S. Holocaust Memorial Museum is such a rewarding experience for us all." Included are photographs of Dachau inmates smiling and waving for the camera while grasping at barbed wire; a note explains that they are cheering the U.S. Army liberators. Enclosed is a letter from a certain Curtis R. Whiteway, of which I quote the following:

Dear Friend,

When I was only 19 years old I was one of the American soldiers who liberated a Nazi concentration camp called Dachau. Now, I don't know if you've heard of Dachau. In 1944 I sure hadn't. Neither had most of my Army buddies. So we just weren't prepared for what we saw that day. . . . Now I'm not going to make you sick by telling you the details, but let me just say that it changed my life forever. Ever since, I've considered it my patriotic duty to this great country that I love so much to share my memories with others. . . . I've heard some say that this is just a Jewish museum—that it's mostly about what happened to the Jews and should be built by the Jews. Well, I'm not Jewish, and I disagree. This is a memorial about man's inhumanity to man. And there's something else: the people I helped liberate that day 46 years ago were people just like you and me. But the people who put them there—the people who murdered 6,000,000 Jews and millions of other people they despised—were *not* just like you and me. Think about it.

You may chalk this up to simple vulgarity, as innocent in its own way as the couples who stand on their wedding day in front of the Holocaust monument on New Haven's Whalley Avenue, a smallish metal statue depicting a hand grasping barbed wire, which is enhanced, if anything, by those occasional white gowns and top hats posed for photos before it. With a little effort, I can understand the intention behind the custom, even if it moves me to mutter the only quote I know from Gottfried Benn: "Das Gegenteil von 'gut' ist 'gutgemeint.'" This is easy abuse, as George Bush's invocation of the Hitler of Baghdad is just a piece of the political appropriation of the Holocaust on which U.S. policy has depended for years.

Things get murkier when I think of the attempts I helped undertake to organize the local Jewish community in defense of besieged Sarajevo. A vocal member of the group refused, with increasing hysteria, to take any action condemning Serbia, for her mother had been in Auschwitz, where she survived with the help of a Serb. The logic of her response was as baffling to me as it was acceptable to others: "My mother was in Auschwitz; *ergo,* I'm incapable of thinking about fascism." That, and a bit of government propaganda provided by a Serbian student, was enough to prevent the group from making any statement stronger than that we, as Jews, were definitely against concentration camps.

A number of people have lamented the fact that postwar Jewish identity is far too dependent on the Holocaust. I share these concerns, a curious mirror image of a German phenomenon: instead of learning and renewing Jewish traditions, we are fascinated with the details of their near destruction. And of course, even to bemoan this phenomenon is to partially participate in it. Risking such participation once again I wish to reflect on a couple of its aspects.

The fact is that for many Jews in America (and I suspect elsewhere) being Jewish is not merely reduced to being a possible victim of a future Holocaust. The reduction goes even further: being Jewish means being an implacable enemy of all things German. This phenomenon is most common in those Jews whose own lives were untouched; whose parents, even grandparents, were born safe in the New World. So safe, perhaps, that in clinging to the reminder of what happened elsewhere, and condemning those German Jews who failed to foresee it, they risk overseeing the parallels between that assimilation and their own. This is not to suggest that American Jews may be threatened by a repetition of history; I believe the dangers lie elsewhere. But it is frightening to see that just those Jews whose observance of the commandment to teach one's children diligently is often confined to the precept: Never forget the Holocaust! Recoil from the confrontation with what really happened, and is happening now.

We know about the tsuris Hannah Arendt suffered for *Eichmann in Jerusalem,* but at least the book was published, and remains in paperback. Despite the positive boom in Holocaust literature in America, the available material is sorely impoverished. Though you cannot enter a respectable bookstore without finding a good-sized section devoted to the Holocaust (often, grimly enough, labeled "Jewish Studies"), you will see no volume of, say, Hilsenrath or Becker. It may not be surprising that a book that begins with the words "Prologue or: Fuck America" was unable to find a New York publisher. But it is unconscionable that, where Wiesel's *Night* is virtually required reading at any good suburban high school, Hilsenrath's much subtler book of the same name is practically unknown.

There are reasons for this. Americans are in danger of losing that great Jewish gift, the capacity for irony. It has been confused, alternately, with sarcasm, bitterness, and slapstick, qualities that mar some of the finest contemporary American Jewish writing. But irony is not only more agreeable than these; it raises more questions. The questions raised in the works of postwar German Jewish literature are moral ones, and they are rarely if ever answered. I submit that it is this fact which makes them seem intolerable.

In Israel for certain reasons, in America for others, Jews want their Nazis dirty, their victims pristine. Those who stayed, or went back to Germany, cannot oblige them. They know it wasn't like that. Which isn't to say that their message is: nobody's perfect, or: nothing matters. That isn't literature, but kitsch or despair. Where contemporary German Jewish writers are good, sometimes great, is in their insistence that it matters a great deal to get moral details right: to describe temptation, complicity, and self-deception, small resolutions and real choices. If these things matter wherever we are, how much do we need them when portraying the event that can be seen as the century's most decisive? Yet in refusing to turn the Holocaust into melodrama, German Jewish writers remain unheard.

Even when something which cannot be fit into the usual schema does reach the public, reactions are troubling. The German academy's response to the film here titled *Europa, Europa* is well-known and disgraceful, but its American reception is no less problematic. It was seen, praised, and thoroughly disregarded. Review after review found the story incredible, a freak accident of history which has "no lessons to teach us, since it concerns an episode which—even if true—was completely anomalous." (These, by the way, were the better reactions; others took it on themselves to castigate Perel as a moral misfit who'd betrayed his people.) Now I know of two published accounts of survival in Germany which are almost as incredible, or more so; and if two have been published, how many remain untold? That victims and criminals were closer, and remain closer, than official versions would have us believe, that heroism and betrayal were, and remain, delicate matters, are facts that place moral ambiguity at the heart of just that historical event which one hoped would be clear.

What all this adds up to are pieces of an argument for the absolute need for a contemporary German Jewish culture. I cannot address the nature of that culture in the past, or to what extent the legendary symbiosis was just legend; that is a task for historians. Nor can I judge whether such a culture is possible; let those with the nerve for prophecy take my place. I only claim that such a culture is sorely needed, now. This claim should not be confused with a nostalgic one. Whether we view prewar German Jewish culture with desire or derision, we know it cannot be revived. What I am imagining, precisely, is a postwar culture in which nostalgia, surely, would place high on a list of original sins. For if postwar Jewish identity is conditioned by the Holocaust—and however we may regret this fact, it is one—then we'd better have some people who are capable of getting it right. (This, by the way, is why Jews need German Jewish culture; Germans may need it too, but I let that be, for the moment, their problem.) Getting it right means not only reflecting, with precision and nuance, what happened during the war, but everything that took place thereafter. This means examining the residues, and seeds, of fascism, the attempts to obscure them which threaten us all. Philosophically, this work was begun by German Jews like Arendt, Marcuse, and Anders. In literature, one thinks of the outrageously comic portrayal of the retention and abuse of anti-Semitic stereotypes in Israel depicted in Hilsenrath's *Der Nazi und der Friseur*; the uncertain ways of revenge and resignation in Becker's *Bronsteins Kinder* or *Der Boxer*. There are other examples, and much remains to be done, and it is not surprising that German Jews should be particularly placed to do it. For what is important is not only the sensitivity acquired through a set of experiences (a sensitivity, in particular, for fraud, duplicity, and illusion). Even more crucial is the matter of distance, distance required for the clearheadedness and the irony that these subjects demand.

Distance. If anybody has it, it's a German Jew, and two questions remain. The first: from whom can one expect it? The state of Israel may provide a lesson, even for those secular Jews among us, on the perils of trying to feel at home anywhere, before the Messiah comes. But it's one thing to demand that we recognize a certain homelessnes persistent in contemporary Jewish experience, and another to suggest that some Jews ought to live in that radical distance—call it permanent alienation—which Germany provides. Those who are called will choose themselves; few will be able to make a choice they call final. A couple of passports and an eye to the door will belong to every Jew who lives in Germany for many generations, and nobody can do a damn thing about it. Living on the edge is not for most, and it would be outrageous to demand it of anyone. Yet the more common request may be differently outrageous. Perhaps it's too much to ask that the international Jewish community actively support those Jews who live in Germany, but it is long past time that they stop condemning them. If the all too common question, "How can a Jew possibly remain in Germany?" would become a genuine request for understanding, we might share in the insight that such people make possible.

This brings me to a final question. It may seem paradoxical that while condemning the fact that modern Jewish identity is focused on the Holocaust, I've argued the need for a revival of German Jewish culture just to make sure the focus stays clear. This is, indeed, a task, but is there any other? One of the harder questions facing any Jew in Germany is whether it is ever possible to do anything else. Here I recall nights spent with my late friend Merve Lowien. Working on a play about Jewish life in Berlin, we would sometimes explode with the sentence: "Wann können wir endlich Schluß mit dem Thema machen?" There was heady relief in echoing the right, but our laughter was uneasy too. Lord knows it wasn't a normal life we sought, just an occasional moment in which to escape the ever-present probing of wounds.

There are internal reasons for Jews in Germany to feel obliged, or condemned, to eternal vigilance, but external ones may be sufficient. Germans make other tasks so difficult. A walk past a bookstore (where, for instance, a particularly offensive poster accompanied a display of Jewish literature) can be a provocation demanding response; if one has a penchant for *Aufklärung* the confrontation can take up several days. In my own case what seemed finally choking was not the occasional expression of anti-Semitism but the inability to cope with living Jews, which often enough takes place under the pretext of paying tribute to dead ones. Those present will know the slight shudders, the swallowed questions, the muffled stares that accompany the announcement, in Germany, that one is Jewish; which turn that announcement into a veritable event, a revelation, for those who ought to know better. But the inability begins even earlier, with the words "jüdischer Herkunft," "jüdischer Abstammung"—to say nothing of the formulation "jüdische Mitbürger," *lieb* or otherwise. On good days, the failures can seem comic. Once a German with whom I was making unusually hearty small talk ventured to express his affection with the speculation that I came from the southern part of the United States. I wondered how he'd guessed. He couldn't quite explain it; he'd just sensed something southern. The gestures, the intonation; he supposed it was rather like the difference between northern Europeans and Mediterranean peoples. Suddenly I smiled. "I was born in Atlanta," I told him, "But that's not what you mean. I'm an atypical Southerner. What you're noticing is that I'm Jewish." The poor man was utterly distraught. "Oh *no*," he protested, "That's not something I would *notice*. That plays no role at all for me!"

It is common to talk of the repression of history, but the question of whose history is less often posed. Small towns in West Germany may present another story, but my first, and strongest impression of Berlin was of how much time was spent remembering. Early on, I found it moving, the searing struggle of a generation to come to terms with its parents. As time wore on it came to seem eerie, and the reasons for my discomfort were clarified when a group of well-meaning Berliners chose to meet on Rosh Hashanah to plan their annual commemoration of *Kristallnacht*. Attempts to explain why the date should be changed were met with incomprehension: the group, said a spokesman, was not interested in religious matters, but cultural and historical ones. What it meant was that this group, like so many others, was not interested in Jews but in Nazis. Now I've nothing against self-knowledge; quite the contrary. But the repeated attempts of the best of Germans to "come to terms with the past" and to mean only their own often struck me as less harmless than the right-wing attempt to forget the whole thing. If forced to choose between them, I'd prefer indifference to fascism to fascination with it.

And all this was in the 1980s, when life was simpler. By 1990, without much notice, the reference of the word *Vergangenheitsbewältigung* had swiftly and dramatically changed: what sighs of relief accompanied the suggestion that the DDR too had a past that required overcoming! Even more dangerous than the ever-threatening attempt to identify Nazism and Stalinism was the implication that the old sense of *Vergangenheitsbewältigung* had already been realized. If the confrontation with that other past wasn't quite completed, it was certainly old hat: tasks more fresh and more important lay closer to hand.

If the events of the last months have shown anything with certainty, it's the folly of that relief, another attempt to divert, to repress, to flee. Now I believe that the last thing which would help matters is another litany of the camps, another monument to the victims, another list of murdered Jews. But the *best* prospect facing Germany today is probably another round of *Vergangenheitsverarbeitung*. And Jews living there will be forced to live with that: to call out the failures, the misconceptions, the ways in which the plans will miss the point. At the very least, they will be unable to avoid the new series of subway posters adjuring "Miteinander leben!" and featuring insipidly smiling *Ausländer* under rubrics like "Toleranz hat Tradition." And this, of course, is if everything goes well. Faced with that prospect, who can avoid a sigh of overwhelming weariness: what about the other interests which make up a life?

Yet there is another task for German Jews, and one hardly less important: the confrontation with our own past, a confrontation that would bracket those fatal twelve years and come to terms with others. That the same people—some of them famous, well-read and published—who hold it to be a religious obligation not to set foot on German soil are often those who hold the other component of Jewish identity to be pride in belonging to the tribe that produced Marx, Freud, and Einstein may require little comment. But even thoughtful people have sought to avoid the ways in which Jewish identity is still, despite everything, German Jewish identity. The fact that until very recently, all great Jewish secular contributions to Western culture, and not a few of the religious ones, were also German contributions is a fact which has been studied, and mourned, but too rarely explored. The wealth of scholarly material available about just how many German Jewish cultures there were does not erase the fact that, for the general Jewish public, all of them remain taboo. And the connections go deeper: most of us feel strangely at home not only in that mixture of irony and enlightenment that marks German Jewish thinking, but in the very cadences and structure of the language which spawned the *Mamaloschen*. (I have noticed this phenomenon in those, like myself, who grew up in homes where Yiddish was no longer spoken. What remained, next to scraps of expression, were rhythms and grammatical phrasing that are, exactly, German ones.)

Strangely at home: an understatement if there ever was one. To be drawn, or tied, to the place that left the luckiest of our families merely homeless can seem simply perverse. More precisely, masochistic, to name the gentlest reproaches of the cleverer Israelis I know. Without doubt, there are four thousand years to be cherished and explored. Yet those who seek to deny those crucial ones that were so distinctly German deny and maim us just as surely as those who once saw nothing else. Odd as it may seem, part of getting through the ways in which modern Jewish identity is determined by the Holocaust would be to face, squarely, the ways in which that identity was, and still is, very German.

This confrontation, again, would be a task for contemporary German Jewish culture. It cannot be an easy one, and it will be shot through with doubts. Complex and unpleasant motives are always a risk. Jews inside Germany will suspect themselves; Jews outside will not want to hear them. When one knows that the word "Jew" still cannot be spoken, in German, without panic, the call for such a confrontation may sound positively utopian.

But I wouldn't be the first Jew to believe that utopian thinking is needed at just those moments when it seems most absurd.

12. No Exit from This Jewry

Esther Dischereit
Translated by Michael Roloff

My God, where are my shoes? Here's one. There's the other. And my keys? Shit. Where are the keys?

These are the opening lines of my play *Red Shoes*—which then continues:

I hate parks. And these constantly smiling mothers with their strollers. I don't want to see them anymore, these playground mothers with their sliced apples and sugarless tea bottles. I've got to get out of here. Out. Look at me. I'm literally shaking with unhappiness. Can't you see it? My hairs are bristling in this darkness. Everything looks dark to me. The daffodils disgust me. The red of the tulips won't let me alone. No, I don't want to see it. Where should I put my eyes?—A pack of cigarettes please. Sorry, make it three packs. Those over there. Yes, thanks. How much is that? Of course. Yes, matches. How much does that come to? He made me a present of them. I'm insanely happy that he made me a present of a pack of matches. I feel around my pocket for the matches. As though he had said: what a beautiful woman you are. Now I am a woman because he's made me a gift of a pack of matches. At some point I must have gone crazy, right? Mad. Yes. Therapy said my last lover. You should give therapy a try. Yes, therapy about the fact that I am a broken piece of glass, a shard of glass on a ghetto site. He found it. Picked it up, the way you pick something up that catches the light, refracting it interestingly. Then the light took on a different color, and he tossed the piece away again, not even back to the same spot. Not even back to the same spot! Thus: therapy.

Because that piece of broken glass business, that's pathological. Of course it is pathological. And so I ought to give therapy a try. Against what? Against *the* subject of our time. *The* subject of our time is National Socialism. Everyone in my generation is preoccupied with this subject—at least in the West they are. Thus: therapy against National Socialism. Why not?! Actually, it's possible to try therapy against just about anything: my lover, too, was therapeutically treated. Autodidactically: a second-generation perpetrator. Thus I should try therapy with the second-generation therapists. The play contains these lines:

> No one has told me to be here. No one. It is like with social welfare. Two children and the father is broke—how could you let that happen?! And to bring children into this world. The indecency—of being born or to have stayed alive; whichever, it amounts to the same thing. You know the H, the Hebrew H—I always loved this letter of the alphabet more than any other—there's a little vertical line, you can catch hold of this line, then it seems to hover, it has a roof over it after all. This little line is me. Except that the roof and side-walls have broken away. I could decorate the walls of my room with tapestries made from these broken-off walls. I want to see something else besides my shitty room.

An editor comments that he finds the piece, of which I read an excerpt, successful; he congratulates me. But he also has reservations: what about those passages that are specifically Jewish, why not cut them? The Jewish theme disappears anyway as the action continues, and is perhaps minimized. On the other hand, the audience has been led to expect a continuation of the Jewish theme. It is a very German reservation, that of most Germans. The Jewish ought to be, yes, but as a pure piece, as contemporary history, a piece of contemporary criticism as they say, a sociopolitical discourse against National Socialism as part of the great *spiritual* conflict of our days. The position should be articulated as a theme, not so much as in the form of action within the categories of guilt please only pure. As a sociopolitical theme for a discourse, nothing less, all other conditions of being Jewish minimize Jewishness. and non-guilt: a very premature burial of the guilt question when I think about the fact that it was never properly raised. Thus: Jewishness ("Jüdischkeit") in the Federal Republic—

Dramaturges from two radio stations make similar comments about my radio play, *I am pulling the color out of my skin,* and I quote: "a sloganeering and simplified causal chain of events of a sexual, private and politically violent nature"; and "thrillingly drawn parallels between perpetrator and man, victim and woman, the past and the present, murder and sex seemed somewhat questionable to us." I am told to write a straightforward, unadorned report—I emphasize—report. Here the same basic idea seems to recur: please don't sully Jewishness by mixing it up with femininity, with sexuality, with fantasies of violence and violent realities. Meanwhile a different station is producing the plays.

The reality of the Federal Republic entails a stock-taking of Jewishness as though there had been born unto the Germans, recently, a collective patient whose illness still needs to be identified—felt for, hesitantly—a process that is accompanied by a lot of talk and a lot of understanding. But this must be done the way professional medicine conducts its craft: with a picture of human being lacking in a sense of wholeness, with dissections, a search for symptoms, not for causes; and the certainty that we know who really is the patient. This state of affairs dates back, probably, to the time "years ago," and that, it seems to me, in Germany, must be thousands of years before we started counting time, and is very far removed from the life of our grandmothers and grandfathers, of our mothers and fathers. For a long time there was no need for Raul Hilberg's works. Two decades passed until they were translated into German.

I—a Jewess—am by definition not a member of the species. or: why should a Jewess not have problems with public assistance and with her children? The postwar German Jew, to the extent that such a being even exists, was born after 1945, and his or her children have different problems with public assistance than other people do. These Jews will encounter officials who register and make notes; state officials who, as best as such a Jew remembers, were accessories to the terror, not providers of succor to citizens. The book *Merryn* contains these words about its protagonist: "The forms are burning between her fingers. These documents have been burning her fingers ever since. This people who stamp and shuffle papers smell no smoke but only smelled the ink of their stamp pads and perhaps also smelled their own displeasure at having to deal with a heavy work load—once the wave got rolling." More than likely, any doctor who officially inspected someone after 1945 had already seen service long before that date. And the judge's daughter? She too painted a swastika onto my school desk. In other instances, those who administered the West German restitution program to the victims—let me call them restituters—were the same persons who, prior to 1945, had been designated to confiscate the property that was to be made Aryan. Thus, a Jewess who is on public assistance will be the same as any other person and yet will be a Jewess. German, as a language, is the same to me too, and yet not the same. Not all words are equally available to me; for example, the word "ramp." I simply cannot use that word any more, not for anything. You know, furniture is usually sold from a store and is picked up from a ramp or transported to and from the truck on ramps. It is impossible for me to hear someone say that he is fetching his furniture from the ramp. My hair and my hands become Jewish. However, in the other German presence, Jewishness is the occasion for commemorative hours, for sociopolitical reflections. The Jewish human being in public perception has again become a Jew and nothing but a Jew. As though he were dead, inasmuch as he belongs to the species. In some respects this designation is not even wrong. Survivors—the children of survivors—concepts of life or concepts of death?

The German of the majority, the healer, the Savior—and the patient. The Jewish patient is actually forgiven for being ill. Germans assume this pitying attitude by definition toward each and everyone who does not belong to the majority. What is different is what is un-German, deficient with respect to being German. And it is the same with the representation of man as mankind as such, and woman as his deficit. Thus the German Roma and Sinti—so-called Gypsies—do not represent a recognized group of Others that is deserving of protection, because of their Christianity, which, being unexceptional, calls no special attention to itself; are not regarded as a community, nor as in need of state support. But it is different with the Jews because of their religious non-Christianity, and/or do they rank higher on the scale of victims? Germans define themselves as citizens, the Jew as a "fellow citizen" ("Mitbürger"). "The loss of the Jewish contribution to German culture is painful," is a sentence you frequently hear, say, on the occasion of memorial days. And while this regret is supposed to make one think about the loss of Jewish representatives of culture I think of the many dead Spiegelman-fathers, and of the Jewish good-for-nothings, and of the ease with which one differentiates between what is valuable and invaluable. What else occurs to me about this sentence? German culture, in other words, *is there* to begin with, Jewishness is added, and, according to the dominant opinion—as long as it is—enriches it; but what I never hear is: Jewish culture is German culture or, say, the formulation: culture is German. German culture embraces the products of cultural producers of different kinds and of different origins. That sentence is not uttered. But: Jewish culture came to German culture and made it blossom, which is why an untold wealth of spiritual goods was destroyed. That sentence, which betrays a great deal, is uttered by the good ones, those who mean well in the Republic.

This *völkisch* German way of thinking even enters the legal definition of citizenship. Blood remains German, and this has to be proven by your family tree. German citizenship is difficult to obtain without it. The civil rights conferred by citizenship are not to be found in the existence of the many who are different from each other, but in the one quality that the majority shares, the quality of being German, of being the "norm"—and this is a contradiction of democracy, this is a *völkisch* concept of statehood, which has led today to the exclusion of whole generations of different peoples from political life of the Federal Republic.

The Jewish question has been *the* taboo subject in a young Republic that seeks to polish its reputation. The only way for Germany to be able to regain its place among other nations was to "behave correctly" in this question and to fit in within the camps of the East/West conflict. Democracy was installed by the Allies; for most Germans it was a defeat. When I was born most of the few convicted Nazi bigwigs were marching out the prison gates into freedom, right into public life. There was no shame. Millions of people had been denazified in a process that resembled the handing out of Green Stamps. There was no need for shame. Democracy became the "buzzword," the language regulation for representatives with sullied biographies. It became a prerequisite of democracy that those who were its pillars would function sturdily in its behalf because they could be blackmailed into doing so. Willy Brandt was once chancellor, although he did not partake of this quality of being open to blackmail. I emphasize the word "although" and not the word "because." Josef Neckermann led the Federal Republic's horse equipage to international acclaim, a symbol of the regained reputation—and at home led a blessed mail-order business as a profiteer of the forced sales of wealth that had been made Aryan. Who thought of giving anything back? To whom, after all? The "Roma" and "Sinti" still are not even allowed to ask for restitution: they were not criminally persecuted for racial reasons, but rather because their "race" is "criminal"! Industrial concerns refuse to make any form of restitution to the forced laborers who had to work without pay but paid with their lives. The result: a failed denazification; and an enforced democracy. The postwar fathers built the legendary Volkswagen model, but did not work on the truth. It was left to the '68ers—the generation of the student revolt, twenty years later—to doubt the honorableness of this postwar democracy. If that was democracy, they would spit on it. I spat along, secure in the knowledge that these perjurious state representatives would soon be brought to their senses by the "cleansed" German worker—a totalitarian reply to the post-totalitarian condition. Lacking any personal concept of democracy, a part of the Left reached eagerly for Stalinist or Maoist solutions, and did so with such ease because, morally, they seemed to have the Communists, who as Hitler's opponents had also been exterminated and victimized, on their side. This morality was developed into a state religion in the GDR that not only did not permit an open biographical discussion about the question of who anyone had been during the period of National Socialism, but which strangled its political opposition ideologically and existentially. Even today, Honecker is being partially exonerated because he was imprisoned by the Nazis—an exoneration that the entire GDR elite used to legitimize itself and the injustices it committed. In the West, too, one would routinely introduce the fact that one had been persecuted by the Nazis into political discussions; as a consequence of the former victim's political impotence this lacked the kind of consequences it could have in the GDR, but nonetheless it partly paralyzed the peace movement. This is one reason among others why political human rights positions have been scarcely developed in West Germany. Meanwhile we can presume that the agreements between those who bore responsibility in the East and in the West coincided far more systematically than we could ever have dreamed—and corresponded to the United Front idea by no means only with expelled Communists. If matters had been different, reference to the Human Rights Charter would not only have been made in the case of the situation in Nicaragua, but also to life behind the Iron Curtain, which the West German Left by and large greeted with indifference, so that as a cause it was left to the conservatives to pursue.

The discussion about the Shoah, too, was repeatedly used from a variety of perspectives for other legitimizing purposes. Thus the justified refutation of the belittlement that comparing different kinds of atrocities simultaneously introduces has actually assisted an ostrich policy. Stalin's gulags were "not good either" from our point of view, or "were horrible but" is how the phrases go. From this perspective, the perpetrators' children, once they had given it some thought, had little choice but to find the Gulf War right. There is a taboo on a discussion of Israel as a state with racial politics of its own. There are think and talk taboos, which have been imposed on Germans by history, as it were—yet one more result of the years of "the overcoming of the past." Meanwhile we are experiencing an odd sanctification of the dead Jews. Debates about memorials—for example, "May we mention 600,000 murdered Roma and Sinti in an admonitory memorial together with the dead Jews?"—recollections of different kinds of death, uniqueness among the unique. These death debates have led away from the question about the mentality that committed the atrocities, the kind of concept of the state, the kind of conscience of those who were the perpetrators, the agents of death. Their actions cease being comprehensible, politically, legally, or psychologically and, instead, seem to belong to the most esoteric realms. To hold "no one responsible" but " to enlighten" is a frequently expressed intention. It's me, who, instead, wants to assign guilt where guilt is, and to determine responsibility where it exists.

To restitute illegally acquired wealth—isn't the generation that succeeded the student revolt, isn't it free to return the stolen property? Aren't they in a position to behave differently from the silent fathers? Unexpectedly the question of making restitution has become a topic of intense current discussion, because property in eastern Germany is being returned under the reprivatization laws. Who will register a claim? Most probably it will be the post-1945 owner. But what happens to the one who owned it before 1945? From 1933 to 1945—in the event there was a different owner. The Federal Republic corrected this legal situation which, during the first reading of the law, had considered only legal claims for restitution for post-1945 owners. Incidentally, the office that administers these affairs bears the name "Treuhand" (faithful hand!), "trustee" in English, and a word rich in associations in German. Raul Hilberg writes in his book, *Perpetrators, Victims, Bystanders* (1992), that "the concept of 'Treuhand'" was customary usage "in connection with the confiscation of the wealth of emigrated or deported Jews." The often busy and eager public efforts to demonstrate historical awareness strike me as facile attempts to placate other countries rather than as genuine efforts to establish political morality. Alfred Grosser paid his respects to a government which publicly assumed responsibility for crimes of state as something unique among democracies; yet this did not keep the same government from suggesting in 1989 that the day which in 1988 had been designated to commemorate the *Reichskristallnacht* ("Night of broken glass") should also serve as a national day of celebration of the fall of the Berlin Wall. That was averted in the nick of time. What is less easily averted, however, is the fact that German politicians frequently screw up matters, especially on occasions when German-Jewish reconciliation is being demonstrated, and usually they screw things up for good—so that they have to resign. Their mistake is usually that they use vocabulary from the Nazi period in talking about the position, honor, and legal status of the Jews currently living in Germany; or they communicate with German Jewry as though it were an affair of state between two nations, that is between Germany and Israel. The representatives of German Jewry in an instance such as this are understood to be middlemen; this is yet one more attempt to overcome history and to restore a normality that has never existed—the kind of normal state of affairs that exists between the citizens of two nations. Such attempts represent the only way contemporary Germany knows how to deal with Jews, or with any German who is not of the *majority*.

Germans generally regard Israelis as capable and militarily admirable. The shadows of the West Bank and Gaza Strip barely graze German consciousness. A good relationship to Israel is useful in a variety of ways for building bridgeheads in the Middle East. All this potential is increased by Israel's loud protestation that it is they who represent Jewry as such, and by the Federal Republic's position of deep loyalty to Israel, which the Jewish Communities never tire of asserting. It is important to have friends there, to be known—children of victims as well as of perpetrators will eagerly profess this. Incidentally, an interesting constellation is how this solves the question of Jewishness for Israel too, by means of conducting normal relations between two nation states. This point also seems of great import for Israel's concept of its own self. If I take a critical position in this respect, I nevertheless acknowledge what it means for a Jew to know of the availability of an Israeli passport. I, too, have become more keenly aware of this since the recent pogroms in Germany. But before it comes to that, I would not leave anything undone to obtain a different European—or maybe American—passport, because I fail to associate anything positive with the idea of a nation state based on a homogeneous people, and would prefer to belong to a society that is less informed by militarism and religion. Besides, I admit: the passport question preoccupies me constantly, even when it seems less pressing than now. My whole life I have tried to acquire qualifications that are less language-bound than poetry—with only meager success.

Now I want to tell the story about my first boyfriend. He was big and good-looking, as they say. Took me out to dinner and brought my mother flowers. That flower business was important. For my mother had saved not only her life but also her etiquette, which probably had been in vogue under Emperor Wilhelm among the German bourgeoisie. But she ignored the flowers and asked the young man for his last name. While they were talking she asked a second time, and later told me: too old, simply too old for you. The friend's last name was Mengel, and I didn't think anything of it at age 14. She had been unable to shake the suspicion that the last might just have another *e* at the end—you know, this *e* of the physician who did the selecting at the camp in Auschwitz, of the man who experimented on human beings. It was always like that in Germany. You never knew to whom you were talking. The probability of having a murderer, a killer, an accessory in front of you was very high. Still in 1989 I noted a brief poem:

I am not allowed
to say Jewish
when I say "Jewish"
that means war,
says my child.

I often had the feeling that human beings in the new communities are at ease with each other. They wear the Mogen David (Star of David) above their shirts, I wear it underneath. Was I a coward or pathological? Finally I noticed the difference between the survivors. Those who had emigrated to Germany had not lived among "normal" Nazi Germans; those dispersed refugees who had come to Germany from elsewhere after the end of World War II hadn't either—nor finally, had those few who had survived the concentration camps—none of these groups had experienced the normalcy of a Nazi German everyday. I, on the other hand, am the child of a woman who survived Nazi Germany right among the Nazis, one of those improbable 5,000. My mother heard an accountant's "normal" prejudices which could have had deadly consequences, felt the power of the owner of a ration card, the eyes of the legalized vigilantes who had been installed in every city block to watch over it (*Blockwarte*). I never became unselfconscious about being Jewish in Germany. When we take the streetcar my daughter tells me loudly, much too loudly, about the Passover preparations in kindergarten, and I look right and left. I always look over my shoulder.

With Hoyerswerda, Hünxte, Rostock in 1991 and 1992, my latent daily fear crystallized, stepped forth from the smouldering invisibility; in my historical memory there arose the images that

Albert Memmi, Eli Wiesel, Heinrich Heine had drawn. A pogrom, I thought, that is a pogrom, I have heard about pogroms—that they pass. Leading politicians had made names for themselves with virulent attacks on those seeking asylum, had started doing so precisely since the time that the number of those seeking asylum in Germany from the so-called Third World countries surpassed the number of Cold War refugees from the former Eastern Block. While Iran took 1.4 million refugees in 1991 from Iraq, and the African state of Malawi took in 940,000 refugees, with a population of around 8 million, the well-to-do Federal Republic seemed to disintegrate from the influx of 256,000. Even while the attacks, firebombings, and murders were happening, the Bundestag was discussing how these people who at that time were victims of the attacks were to be kept out of the country—a political wasteland, as Habermas calls it, and a frightening brutalization. At a time that the former political refugee Herbert Frahm, alias Willy Brandt, was dying, the very right of asylum that constitutes the Federal Republic's historical responsibility and with which it faced this responsibility was being demobilized.

The German chancellor kept warning about the terror from the Right and from the Left while the terror from the Right—I am using this now quite useless coupling of concepts once again—ruled the street and the democracy, and the Left was imprisoned by the police. The other protests by the citizens did not impress this government. One thing that did impress it, however, was the engagement of German industry against the vigilante attacks. German business is highly export-oriented, and feared the repercussions from bad publicity. The outrage this caused abroad, especially at German consulates and Goethe Institutes—made an important difference in helping the other Germans find a public hearing again. They must remain on guard and outraged. After all, hundreds of thousands are in the meantime demonstrating against Rightist radicalism and hatred of foreigners. A mass circulation tabloid appropriately ran a headline about the right-wingers: these madmen are destroying our democracy for us. But there is no ignoring the fact that these citizen's demonstrations are not dominated by demands for legal equality, but by slogans to be friendly and nonviolent. For other minorities—the disabled.

Jews, gay men and lesbians the excesses are equally threatened. How interchangeable the object of hatred is! As far as I am concerned, no Jew can believe that he or she can live as a citizen among citizens in Germany as long as nothing is done about all the others who are excluded from the exercise of their civil rights. And this is something that the Jewish communities seem to have understood in the meantime, because, for the first time, their representatives have been moved to communicate their dissent—at least on the asylum question—to the government.

The option for a different, culturally open, Federal Republic would raise the question "Jew" and/or "German" to a somewhat different level. For we seem to be able to be neither German Jews nor Jewish Germans; rather, we remain both simultaneously—alongside and against each other. Jews and Germans. Whether we regard ourselves as such or are so designated by the majority makes a definite difference. Thus German public life stands in need of a regular enlightenment about the fact that Jews were and are Germans. A conscious rational effort is necessary, there is nothing self-evident about our status. From a Jewish perspective, from my perspective, there is nothing self-evident about it either, not any longer: there is no recourse left to the historical context. It may be better for a Jew to be conscious of the temporality and evanescence of any kind of belonging to a nation—to forego the certainty of any set locality, to accept it as long as it lasts, but not to be too attached to it, or to believe in it. Citizen / Farmer / Beggarman—Emperor / King / Nobleman . . . if ever we become part again of an existing order; despairing, deceived like the Jews of the Weimar period—or wouldn't it be more sensible and dignified to find one's place outside, alongside, the order—to be a disorder and to create a new order?

New orders and disorders have been forming in Germany in any event since the fall of the Wall—also dangerous ones. Mass and might, nation or freedom. In the overcrowded days of November '89, I happened to walk a ways with a man from the other side, a young man, a worker for the railroad. The sky, unimpressed by the fact that world history was being made, was draggy gray. The street next to the S-train tracks led in foreseeable time to the less boring city center. "I can't get over it, I just don't get it that I can just walk here. I kept seeing this on TV all the time. And couldn't get over here. It's beautiful here, so beautiful." I was somewhat astonished and made an effort to see the beauty. We didn't quite know what we should talk about. Before I left him he said: "Is it true that you got all these Turks over here?" The unification of the GDR and the Federal Republic is costing thousands of Mozambiquans and Angolans and Vietnamese their work and study places. They were sent back. That was the morality of the foundation. But many people from the West, comparatively speaking, treated the SED old-boys network rather tactfully. Those who hadn't managed the denazification did not feel entitled to make a judgment now. Really, very tactful!

The lawmakers so far have not devised a legal instrument to bring those to trial who were responsible for human rights violations. All the Gauck commission can do is research whether a person was affiliated with the state security apparatus, Stasi, an organization that conducted its spying operations in brushfire fashion. In terms of numbers, it was better staffed than the Gestapo in its time. Approximately 85,000 employees belonged to the Ministry for State Security. In addition, the number of unofficial collaborators is estimated at about 100,000—for a population of 16 million. The "shield and sword of the Party" had data on 6 million citizens, 4 million in the GDR, 2 million in the West. For example, in a city like Dresden between 4,000 and 5,000 letters were opened daily. Even if I don't believe that the Stasi was a secret service like any other, I nonetheless want to provide the number of people employed by the BND, the secret service of the Federal Republic: 15, 560 for 62 million people, compared with 85,000 for the Eastern inhabitants who numbered 16 million (figures according. to K.W. Fricke). The most interesting files, largely unobtainable today, pertain to Main Section (*Hauptabteilung*) XX. These files might afford an insight into Stasi relations to the West, which seems more than ready to spread the coat of forgetfulness even before the public knows what ought to be forgotten. Unfortunately, the Germans will have to conduct their denazification on their own. The attempt at enlightenment and at bringing the culprits to justice once again is dissipating into the scream of the individual victims who cannot forget. Intellectuals of note detect a denunciation climate à la 1933. Heiner Müller sees East Germans one and all as victims—now of the West. He is calling up the picture of a dead Jewish boy in the ghetto. The boy is supposed to have carried a notebook under his arm with his final sentence: I want to be a German. And that is what should concern all of us now. Presumably there existed a heartfelt closeness that reached from the SED deep into the West-democracy. Political prisoners were regularly exchanged for hard currency by one state, bought by the other, and then maneuvered to the political outside by the buyer. Anyone who went hunting for hare with Honecker, as Chaim Noll—a dissident author in the GDR and a Jew who was placed into a psychiatric ward, but the son of a very prominent, very GDR establishment author—asked, why would such a guest be interested in enlightenment?

Conclusion

"Isn't there anything that's o.k. with us?" an East German educator once asked me. No, to be honest, no, for that way of looking at things is not mine. Or should I ask with Adorno: "Is there a right life in the wrong one?" The woman was talking about her work: she had been employed in a children's home once. In Bad Saarow. Near the border. Often they brought children at night and fetched them again the next morning. "When a woman next morning said that she was the aunt, I didn't ask her whether she really was and gave her the child." The right life in the wrong one? Now she is working in another children's home. Near Berlin. After the "change" she stopped separating siblings from each other and bringing them into different homes. In the dining hall for the children the tapestries are hanging in tatters from the wall. Meanwhile, in the office, computers have been installed in "rooms" with a view of the lake and with parquet floors. In the dining hall the tapestry is hanging in tatters, the renovation was stopped halfway. Actually, for the children, paint is available everywhere now after "the change." Do you know for how long? It has been like that for one year.

I will quote from the work plan for a kindergarten group—

Krostitz is the name of the place: "The means I used on my children to convince them of the need for the armed organizations." The individual steps anyone took envisioned educational measures, every month educational measures, educational measures, monitoring, the control of the daily routine cleanliness, order, greeting, and the expression of love for the socialist fatherland had to be learned, the envisioned series of steps by means of which the socialist personality would develop: going to the toilet, eating, behavior in the forest was regulated, there was even a socialist way of dealing with flowers: there was a socialist size for flowers. Only this one size was correct when the children painted. The right life in the wrong one? Who are these children, this youth, these adults? The way they were kept in the real socialist arrangements formed the personality from crib to vacation spot—there was no room for plurality, no room for individuality. For roughly sixty years the people in what used to be East Germany lived under a dictatorship, and now they have a freedom, which they imagined as different, less demanding. It's idiotic, this scream for freedom, a nurse told me in 1991. People in the West say derisively, "Banana refugees," of which they of course had more than enough. At the moment this struggle for democracy hangs in the balance in the Federal Republic, and the proportion of the citizenry who hardly know what democracy means has probably not been as high as this in this not-very-old republic since right after World War II. There is no telling the outcome of this effort. I myself never carried the West German constitution as frequently and consciously under my arm as I do now. The landscapes of lies, as the writer Jürgen Fuchs called them, make me afraid. With whom am I sitting at a desk and defending human rights and fighting layoffs? Who, please, was my colleague? And one more thing: the pillars of the SED regime: weren't they all armed? There are a lot of weapons around. The representatives of public life from both East and West surely should be open for investigation of their biographies. Why don't they want it?

Thus there is again this dull undercurrent beneath the democratic floor, which warns me: anyway there is little room for Jews in the "prescribed" anti-fascism, and for a Jew this is not much of a concept to fight with, is it?

To write in Jewish in front of a German-German audience has a slatternly prostituting air about it—like a woman getting undressed in front of the eyes of men, I know. But I see no alternative. I will close with a poem from my piece, *I Am Pulling the Color Out of My Skin*:

A woman about herself: "Do I have a history. No better to do without, if possible. No. Not with us. Unfortunately that's impossible. Impossible." And so she thinks—sings a song to her child, a song outside time, without beginning and without end: "Yes it was like that." Then she stood in front or me and sang to me:

Grandma and grandpa take me to America
there it's great and wonderful
uncle and aunt are going to America
there it's great and wonderful.

She has been singing this song into my ears for the past fifty years. I hold my ears closed. How thin she is. I could count her ribs. The hair is shorn of her bare head, her ribs are sticking out through her skin.

Grandma and grandpa,
take me to America
there it's great and wonderful
uncle and aunt are going to America
there it's great and wonderful.

Died over there. Did not take her along. I didn't want to let her go. I am keeping my ears closed.

There it's great and wonderful
Uncle and aunt and grandpa

I gave birth to her
back again into the world
so that she can sing again.

Chava, eye of my eye
mein oigele
you are singing so happily sing
slap the rhythm with your pretty hands
forget grandpa and grandma—they would have taught you
forget grandpa and grandma—they would have taught you
forget and slap the rhythm with your pretty hands
sing happily sing
sing as long as there is song in you
sing as long as there is song in you.

And the child asks: "Where is America?"

Index

Abraham, 235
Adass Isroel, 67, 88, 93, 96, 101, 111n.129, 138
Adorno, T.W., 279
Alberstein, Chava, 119
Allenbach Opinion Poll, 10
Allgemeinde Jüdische Wochenzeitung, 81, 114, 132, 138, 179
Amanda herzlos (Becker), 19
American Joint Distribution Committee, 63
Anders, Günther, 261
Andree, Richard, 213
Antisemitismusstreit, 148, 155–56, 160, 163, 165–66
Arafat, Yassir, 70
Arbeiterkampf, 161, 163
Arendt, Hannah, 259, 261
Assistant, The (Malamud), 240
Augstein, Rudolph, 180
Autenrieth, J.H.F., 219
Azzola, Axel, 55

Babel, Isaac, 100
Babylon (journal), 4, 5, 20, 88, 157
Babylon (musical group), 52
Banished Knowledge: Facing Childhood Injuries (Miller), 238
Baruma, Ian, 15–16
Becker, Jurek, 19, 20, 118, 178, 227–29, 233, 239–42, 259, 261
Beckermann, Ruth, 185
Behrens, Katja, 17, 30–33
Bellow, Saul, 30
Benjamin, Walter, 190, 207n.17
Benn, Gottfried, 258
Benz, Wolfgang, 47
Bergson, J., 221
Berliner Tagesspiegel, 122
Berlin Umschau, 51
"Betrayal" (Biller), 229, 241
Biermann, Wolf, 33, 153, 227
Biller, Maxim, 20, 69, 119, 180, 227, 229–31, 241–42
Billings, John S., 236
Bitburg affair, 1, 19
Bitter Harvest (Holland), 37
Block, Iwan, 217, 237
B'nai B'rith, 85
Bodemann, Y. Michal, 7, 123
Bohrer, Karl-Heinz, 156
Born (Schindel), 234, 241
Böse Onkelz, 122
Boxer, The (Becker), 233, 261
Brandt, Willy, 271, 276
Brauner, Artur, 37
Brenner, Michael, 123
British Medical Journal, 215
Broder, Henryk M., 18, 21, 58, 69, 91, 111n.129, 120, 129n.46, 150, 242
Bronsteins Children (Becker), 20, 178, 227, 261
Bruhn, Joachim, 164–65

Brumlik, Micha, 21, 69, 86, 151–52, 157, 159
Bubis, Ignatz, 48, 56, 82, 93, 106n.38, 112n.135, 114–18, 123, 130–32, 134, 136, 145–46
Bundesrat, 4
Burton, Richard, 214
Bush, George, 154, 258

ça ira Verlag (publishing house), 165
Cannibals (Tabori), 33
Carlebach, Julius, 89
CDU (Christian Democratic Union), 72
Celan, Paul, 18
Central Committee of the SED, 63
Central Council of Jews in Germany. *See Zentralrat der Juden in Deutschland*
Chabad Center (London), 101–2
Christian Democratic Union (CDU), 72
Christian-Jewish Brotherhood Week, 177
Christlich-soziale Union (CSU), 121
CIS (Community of Independent States), 122
Claussen, Detlev, 156
Cohen, Hermann, 256–57
Community of Independent States, 122
Conference on Jewish Material Claims Against Germany, 65
Crawley, Ernest, 218
CSU (Christlich-soziale Union), 122
Cultural Association. *See Jüdische Kulterverein*

Dachs, Gisela, 132
Darwin, Charles, 217
Deleuze, Gilles, 17, 21–29, 39–41, 206n.8
de Maizière, Lothar, 72, 101
Denkbilder (Benjamin), 190
Descent of Man (Darwin), 217
Describing the Holocaust (Young), 119
Deutscher, Isaak, 53
"Deutschtum und Judentum" (Cohen), 257
Dies ist nicht mein Land—Eine Jüdin verläßt die Bundesrepublik (Fleischmann), 18
Diner, Dan, 3, 21, 55, 69, 81, 157–59
Dische, Irene, 9, 179–80, 185–86, 191, 200–204, 206n.9, n.11, 209n.31, 223–25
Dischereit, Esther, 3, 6, 8, 9, 17, 20, 30–33, 119, 128n.27, 185–204, 206n.11, 222, 224
Domin, Hilde, 18
"Doppeltes Grab" (Honigmann), 192
Dorfman, Ariel, 182
Dörrie, Doris, 226
Drach, Albert, 211
Dybbuk, The, 100

Edvardson, Cordelia, 177
Ehrlich, Avraham, 123
Eichmann, Adolf, 16
Eichmann in Jerusalem (Arendt), 259
"Einheitsgemeinde," 79, 89, 101
Einstein, Albert, 264
Ellis, Havelock, 217
Ende der Lügen, Das (Margolina), 53, 59
Enzensberger, Hans Magnus, 153–54
Erasmus, Desiderius, 216
Erikson, Erik H., 238
Eschwege, Helmut, 71, 94, 96
Europa, Europa (Holland), 17, 20, 36–39, 223, 260
Eusebius, 216

Fassbinder, Rainer Werner, 1, 19, 116

Ferenczi, Sándor, 237
Fink, Heinz, 70
Fischer, Eva Elisabeth, 180
Fischer, S. (publishing house), 182
Fleischmann, Lea, 18, 185, 222
Forel, August, 218
Fortzeugung des Behemoths (Spehl), 164
Foucault, Michel, 189, 207n.14, 208n.22
Frahm, Herbert, 276
Frankfurter Journal, 220
Frankfurter Jüdische Nachrichten, 53
Frankfurt Jewish News, 4
Free University (Berlin), 225
Fremdes Gefühl, Ein (Dische), 186
Fremd im eigenen Land (Broder and Lang), 18
Freud, Sigmund, 33, 235, 237, 239, 264
Friedländer, Salomo, 229
Friedländer School, 97
Fritz Bauer Institute, 92
Fromme Lügen (Dische), 186, 200–201
Frye, Northrop, 70

Galinski, Heinz, 51, 56, 84, 104n.19, 127n.25
Garbage, the City and Death (Fassbinder), 1, 116
General Paper of the Jews in Germany, 4
Genscher, Hans, 162
German Export Film Union, 37, 39
German Military College, 58
"Geschlossene Vorstellung. Der jüdische Kulturbund in Deutschland 1933–1941," 21
Gethsemane Church, 71–72
Gilbert, Jane E., 224–25
Gilman, Sander L., 9, 48, 191, 207n.13, 208n.24
Giordano, Ralph, 21, 59, 116, 132
"Glasses, Lara, and the Bells of St. Ursula" (Biller), 230
Glucksmann, André, 59
Goldberg-Variationen (Tabori), 20
Goldstein, Sidney, 48, 60n.7
Goldstein, Theo, 66
Gorelik, Michael, 119
Gorki, Maxim, 53
Green Party, 121, 156, 160
Gremliza, Hermann L., 150
Griner Aquarium (Sutzkever), 119
Grosser, Alfred, 59, 273
Grötzmacher-Tabori, Ursula, 34
"Gruppe-K," 163
Guattari, Félix, 17, 21–29, 39–41, 206n.8
Günzel, Bernd, 20
Gysi, Gregor, 68, 70, 153, 162

Habermas, Jürgen, 276
Ha-Ikar, 54
Hartung, Klaus, 150
Hatikvah, 52
Heenen-Wolff, Susan, 212
Heine, Heinrich, 34, 275
Heller, Joseph, 229
Hermann, Matthias, 20
"Herr Moriz Deutschösterreicher," 212
Herzberg, Judith, 20
Herzberg, Wolfgang, 68, 71
Heym, Stefan, 68, 119
Hilberg, Raul, 268, 273
Hildesheimer, Wolfgang, 18
Hier wollen wir leben (Günzel), 20
Hilsenrath, Edgar, 18, 118, 203, 259, 261
Hirschfeld, Magnus, 217
Historiker-Debatte, 19
Historikerstreit, 1, 58, 155
Hitler, Adolf, 68, 137, 151, 154–55, 173, 176, 232, 258, 271
Hitlerjunge Salomon. See Europa, Europa

Hitschmann, Eduard, 237
Hochschule der Bundeswehr, 58
Hochschule für Jüdische Studien, 81, 83, 89
Hoffman & Campe, 179, 181–82
Hölderin, Friedrich, 33
Holdheim, Samuel, 220–21, 241
Holland, Agnieszka, 37–39, 41, 223
Holocaust (film), 16–18
"Holocaust Documentation Center," 92
Holocaust Museum, 257
Honecker, Erich, 64, 145, 271, 279
Honigmann, Barbara, 9, 17, 20, 30, 32–33, 68, 71, 119, 185–92, 197–201, 204, 206n.11, 222
"How Yiddish Do We Germans Speak?" 121
Hygiene of Love (Mantegazza), 216

I Am Pulling the Color Out of My Skin (Dischereit), 281
Ich war Hitlerjunge Salomon (Perel), 17, 36, 39. *See also Europa, Europa*
If I Became a Rich and Dead Man (Biller), 180
Initiative Sozialistisches Forum (ISF), 164–65
Ins Freie (Janeczek), 20
Institute for Studies of Anti-Semitism, 47
Institut für Sozialforschung (Hamburg), 149
Interrogation, The (Sinakowski), 231
ISF (Initiative Sozialistisches Forum), 164–65
"Israel-Palestine and the Federal Republic," 163

Jacob the Liar (Becker), 178
Jacoby, Jessica, 166
Janeczek, Helena, 20
Jenninger, Philipp, 1
Jesus Christ, 58, 218
"jetzt weider zu den Fremden im Land zählen" (Silbermann), 132
"Jewess for Charles Allen, A" (Dische), 191, 202, 223
Jewish Communities. *See* Jüdische Gemeinde
Jewish Cultural Association, 67, 70
Jewish Cultural Festival. *See* Jüdische Kulturtage
Jewish Life-Worlds, 120
Jewish Publishing House, 119
Jewish Theological Seminary (New York), 90
Jewish Welcome Service (Vienna), 102
"Jewish Women in Berlin," 93
jiddische Mamme, Die (Seligmann), 19, 20, 29
Joëmis Tisch: Eine jüdische Geschichte (Dischereit), 20, 186, 189, 191–95, 198, 222
Juden in Deutschland (Müller), 20
"Juden und Deutsche," 114
"Jüden für Charles Allen, Eine" (Dische), 191, 202, 223
Jüdische Allgemeine, 254
Jüdische Forum e.V., 106n.43
Jüdische Gemeinde: Berlin, 5, 49, 51, 84–85, 87–89, 101, 108n.83; Cologne, 87, 90, 106n.45; Düsseldorf, 80, 87; East Berlin, 94, 97; Frankfurt, 81–84, 87, 108n.83; Koblenz, 85
Jüdische Gruppen, 49, 80, 86, 87, 96, 157
"Jüdische Identitat im Spiegel der Literatur vor und nach Auschwitz," 21
Jüdische Kulturtage, 5, 52, 118, 119, 121–23
"Jüdische Lebenswelten," 21, 57–58, 120–21
Jüdischer Kulturverein, 80, 96–101, 123

Jüdischer Verlag, 119, 123
Jüdisches Forum Köln e.V., 87, 123
Jüdisches Kulturmagazin, 118
Jüdisches Lexikon, 119
Jüdische Volkshochschulen: Berlin, 81, 85, 116; Frankfurt, 81–83
Jüdische Zeitung, 179
"Junge Juden in Deutschland," 21
"Jürgen," 161–62

Kafka, Franz, 28, 33, 34, 41
Kafka: Toward a Minor Literature (Deleuze and Guattari), 21
Kahane, Anette, 68, 71, 72
Kaniuk, Yoram, 177
Kant, Immanuel, 257
Kaplan, Marion, 8
Katz, Jacob, 49, 57
K-Gruppen, 162, 164
Klezmatics, The, 119, 122
Koch, Gertrud, 69
Kohl, Helmut, 54, 72, 115, 116, 149, 151
Kommunistischer Bund, 162–63
Konkret, 150, 152, 154
Krafft-Ebing, Richard, 217
Kraft durch Freude, 122
Krause, Peter Moses, 123
Kritik und Krise, 165
Kugler, Anita, 52, 55
Kulturverein. See Jüdischer Kulturverein

Lang, Michel, 18
L'Chaim, 93, 108n.80
Leas Hochzeit (Herzberg), 20
Leo, Annette, 68, 71
Leo Baeck Institute, 47
Lessing, Gotthold Ephraim, 176
Levi, Primo, 177
Liebe aus nichts, Eine (Honigmann), 20, 32, 189, 197
Limited Hope: Germans, Jews, Israelis (Seligmann), 181
Lind, Jakov, 18, 244n.19
Lombroso, Cesare, 217
Louvish, Simon, 235–37
Löwenfeld, Leopold, 236
Lubbock, John, 219
Luther, Martin, 216
Lwanga, Gotlinde, 166

Magic Mountain, The (Mann), 34
Maimonides Society, 81–82
Malamud, Bernard, 30, 240
Mantegazza, Paolo, 216–18, 236
Marcus, Jacob R., 213
Marcuse, Herbert, 261
Margolina, Sonja, 53, 56–59
Marx, Karl, 264
Melzer, Abraham, 149
Memmi, Albert, 275
Menengoz, Margaret, 37
Merryn (Dischereit), 3, 20, 31, 186, 189, 191, 196, 268
Michaelis, Johann David, 220
Miller, Alice, 237–40, 242
Mit beschränkter Hoffnung (Seligmann), 29
Morris, Desmond, 238
Moses, 218
Moses and Monotheism (Freud), 239
Mull, die Stadt und der Tod, Der (Fassbinder), 1, 116
Müller, Heiner, 278
Müller, Jürgen Martin, 20
Musica Judaica e.V., 92
Mynona (Salomo Friedländer), 229

"Nach Innen Ausgewandert" (Behrens), 30
Nachmann, Werner, 56
"Nation of Readers Dumps Its Writers, A," 72
Nazi und der Friseur, Der (Hilsenrath), 261
Neckermann, Josef, 271
Neiman, Susan, 6, 225–26

Neues Deutschland, 153
Neuman, Rabbi Isaac, 91, 95
"New Synagogue," 94
"New World Order," 155
New York Review of Books, 15
New York Times, 72, 132
"Nie Wieder Deutschland," 160, 161
Night (Hilsenrath), 259
Night (Wiesel), 259
Noll, Hans (Chaim), 71, 279
Nolte, Ernst, 58
Nozizwe, 166–67
Nudnik, 4, 88

Ochse, Katharina, 7
Offenberg, Mario, 101, 127n.21, 138
Olsen, Charles, 213
On Human Love (Mantegaaza), 216–17
"Opfer des Faschismus," 49
Origen, 216
Osler, William, 218
Ostow, Robin, 7

Palestine Liberation Organization (PLO), 70
Partei demokratischer Sozialismus. *See* Party of Democratic Socialism
Party of Democratic Socialism (PDS), 98, 121, 153, 162
"Patterns of Jewish Life," 92
Paul, Saint, 216, 227
PDS. *See* Party of Democratic Socialism
Peck, Jeffrey, 8, 11
Perel, Salomon (Sally), 17, 36–39, 223, 260
Perpetrators, Victims, Bystanders (Hilberg), 273
Persian Gulf War, 8, 148–67
Pestalozzistrasse Synagogue (Berlin), 88
Philo, 219
Physiology of Love (Mantegazza), 216
Pious Secrets (Dische), 179
Pisar, Samuel, 177
Plank, Karl, 193
PLO, 70
Pound, Ezra, 213
"Promised Land, The" (Sinclair), 240

Radikale Linke, 160–62
Radio Dreyeckland, 163–65, 168n.39
Radziewski, Hans, 212
Rebling, Jalda, 68, 71
Red Shoes (Dischereit), 266
Reemtsma, Jan Phillip, 149
Reichenbach Synagogue (Munich), 233
Reich-Ranicki, Marcel, 174, 178
Remmler, Karen, 9
Rheinz, Hanna, 123
Richler, Mordechai, 240
Riesenburger, Martin, 94
Roman von einem Kinde (Honigmann), 186, 191–92
"Rooted in Nowhere" (Rosenstrauch), 185
Rosenstrauch, Hazel, 185
Rosh Chodesh, 90
Roth, Philip, 30, 240
Rubenstein's Auction (Seligmann), 178–79, 227, 232–33
"Rundbrief für jüdische Lesben und Feministinnen," 92–93
Runge, Irene, 68, 70, 72, 99

Sabbatai Zevi (Scholem), 119
Sachs, Hanns, 236
Sachs, Nelly, 18
Saddam Hussein, 150, 153–55
Salinger, J.D., 228
Salomon Ludwig Steinheim Institute, 9
"Schabbeskreis," 92

Schiller, Friedrich, 241
Schindel, Robert, 241, 234
Schlagkamp, Franz-Dieter, 115
Schmidt, Karl Heinz, 136
Schneider, Richard Chaim, 58, 123, 128n.44
Schneider, Wolfgang, 152–53
Schoeps, Julius, 59
Scholem, Gershom, 3, 83, 119, 192
Schönhuber, Franz, 179
SED. *See* Sozialistische Einheitspartei Deutschlands
Seebacher-Brandt, Brigitte, 156
Seligmann, Rafael, 3, 6, 8, 17, 19–20, 27–28, 33, 41, 58, 119–20, 123, 178–82, 227, 232–34, 239–42
Semittimes (Semit), 4, 5, 20, 88, 149
72 Buchstaben (Hermann), 20
Shamir, Izak, 180
Silbermann, Alphons, 132
Sinakowski, Andreas, 231–32, 234
Sinclair, Clive, 240–41
Singer (Dorfman), 182
Socialist Unity Party, 153
Society for Christian-Jewish Cooperation, 176–77
Sontag, Susan, 132
Sozialistische Einheitspartei Deutschlands (SED), 62, 98, 121, 278–80
Spehl, Helmut, 163–65
Sperber, Manès, 18
Spiegel, Der, 9–10, 47, 72, 114, 116–17, 132, 140, 153, 180, 256
Spiel, Hilde, 173
Spies, Gerti, 177
Spinoza, Baruch, 217, 246n.28
Stalin, Joseph, 53, 56, 64, 71, 272
Stein, Ernst M., 88
Stella (Wyden), 117
Stern, 132
Stern, Frank, 21
"Stiftung zur Förderung jüdischer Frauen in Wissenschaft und Kunst," 92
"Straight to the Heart" (Dörrie), 226
Streithofen, Basilius, 115
Strobl, Ingrid, 154
Stuyvesant, Peter, 139
Süddeutsche Zeitung, 121, 180
Suhrkamp Verlag (publishing house), 119, 178
Sutzkever, Abraham, 119
Szene, 256

Tabori, George, 17, 20, 33–37, 41
Tachles, 4, 123
Tacitus, 236
Tageszeitung, Die, 52, 121
Talkshow: Good Night, Germany (Seligmann), 182
Taubes, Jacob, 225
taz, 55, 150, 153, 254
Technical University (Berlin), 47
Thompson, Jerry E., 73n.2
Thousand Plateaus, A (Deleuze and Guattari), 39
Thränhardt, Dietrich, 136
Three Years in Theresienstadt (Spies), 177
Tolmein, Oliver, 160
Torberg, Friedrich, 173

United States Academy of Motion Picture Arts and Sciences, 37, 39
University of Freiburg, 163
University of Tübingen, 219

Verband der jüdischen Gemeinden der DDR, 95
"Verwurzelt im Nirgendwo" (Rosenstrauch), 185
Vienna Psychoanalytic Association, 237
Virchow, Rudolf, 215
von Luschan, Felix, 215
von Weizsäcker, Richard, 114, 140

Vorsitzender des Innenausschusses der Rostocker Bürgerschaft, 136
Voss, Thomas, 156

Waks, Moishe, 128n.45
Waldheim, Kurt, 234
Walker, Kizer, 8
Washington Post, 132, 135
Wassermann, Jacob, 211
Weigel, Hans, 173
Weisman und Rotgesicht (Tabori), 17, 20, 34
Weiss, Konrad, 68
Weiss, Peter, 18
Wenn ich einmal reich und tot bin (Biller), 19
Westermarck, Edvard, 217–18
Whiteway, Curtis R., 257
Wiesel, Eli, 180, 259, 275
"Wir für Uns," 96–97
WIZO, 81, 85
Woche, Die, 117
Wolffsohn, Michael, 58–59, 120, 123
Women against Racism and Anti-Semitism, 93
Woolf, Markus, 231
World Jewish Congress, 132, 138
Wundt, Wilhelm, 219
Wyden, Peter H., 117

Yiddish Mama, A (Seligmann), 180
Young, James E., 119

Zeit, 132, 153
Zelman, Leon, 102
Zentralrat der Juden in Deutschland, 18, 26, 54, 55, 65–66, 82, 88, 95, 114–15, 118, 125n.6
Zipes, Jack, 6, 7, 203
zum Winkel, Detlef, 160
Zweig, Arnold, 173
ZWST, 54